IN SEARCH OF
VAN GOGH

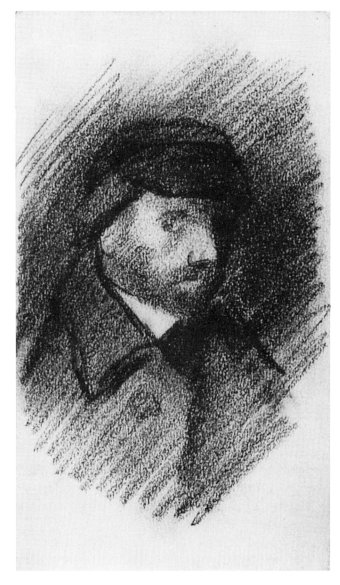

One of Vincent's first self-portraits, Antwerp, Winter 1885. He had just been told the nature of his illness. *Vincent van Gogh Foundation/National Museum Vincent van Gogh, Amsterdam*

IN SEARCH OF
VAN GOGH

KEN WILKIE

'The germinating seed must not be exposed to a
frosty wind—that was the case with me in the beginning.'

From Vincent to Theo
Drenthe, November 1883

**Vincennes University
Shake Learning Resources Center
Vincennes, Indiana 47591-9986**

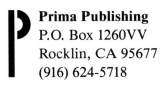

Prima Publishing
P.O. Box 1260VV
Rocklin, CA 95677
(916) 624-5718

For Laura

Copyright © 1978, 1990, 1991 by Ken Wilkie

First published 1978 by Paddington Press as *The Van Gogh Assignment*

Reprinted with permission of Souvenir Press Ltd, 43 Great Russell Street, London WC1B 3PA

Prima Publishing
Rocklin, CA

Library of Congress Cataloging-in-Publication Data

Wilkie, Kenneth, 1942-
   [Van Gogh assignment]
   In search of van Gogh / by Ken Wilkie
      p.   cm.
   Reprint. Originally published: The van Gogh assignment. New York:
Paddington Press, © 1978.
    ISBN 1-55958-101-8
    1. Gogh, Vincent van, 1853-1890.   2. Artists — Netherlands-
-Biography. I. Title.
[ND653.G7W54   1991]
759.9492 — dc20
[B]
                            91-2069
                            CIP

91 92 93 94 RRD 10 9 8 7 6 5 4 3 2 1

Printed in the United States of America

How to Order:

Quantity discounts are available from the publisher, Prima Publishing, P.O. Box 1260VV, Rocklin, CA 95677; telephone (916) 624-5718. On your letterhead include information concerning the intended use of the books and the number of books you wish to purchase.

U.S. Bookstores and Libraries: Please submit all orders to St. Martin's Press, 175 Fifth Avenue, New York, NY 10010; telephone (212) 674-5151.

Contents

List of Illustrations

Acknowledgements

Most of the people I am indebted to for the content of this book appear in the text itself—not least the descendants in England of Eugénie Loyer and Dr Cavenaile, who entrusted their rare photographic and art material to me on my journey.

For their individual help, I should like to thank particularly Fieke Pabst, Chief Librarian at the Rijksmuseum Vincent van Gogh in Amsterdam, and Han van Crimpen, Head of the Museum's Conservation and Documentation Department, as well as the Van Gogh Foundation for giving me access to certain previously unpublished Van Gogh family correspondence.

For allowing me to study relevant medical documents I am grateful to Dr W.J. Hardeman, Director of the Willem Arntsz Huis Psychiatric Centre in Utrecht, Bernadette Molitor of the Bibliotheque Interuniversitaire de Médecine in Paris, and Judith Barker of the Wellcome Institute in London.

Thanks also to Vernon Leonard, my old editor who started it all by assigning me to the magazine story in the first place, and to my colleagues at *Holland Herald* today—Penny Fisher, Roderic Leigh and Paul Zonderland—who have all helped me out in different ways. I appreciate also the help of my friend Kees van Kooten, who joined me enthusiastically with essential equipment at a crucial time in my researches, and of Jim and Nel Mailer who helped me with a bed and transport in London.

My understanding of Vincent van Gogh's life has evolved from sources as diverse as Charlie Parker and the effect that nature can have on my feelings. But there are five books about Vincent, which, for different reasons, have given me much food for thought. They are Marc Edo Tralbaut's *Vincent van Gogh*, Humberto Nagera's *Vincent van Gogh, a Psychological Study*, *Stranger on the Earth* by Albert J. Lubin, Bruce Bernard's *Vincent, by himself*, and *Lotgenoten, the lives of Vincent and Theo van Gogh* by Jan Hulsker. I should also like to thank New York Graphic Society Books, Little, Brown and Company, Boston, for permission to reproduce extracts from *The Complete Letters of Vincent van Gogh*.

Preface

Travelling and the lives of artists have always played a central role in my writing career. My early profiles of Rembrandt van Rijn and Piet Mondrian involved as much time on the road as among reference books. In the 1970s, however, I was given an assignment that took me farther and deeper into my subject and myself than I had ever ventured before. It happened at a time when I was absorbed in the writings of Tom Wolfe, Gay Talese, Hunter S. Thompson, Truman Capote, Charles Dickens and other writers for whom realism lay at the root of emotional involvement, in the most powerful prose, whether fiction or non-fiction.

I was asked by my editor on the magazine *Holland Herald* to write a feature article on the painter Vincent van Gogh. Its publication was to coincide with the opening of the Van Gogh Museum in Amsterdam, the nucleus of which was the collection of hundreds of paintings and drawings sold to the Dutch government by the engineer Dr Vincent van Gogh, the painter's nephew and son of Vincent's brother, Theo. In 1890 he was the baby for whom Vincent painted a romantic picture of an almond tree in blossom against a baby-blue sky.

I embarked on a journey that led me, often unintentionally, into some of the secret sources of Vincent van Gogh's misery, a journey that was to extend far beyond the boundaries of the original magazine article. I tracked down people all over Europe who had some kind of connection with the painter—from an old miller in the south of Holland to a doctor in Antwerp and the descendants of Vincent's first love in London. My quest demanded hours of tedious telephone calls, long car and train journeys and sleepless nights, but it brought fascinating glimpses into the lives of people who had no idea that they were in any way linked to the painter. I became involved in some difficult interviews concerning the suppression of information about Van Gogh and his brother Theo, discovered controversial claims by illegitimate children and even found myself breaking into a mental hospital in the cause of photographic truth.

I found myself totally absorbed in the life of a man whose footsteps were dogged by unhappiness, who failed repeatedly to establish lasting relationships with women, but who succeeded in channelling his repeated lapses into depression, first into religion and then into art, expressing it in the most sublime words and images. For in both his letters and his art, Vincent's personality leaps off the page or canvas in an amazing symbiosis of nature and humanity.

The pattern of the book has been instinctive. Whether I am following in the footsteps of Van Gogh in England, of Darwin in the Galápagos Islands or of Flaubert in Egypt, I follow my nose: a journey becomes an adventure, leading me along constantly diverging paths to new and unexpected sidelights on my quarry. I could not possibly categorise this book. Paraphrasing Groucho Marx, I would never be a member of a movement that would have me as a member, anyway.

I wrote the story in the way I did because of the way I am, and I hope that some of the enthusiasm and excitement I experienced in my quest will be shared by the reader.

Ken Wilkie
September 1989

1 Go

On an icy morning in January 1972, I found myself lying face up in the middle of a narrow canalside road, wedged between my bicycle frame and the legs of an American tourist.

I had been pedalling sleepily to work. He had run out from behind a tree.

'I'm sorry,' we said simultaneously, having cursed each other inwardly for a second. I cracked a feeble joke, trying to make light of the slapstick situation. As we disentangled—slowly, and with great difficulty—he spoke: 'I'm looking for the Van Go Museum. Can you tell me if I'm near it?'

'The what museum?' I thought fuzzily of Go . . . Stop . . . green light . . . red light . . . red light district . . . red . . . blood! There was blood trickling from his nose into little red icicles in his moustache. Had he damaged his head? Did he mean the Transport Museum?

He repeated: 'You know, Van Go—the guy who cut his ear off. The painter.' There was a note of impatience in his voice. Then it dawned on me. The problem was one of pronunciation.

'Oh, sorry . . . you mean Vincent van Gogh?' ('G' in Dutch is pronounced like 'ch' in the Scottish 'loch'.)

'Yeah, that's him. You've got it.' The American had forgotten all about the accident. He looked amiable when he smiled. After all, it was early in the morning, when most tempers are easily frayed and many people would have taken exception to being bowled over by a hairy Highlander pedalling at full pelt.

'Are you sure you're all right?' I asked. I felt it was about time one of us said that. 'You have a nasty bump on your head.'

11

'I'm fine. The bump? That's my nose . . .' We laughed as car tooters pierced the morning air. In a manner reminiscent of Laurel and Hardy we were holding up traffic.

'And you?' he asked as we shuffled over to the side of the road.

'It's woken me up,' I replied. 'I've learnt to live with the unexpected in Amsterdam. It's around most corners. A morning's not the same without a multiple fracture.'

Now that we were standing at the clear side of the road I got my first good look at the man. He was tall and lean, dressed in neat blue jeans and turtleneck sweater. Nothing unusual apart from the scarlet stalactites in his moustache. That, and a strange look in his eyes. As we chatted, I realised what it was: when he talked about Van Gogh, he acquired a look of mild-mannered fanaticism. He told me that he studied psychiatry and painted in his spare time, and had come to Amsterdam primarily to see the Van Gogh Museum.

I hated to disappoint him, but had to inform him that all he would see of the Van Gogh Museum at this stage was its foundations. Van Gogh's paintings were still being housed in the Stedelijk (Municipal) Museum next door in Museumplein. This didn't matter, he said. As long as he could see some paintings. He was only interested in the paintings.

As I would be passing through Museumplein on my way to work, I offered him a lift on my bike. With a look of subdued terror in his eyes, he said he would prefer to walk. I told him how to get there and we said goodbye.

I never forgot that look of fanaticism when he talked about Van Gogh. I would encounter it again and again among people who in some way related to this painter. It was a look that Van Gogh himself would easily have recognised. As I cycled on, I contemplated the power of this painter. That incident had kindled my curiosity.

By the time the spring crocuses were out in Museumplein, the Van Gogh Museum had really begun to take shape. The massive concrete cubish structure rising above the trees had been designed by Gerrit Rietveld, the 'De Stijl' architect, shortly before he died. Its stern angularity reminded me more of a monument to Piet Mondrian than the building destined to house over 600 works by a passionate post impressionist.

As spring was giving way to summer, the name Vincent van Gogh appeared on the museum's façade in large white letters. I became used to seeing his name up there in concrete. It served as a reminder of how little I knew about him.

A few years before, when I was living in a cottage in the Scottish Highlands, a friend had given me a copy of Vincent's letters to his brother Theo. I remembered being struck by their human insight, clarity of expression and intensity of feeling. Later, when cycling through Provence, Vincent's descriptions of the landscape echoed in my mind. But that was all—and here I was living in his native country, cycling every morning past his name in concrete.

The museum was to open officially in March the following year. A story about the life of Van Gogh to coincide with the opening seemed appropriate for *Holland Herald*. I mentioned the idea to my editor, Vernon Leonard, who gave his approval. In our discussions of what form the article should take, he suggested that I try following in Van Gogh's footsteps—visit the places where he had lived—and see what I found. The approach sounded right, being essentially similar to the way I had done an article a few months before on the painter Piet Mondrian. I was not a complete stranger to articles on painters. In the course of my research on Mondrian I had found one of his old flames in Amsterdam—my landlady.

For the Van Gogh assignment Vernon gave me 1,500 guilders (about £375) and three weeks for research. This sum was based on the price of a rail ticket: Amsterdam—Eindhoven—Nuenen—Eindhoven—Tilburg—Breda—Antwerp—Brussels—Ostend—Dover—Calais—Mons—Paris—Arles—Paris—Amsterdam (450 guilders), plus 75 guilders a day for the last two weeks. No specific goal. No detailed briefing. Just notebook and camera.

Even if the trains were running on schedule, I reckoned that most of my two weeks could be spent on trains and in railway stations. In his 37 years, Van Gogh lived in 18 different places in Holland, England, Belgium, and France. I soon realised that, taking in travel time, I couldn't go everywhere. I had to budget my time carefully. Poring over maps of Europe, I decided that train travel would be too inflexible, so I would take my car. But even then it would be impossible to cover every place where Van Gogh had lived.

First I wanted to meet the people who were involved with the museum. In 1972 the Van Gogh family archives were being temporarily housed in a little office in Honthorststraat, a side street off Museumplein. I went round there one morning and introduced myself, and received a very warm reception from the people who were running it: Lily Couvée-Jampoller, Loedje van Leeuwen and museum director Emile Meijer. Their dream was to make the Van Gogh Museum a total, living concept: not only a museum to exhibit the largest collection of Van Gogh's work, and a major study centre for students and scholars, but also a place where people could walk in off the street, pick up a brush and start painting.

Everyone I talked to there was interested in my assignment, and several people went out of their way to be helpful.

Lily Couvée-Jampoller lent me a copy of the definitive study of Vincent's life and work by Dr Marc Edo Tralbaut. 'Tralbaut spends a lot of his time in the south of France,' she said. 'He has a house in Maussane, near Arles. I'll give you his address. And when you're in London you may be interested in contacting Paul Chalcroft. He's a postman who came to visit us last year. In his spare time he paints and is totally inspired by Van Gogh. He's also been doing some research into Vincent's life in London.' I made a note of Chalcroft's name.

Lily then showed me to the archives, where I had plenty of background reading to do. I was confronted by shelves of books on Van Gogh: psychological studies, rows of critical works, potted biographies. My initial reaction was bewilderment. I could spend my three weeks reading and never leave Amsterdam. And besides, with Van Gogh's life apparently so well researched, I would never come up with anything interesting, let alone original. But as I leafed through volume after volume, I realised there was more to be done than I had anticipated. Parts of the painter's life seemed to be only superficially charted. His years in Paris, London and Belgium had been overshadowed by his latter days in Arles.

I made notes: Who was landlady's daughter London? Rejected him. Turned him towards religion. Descendants? Photos? Paris—Few letters. More on V living with Theo and Andries Bonger.

I was downing my fourth cup of coffee and looking at a self-portrait of Van Gogh when the door creaked open. I looked up and did a double-take. Standing in the doorway was an elderly white-haired man. He wore a neat dark suit and a striped bow-tie. He looked remarkably like the face on the page in front of me.

'Van Gogh,' he said, extending his hand in my direction. Is this a password? I wondered. Then I remembered the Dutch custom of introducing yourself by announcing your name as you shake hands. I grabbed his hand and blurted out, 'Wilkie.'

Lily was standing nearby and noticed the look of bewilderment on my face. Hurrying over, she introduced me to the man who was Vincent van

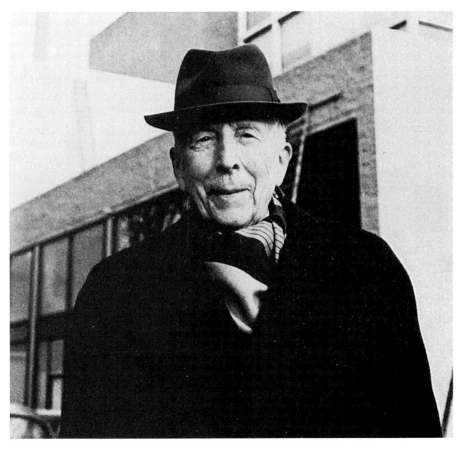

Theo's son, Dr Vincent van Gogh, 'the Engineer', in 1973. *Photo: the author*

Gogh's namesake nephew, Dr Vincent Willem van Gogh. With his high forehead and Roman nose, Dr Van Gogh—or 'the Engineer' as everyone at the museum referred to him—looked more like his uncle Vincent than his father Theo, Vincent's devoted brother who inherited so many of Vincent's paintings and drawings. The Engineer had been only a year old when Vincent held him in his arms, a couple of months before the painter died of a bullet wound in July 1890.

Now, 83 years old, he was standing next to me. He seemed willing to talk, so I took the opportunity to ask him how it had felt to grow up with 200 paintings and 400 drawings by his uncle Vincent. We sat down facing each other and he replied in a business-like manner: 'Our house was stacked full of them—under beds, on top of wardrobes, under the bath, and, of course, on the walls. My father kept them all. Although he couldn't sell any when Vincent was alive, he was convinced that one day his brother would be to art what Beethoven was to music. When my father died (only six months after Vincent), the collection was passed on to my mother, Johanna van Gogh-Bonger, and then down to me.'

Bonger . . . I had just read that name. I circled it in my notebook.

The collection remained the personal property of Dr Van Gogh until 1962 when, at the suggestion of the Dutch government, a foundation was set up in Amsterdam with Dr Van Gogh as president. The State subsidised the foundation to buy the collection for 5,500,000 dollars while providing funds to safeguard the Engineer's descendants. The government also pledged to erect a special building for the collection in Amsterdam's Museumplein. This was the Van Gogh Museum.

Dr Van Gogh had retired as a consultant engineer in 1966, and lived in a thatched mansion in Laren, a village 15 miles east of Amsterdam. I asked him if being Vincent's nephew had affected his personal life.

'Not in the slightest. In my work I have had to deal mostly with industrialists who are not usually interested in painting. But you know, what happened in Vincent's life happens to us all in a lesser degree. Part of the reason for his popularity today is that others recognise things in themselves that happened to him. You're never the same person after reading his letters. He was so many-sided.'

Later, in the course of my research, I would be talking to Dr Van Gogh again about some family matters that had remained shielded from the world. Now I picked up on the name 'Bonger'. The Engineer's mother was Johanna van Gogh-Bonger. Bonger was the name of a man with whom Vincent and Theo had lived in Paris. I asked the Engineer about this relatively obscure episode.

'Vincent's life in Paris . . . I understand that not much is known about it?'

'True,' replied the Engineer. 'You see, he was living most of the time with Theo then and consequently didn't write so many letters.'

'You mentioned the name Bonger. That was your mother's own name, wasn't it?'

'Yes.'

'Was she related to the Andries Bonger who lived with Vincent and Theo in Paris in 1886?'

'Yes, my mother was Andries Bonger's sister.'

'Is Bonger dead?'

'Yes.'

'Did he marry?'

'Yes, twice.'

'Is either of his wives still living?'

'His second wife, Françoise.'

'Do you know where? Would she be willing to see me?'

'Yes, she lives in Almen, in the east of the country, and I'm sure she'd be willing to talk to you. But I doubt if she would know very much about the Paris period. That took place before she knew Andries.'

I decided to phone her immediately. Even if it was a long shot, it was a start, and surely Bonger had told his wife something about his life in Paris.

Lily showed me a room where I could find the telephone number and talk in private. The directory for Almen listed Françoise Bonger, Baroness van der Borch van Verwolde. Quite a mouthful.

I dialled the number and a soft voice answered the telephone, identifying itself as the Baroness. I explained why I wanted to talk to her.

'Well, you may or may not be interested in my memories,' she replied. But she invited me to her home the following day.

I was full of anticipation as I put down the phone. Here was a woman whose husband had actually known Van Gogh, lived with him. A few

17

moments before I had talked with a man who, as a baby, had been held in the painter's arms. I hadn't expected to find people whose lives were touched (even marginally) by Van Gogh. These people made him seem a little less remote. In their different ways, they shared a living link with him. The possibility that there were others like them made me decide to stop trying to absorb the mountains of literature and concentrate on people. I thanked everyone at the Van Gogh Museum-to-be for their kindness and help.

'I'll be taking photographs as I go,' I told the director, Emile Meijer, 'but can I use photos from your archives to illustrate the article, too?'

'Of course,' he replied. 'But you never know what you'll come back with, do you?'

'That's true,' I said, fully expecting to return with little except eyes like crumpled road maps.

Outside I stopped to watch some workmen assembling a staircase. I admired the strict logic with which they did their work: section by section, piece by piece. Hoping that I might learn something from their example, I tried to collect my thoughts. I still lacked a definite goal, but I had a beginning. Vincent left Holland for the last time in 1884, so any person alive who knew him could only have been a child then, and nearly a centenarian in 1972. It was a long shot, but worth trying. The idea had a strange logic about it.

Vincent's last Dutch days were spent in Nuenen in the south of the country, at that time a weaving village where his father was the local minister. I remembered reading in Tralbaut's book that there were a few little boys who collected birds' nests for Vincent and watched him paint. Back in the 1930s, one of them, Piet van Hoorn, a miller who lived at Opwetten, near Nuenen, had talked to a journalist about the experience. Could Van Hoorn still be alive? If so, he would be well into his nineties, or even older.

Back at the *Holland Herald* office, I went to the telephone directory again—for the Nuenen area this time. There was one Van Hoorn listed, and Laura Kelder, editorial assistant, made the call for me. Laura explained to the woman who answered what I was doing, then turned to me: 'Ken, she says she is Piet van Hoorn's niece and that Piet is still alive. He's 98.'

'Ask her if he remembers Vincent van Gogh,' I said.

'Yes,' said Laura. 'She says that although he is very old he's still very active and there's nothing wrong with his memory.'

'Would he be willing to talk to me tomorrow?' Yes. We arranged a time.

I left Amsterdam just before dawn the next day, September 13th. By the time the sun came up, I was in the countryside. The sky was cloudless, casting long shadows over the dewy fields.

I had planned to make a detour on my way to Nuenen and briefly visit the village of Zundert, where Vincent was born. It took just under two hours to reach Zundert, a small parish south of Amsterdam and about five miles from the Belgian border in the province of North Brabant. The gaunt house where Vincent was born stands directly opposite the old town hall in the village square. I walked the short distance from the manse to the churchyard—the route Vincent must have followed every Sunday as a child.

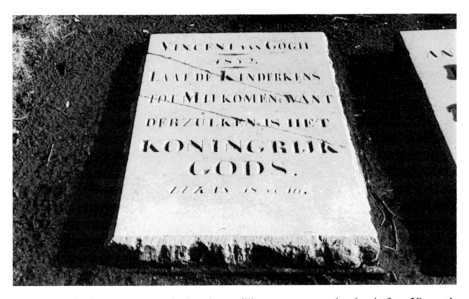

The grave of Vincent's namesake brother, stillborn a year to the day before Vincent's birth. *Vincent van Gogh Foundation/National Museum Vincent van Gogh, Amsterdam*

19

Near the graveyard gate I stumbled on a little gravestone, much smaller than the rest. Inscribed on it was the name *Vincent van Gogh*. This was the Van Gogh family's first child, who was stillborn on March 30, 1852. Their second, whom they also called Vincent, was born a year—to the day—after his baby brother.

Here I was, at the beginning of my journey, beside a forgotten gravestone, already contemplating life and death. What a profound effect it must have had on Vincent every Sunday, as he passed that tombstone with his name engraved on it. A constant confrontation with the idea of death.

When he revisited this cemetery in 1877, at the age of 24, Vincent described the sunrise he witnessed there as 'reminiscent of the Resurrection'. It made me think that the initial grief suffered by Vincent's mother following the death of Vincent I must have persisted as a state of melancholy into the early years of Vincent II.

The warmth and intimacy of a happy mother's loving care certainly appear to have been absent from Vincent II's childhood. He was described as introverted, self-willed, intelligent, difficult, melancholy, not like other children, extraordinarily serious. Deprived of the love his mother could not give him, the foundation for his later depressive tendencies may have been laid at that time.

In simple terms, death became synonymous with being loved and cherished, while being alive was identified with rejection. Did the contrasting themes in his art—sorrow and joy, isolation and togetherness, death and rebirth, darkness and light, earth and heaven—have their roots in the buried memory of his childhood?

As Albert and Barbara Cain pointed out in a relevant article, 'On Replacing a Child', in the *Journal of the American Academy of Child Psychiatry*, people who have been reared as replacements for a dead child tend, like Vincent, to be preoccupied with death, illness and self-mutilation. Like Vincent, too, they tend to believe that they will die at an early age and have an obsessive interest in places of burial. Cemeteries were the goal of many of Vincent's walks, and from his letters we see that he often chose graveyards as rendezvous of reunion. He seemed to regard graveyards not as repositories for decaying corpses but as beautiful places where living things grow out of the ground.

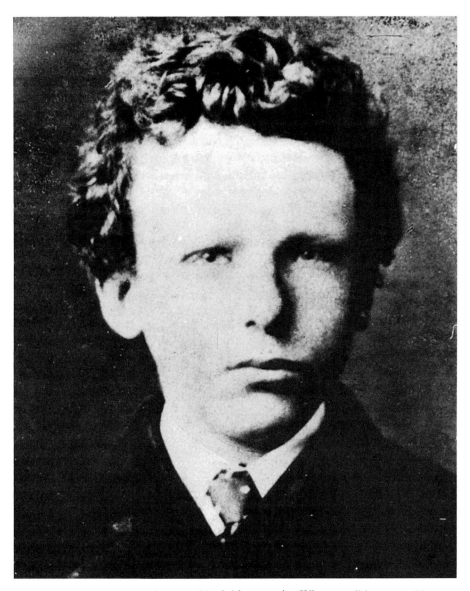

Vincent aged 13. In 1958 Picasso said of this portrait: 'What a striking resemblance to the young Rimbaud, especially the keen and penetrating eyes.' *Vincent van Gogh Foundation/National Museum Vincent van Gogh, Amsterdam*

Vincent's unhappy alliances with women continued throughout his life and they often ended in disaster. Were the seeds of his malaise before me at this grave of his stillborn namesake? I wondered who his first love had been. This must surely have had a crucial effect on him. Had he ever experienced human warmth and affection from a woman? From childhood, was he in the grip of irreversible alienation?

As I walked past the willows of the graveyard, a wave of sadness mingled with the anticipation I felt at the start of my journey. In spite of the bizarre adventures to come, it was a sadness that would deepen as I came closer to the person whom fate had led me to follow.

Conceived in grief, was Vincent II a melancholy man in the eyes of a boy who knew him? I set off for Nuenen to find out.

The country roads from Zundert to Nuenen are lined with poplar trees, the regular patterns broken every so often by a farmstead. I saw a woman at a farmhouse door wearing a poffer, the traditional white head-dress of North Brabant, just like the women in Van Gogh's *Potato Eaters*. Occasionally, in the fields near Nuenen where Vincent had roamed with his canvas and paints, I saw farm workers ploughing or stooping over the furrows—reincarnations of the studies Van Gogh made of peasants in this area 100 years before.

Entering Nuenen, I recognised, from one of his paintings, the little hexagonal church surrounded by a clump of trees where his father had preached. Down the road was the manse where the Van Gogh family had lived, a large detached house, covered in ivy, exuding an atmosphere of mysterious calm. I stopped at the door, remembering that this was the spot where Vincent's father was stricken with a fatal heart attack after a walk in the country.

I knocked on the door and it was answered by a fresh-faced man in his late thirties. I introduced myself and he told me he was the new parish minister, the Reverend Bartlema. He showed me the wash-house at the back of the manse, where Vincent used to paint before he left the household. The back garden which he had drawn and painted had been shortened, but some trees were still there.

Bartlema told me how to reach the watermill at Opwetten, on the outskirts of Nuenen. The old mill remains almost exactly as it was in 1884 when Vincent painted it. Separated from the mill by a line of flat-topped trees is the miller's house, an eighteenth-century building, again with ivy clinging to the brickwork.

Piet's niece, a sturdy countrywoman in her fifties, opened the door. She was expecting me.

'Piet's over at the mill. Although we don't use it for cutting wood or grinding corn any more, Piet likes to keep it in working order. He says you never know when there'll be a power cut.'

We walked over to the sluice. The old man was leaning on the fence, looking thoughtfully down at the mill-pond below. It was Tuesday, but he was wearing his Sunday best—a dark striped suit, black hob-nail boots, collar, tie and cloth cap. A gold watch-chain dangled from the breast pocket of his waistcoat. As we approached he took out his watch to check the time. A smile crossed his face.

'Five minutes late. Not that five minutes either way makes much difference at my age.' There was a glint in his keen old eyes. 'It's just a habit I have.'

He told me he would be 99 in a couple of months. It was hard to believe that on this, the first day on the road, I was probably talking to the last man alive who had talked with Vincent van Gogh. And here he was talking to me in the same village, nearly 90 years on. I asked him about his life.

'I've never strayed far from Opwetten,' he said. 'I stopped working the mill here 17 years ago, when I was a young man of 82, so I have certainly had time enough to recall the people I have known.'

'When did you first meet Vincent?'

'Oh yes, my old friend Vincent. Well, nobody could forget him. I was ten. But I remember it like yesterday, seeing that red-bearded man with the paints. The first time I saw him he was sitting in the road over there. It was a sunny afternoon like today.'

'How did he look?'

'He was short and squarely-built. We called him *het schildermanneke* (the little painter). He was wearing a straw hat and a kind of farmer's smock. Blue. He had a pipe in his mouth all the time. I hadn't seen anyone like him before. My schoolmates and I used to gather round and ask him questions, but he only gave short abrupt answers.'

Piet's path often crossed Vincent's in the fields around Nuenen.

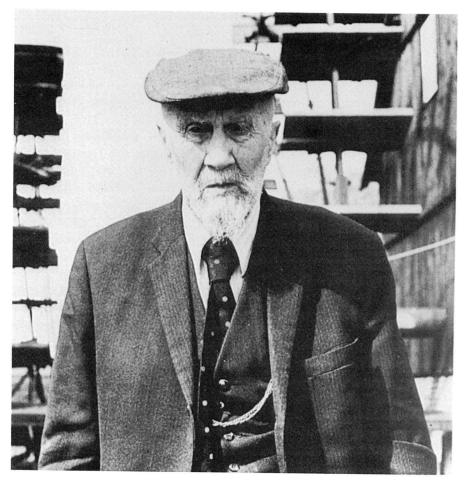

Piet van Hoorn in 1972. At 98 he was still living at his birthplace, the watermill at Opwetten, painted by Vincent. *Photo: the author*

'I used to see him on his knees, holding his hands up to his eyes.' Piet crouched, imitating the painter. 'Then he would sway from side to side, tilting his head from one side to the other. Some people thought he was mad. I can understand why.'

He showed me around the mill, explaining in detail how, until recently, the corn had been ground by water power. After I had taken some photographs, we walked over to the house, where we sat in the dim light of the big Dutch kitchen. Against one of the tiled walls stood an old grandfather clock. In this timeless atmosphere, its slow tick was the only sound. Piet sat in a farmhouse chair by the stove. Every so often he took out his watch and checked the time against the grandfather clock. He looked out of the window towards the cornfields and pointed in their direction.

'One day I met Vincent in that field over there. He asked me if I could find the nest of a golden oriole for him and bring it to where he was living in Nuenen.' The golden oriole was not a common bird, but Piet knew the nesting places and found one high up in an oak tree.

'The nest was wedged in a fork of two branches, so I took the nest and branches together to Vincent's studio. He told me he lived in the house of Schafrath, the caretaker of the Roman Catholic church at Nuenen. When I reached it, the door was open so I walked in. Vincent was painting and didn't notice me. "I found your nest, Mr Van Gogh," I said. But he didn't hear me, or if he did, he paid no attention. The studio was what you might expect. Ashes were piled up around the stove. Shelves and cupboards were full of birds' nests and plants that he had probably picked while out on his rambles. I remember a spinning wheel too and all sorts of farming implements. Some dry bread and cheese lay on the wooden table.

'Vincent was a strange sight. He was dressed only in his long woollen underwear but was wearing his straw hat and smoking his pipe. He was painting trees. He walked three paces one way and then three paces the other. I had never seen anyone like him. "Mr Van Gogh," I said, a bit louder. But he didn't hear. He stood some distance from the easel with his hands folded over his chest—he often did that—and stared at the painting for a long time. Suddenly he would leap up as if to attack the canvas, paint two or three strokes quickly, then scramble back to his chair, narrow his eyes, wipe his forehead and rub his hands. Not until he finally seemed satisfied with the results did he look round and notice me standing there. When he saw the nest and branches, his eyes grew large. He put down his palette and took the pipe out of his mouth and exclaimed: "Well done, lad!"'

Piet filled his own pipe, then demonstrated how Vincent looked at the nest from all angles. 'He didn't give me more than 50 cents for a nest, but that was a lot in those days for a boy of ten.'

'What did you think about Vincent?'

'Well, they said in the village that he was mad, but he didn't give me that impression. He only appeared odd because his way of life was different from other people's.'

Piet refilled his pipe and went on to tell me that a series of events at Nuenen, including the attempted suicide of Vincent's neighbour Margot Begemann (one of the few girls who seem to have fallen in love with the painter), his father's death, and unfounded rumours that Vincent had fathered the baby of Gordina de Groot, the girl featured in *The Potato Eaters*, made him leave the village. The accusation concerning the child was denied by Vincent in a letter to his sister Wilhelmien, and Gordina de Groot, who died in 1927, claimed the father of her child, Cornelis, was a nephew.

Before Vincent left Nuenen, he told Schafrath, the verger from whom he rented a studio, that he would only be away for a fortnight. But he never returned and left behind all his belongings except for a few paintings he had sent earlier to Theo.

Vincent's mother, from whom he felt estranged, ordered some of her son's work to be burned, and bundled another huge pile of pictures off to a carpenter in Breda, called Couvreur. Consequently, a vast quantity of canvases and studies were consumed by a paper mill, while hundreds of drawings and sketches were stacked on Couvreur's pedlar's cart and sold in the local market for five or ten Dutch cents each.

'Poor Vincent,' sighed Piet. 'I remember feeling very sad when I heard he wasn't coming back.'

The old man was getting tired. There were long pauses between his sentences, and his voice sounded a little hoarse. But as I sat there in the failing light of his parlour, I marvelled that this man was recalling experiences he had had nearly 90 years before. And as I was leaving it occurred to me that I was getting a glimpse into Van Gogh's life just before it passed beyond the reach of human memory.

I never saw Piet again. He died on November 25, 1974, a week before his 101st birthday.

I walked across the fields towards a clump of trees that Piet said

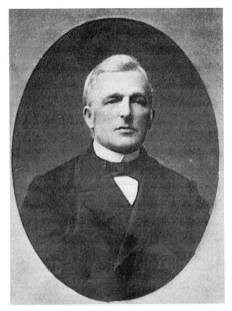 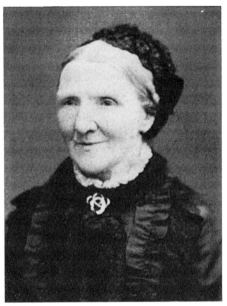

(*Left*) Vincent's father, Pastor Theodorus van Gogh (1822–1885), a minister of the Dutch Reformed Church. (*Right*) Vincent's mother, Anna Cornelia Carbentus (1819–1907). She painted flowers and plants. Several of her sisters married members of the Van Gogh family. *Vincent van Gogh Foundation/National Museum Vincent van Gogh, Amsterdam*

concealed a small graveyard overgrown with moss and ivy. Vincent's father was buried there. The sun was sinking in the sky and cast a sheen of gold over the ripe heads of corn swaying in the warm breeze.

In the graveyard I cleared away the earth and foliage to photograph Vincent's father's neglected tombstone. A forgotten life and a forgotten death. A pattern had already begun to form in the journey. Would every Van Gogh gravestone lead me to a living link with the painter? I hoped not—there were a lot of dead Van Goghs and I had a deadline.

It was a warm, balmy night, and I slept out in my old goose-feather sleeping bag. I awoke with the birds just before dawn and set out for Almen at sunrise.

Almen lies in the Gelderse Achterhoek, an eastern enclave of the

Netherlands. Here the unrelenting flatness of the reclaimed west part of the country gives way to more natural wild woodland.

The Baroness had told me on the phone that anyone in the village would be able to tell me how to get to her home. I took her advice and asked the first person I saw.

'Could you tell me how to get to the home of Françoise Bonger, Baroness van der Borch van Verwolde, please?'

'Who?' The woman looked me up and down suspiciously. I repeated the question.

'Never heard of her. There's a butcher called Bonger down the street, ask him.'

Butcher Bonger was no relation to Baroness Bonger, but he did tell me where to find her.

The Baroness lived in an elegant eighteenth-century manor house at the end of a winding, wooded drive. Sheep were grazing on her front lawn which tapered away into an apple orchard. A river ran through the bottom of the valley beyond. The Baroness was standing in the porch, a slender, elegant lady dressed in black-and-white lace. She was feeding the guinea fowl, who seemed to prefer to peck at the sunflowers outside the house. Once again I was reminded of Van Gogh, who loved these flowers so much.

She extended her hand in an aristocratic manner. I didn't know whether to kiss it or shake it, but decided on the latter. She showed me into the drawing room, where tea was served by her maidservant. The walls were covered with pictures by artists such as Odilon Redon and Emile Bernard, a close friend of Vincent in Paris. The Baroness saw me looking at them.

'Yes, there are some very beautiful paintings here,' she said. 'They were mostly given to Andries, my husband, in Paris. He knew so many painters there.'

'He knew Van Gogh, too?' I asked, hoping she would elaborate.

'Well, he knew Vincent better than any of the other painters,' she said. 'As you know, they lived together for a while. Vincent gave Andries that self-portrait with the grey hat. I'm sure you know it. It's now part of the collection in the Van Gogh Museum. Actually, Andries told me it was Theo's hat, not Vincent's. Apparently Vincent used to wear out all his brother's clothes.'

It didn't take me long to realise that the 86-year-old Baroness had a memory as vivid as Piet van Hoorn for the stories her husband had told her about his time with Vincent in Paris—two years after Piet knew him in Holland.

Vincent's Paris period, as Dr Van Gogh had said, remained a blank largely because Theo and Vincent were living together, so they didn't write the letters which are a primary source of information. Although Vincent completed at least 200 paintings and 50 drawings, only seven letters have been preserved from his two years in the French capital. But how much had Andries Bonger told his wife?

Seated by the window in her Victorian basket chair, Baroness Bonger needed little prompting as she recalled her late husband's stories about the bizarre summer he spent in Paris with the Van Gogh brothers.

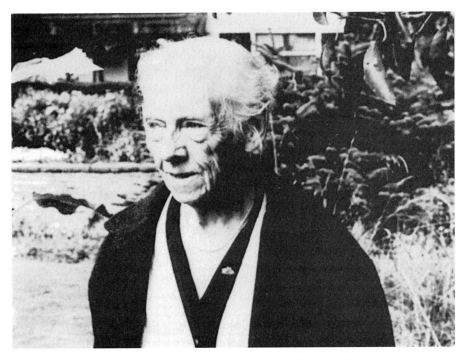

Françoise Bonger, Baroness van der Borch van Verwolde, aged 81. *Photo: the author*

'Andries was an insurance agent. He met Vincent for the first time in Nuenen, where you've just come from. Andries said that Vincent didn't take any part in family life and struck Andries as being decidedly odd. His face was tense, whereas Theo's was calm.

'They met again in Paris a couple of years later. It was the summer of 1886 and Vincent was studying at Cormon's studio in Montmartre, I believe. Vincent had moved into Theo's flat at rue Lepic, and Theo—he was having a terrible time coping with Vincent—asked Andries to come and live there also. Which he did.

'Neither Vincent nor Andries had much money, so they jointly bought the books they wanted to read. Here is one of them,' said the Baroness, pointing to a volume in the bookcase. 'It is Zola's *L'Oeuvre*. It deals with the failure of an Impressionist painter who loses his mind and commits suicide. Andries said that he and Vincent read it together.'

'Did your husband describe the apartment in rue Lepic to you?'

'Oh yes, I remember he said the flat was quite large by Paris standards. But after Vincent moved in, it began to look more like a paint shop than an apartment. Andries said that more than once he stepped out of bed in the morning into pots of colours that Vincent had left lying around. There was a woman living with them too.'

'Did Theo and Vincent get along well together?'

'Theo was ill and Andries said that Vincent was totally inconsiderate of his brother's condition. They were both suffering from bouts of nervous depression but Theo was much worse. Vincent would come home late after drinking all night in the Café Tambourin with Toulouse-Lautrec and others and then keep Theo awake by arguing with him in a very dogmatic way. According to Andries he could be very objectionable, and on one occasion in the Café Tambourin someone hit him over the head with one of his still lifes.'

'Do you know what illness the brothers were suffering from?'

'No. Andries never said. He did say that he used to look forward to the days when Vincent would wander off into the country with his easel. He would get peace then.

'Vincent did have a sense of humour apparently, for when he returned from the country in the evening, Andries said that he would tell hilarious stories about his experiences with the villagers who thought he was a madman. Andries and Theo would roar with laughter as Vincent imitated their reactions to him.

'But these happy moments did not last. Within minutes Andries and Vincent would be at each other's throats again. Vincent could never see anyone else's point of view, he said. When angry, he had an extraordinary way of pouring out sentences, in a wild mixture of Dutch, French and English—then glaring back over his shoulder and hissing through his teeth . . .'

'And Theo?' I enquired.

' "Poor Theo," Andries used to say. He hardly had any clothes left to wear in his gallery. Vincent used them all up and just left them lying around mixed up with canvases and brushes. On one occasion he used one of Theo's clean socks to dry his brushes. You can imagine the effect Vincent's old underwear would have on Theo's business clients when he brought them back to his home.'

I asked the Baroness about the relationship between the Van Gogh brothers and the woman who was Theo's mistress.

'Andries hardly talked at all about this to me except for mentioning once that Theo had a lot of problems with a woman. But I saw from Andries' letters after he died that he referred to this woman simply as "S". I don't know why they wanted to conceal her identity. In his letters to Andries and Vincent, Theo also referred to her as "S". Whoever she was, in his letters Andries described her as being rather highly strung, mentally unstable and also physically ill. Whether she was like that before she moved into rue Lepic or became that way after living with them, I really don't know.'

I asked the Baroness if she learned anything about the relationship between the brothers and the woman called 'S'. She poured another cup of tea and continued.

'It sounded rather bizarre. "S" was originally Theo's woman and I think they were living together when Vincent landed on Theo's doorstep in the spring of '86. I am sure this was why Theo kept trying to dissuade Vincent from coming to Paris at that time. What happened after Vincent moved in I never really found out. But whatever it was, it finally made Theo leave the house. In his letters Theo made it clear that he wanted either Vincent or the girl to leave the flat.

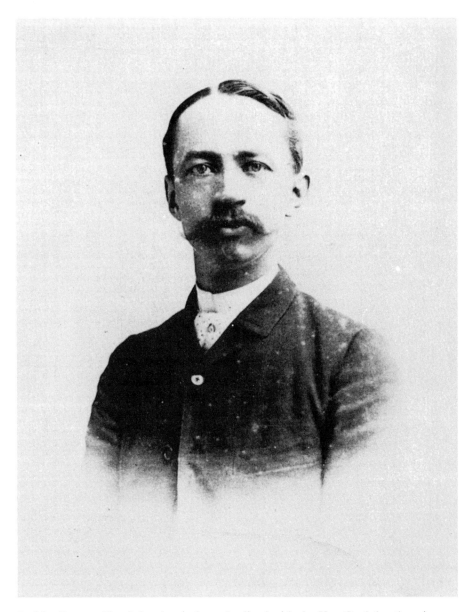

Andries Bonger, Theo's brother-in-law who lived with the Van Gogh brothers in Paris. *Vincent van Gogh Foundation/National Museum Vincent van Gogh, Amsterdam*

'Apparently Vincent didn't approve of Theo's match. Vincent said he was scared that "S" would commit suicide if Theo threatened to throw her out. But instead of offering to leave himself, he suggested to Theo that he take the girl off his brother's hands and marry her if necessary. Andries told both Vincent and Theo that he definitely did not think that was the best solution.'

'What was the outcome?' I asked the Baroness.

'I never found that out. The girl was never referred to again in any letters that have been published. Theo ultimately went back to Paris and Andries left rue Lepic. He said that when he asked the brothers later what had happened to her, the question was evaded by both Vincent and Theo.'

I made notes for Paris: Find Café Tambourin. Who was 'S'? What was Vincent's and Theo's illness?

The Baroness showed me round her garden, where I took some photographs of her. She said she enjoyed talking to me but didn't make a habit of dwelling in the past. She had never told anyone about it all before, mainly because no one had asked. Like Piet, time had nearly forgotten her.

Through two people I had spanned two years of Vincent's life. What a change seemed to have taken place in his character. Piet had seen him as kind and generous, Bonger as temperamental and inconsiderate. This sense of change deepened the mystery for me. Through Piet and the Baroness I had seen him at two different points in his life. As I drove west, I wondered how and why these changes had taken place. I was intensely curious to find out, but that would have to wait. First I wanted to investigate an earlier period in Vincent's life—the two years he spent in London, where he first fell in love.

Not much was known about his life in London. I hoped a visit there would reveal more—if I could find people connected to him. Could there be any living links across the North Sea? I wondered. I drove through the darkness to Zeebrugge in Belgium and took the boat-train to Harwich. Vincent had made the same trip a hundred years before.

2   The Maynard Connection

Vincent was 20 when he first crossed the North Sea to England. That was in 1873. For nearly four years he had been working as an apprentice art dealer with the firm of Goupil in The Hague and in Brussels. He had shown such promise—'Everyone liked to deal with Vincent,' said his boss, Tersteeg—that it had been decided to transfer him to the firm's London office.

Vincent resigned himself to the move but showed an undercurrent of sadness at having to live so far away from home.

Elisabeth Huberta, one of the painter's sisters, described him around this time. He was 'as broad as he was long, his back slightly bent, with the bad habit of letting the head hang; the red-blond hair cropped close was hidden under a straw hat; a strange face, not young; the forehead already full of line, the eyebrows on the large noble brow drawn together in deepest thought. The eyes, small and deep-set, were now blue, now green, according to the impressions of the moment . . .'

As a postscript in a letter to Theo, who was also an apprentice art dealer at this time, Vincent advised him to smoke a pipe. 'It's a good remedy for the depressions I have had recently.'

In London Vincent gave an impression of middle-class respectability. His salary was £90 a year which was much more than his father was earning as a minister in the Netherlands and he would occasionally send money home to Holland. He lodged with a family named Loyer in South London and would walk every morning over Westminster Bridge, past the Houses of Parliament, to the Goupil gallery in Southampton Street, off the Strand. These premises were occupied by Goupil until 1875, when they moved round the corner in Covent Garden to 25 Bedford Street, the Moss Bros. building, demolished in June 1989. He wore a top hat ('You

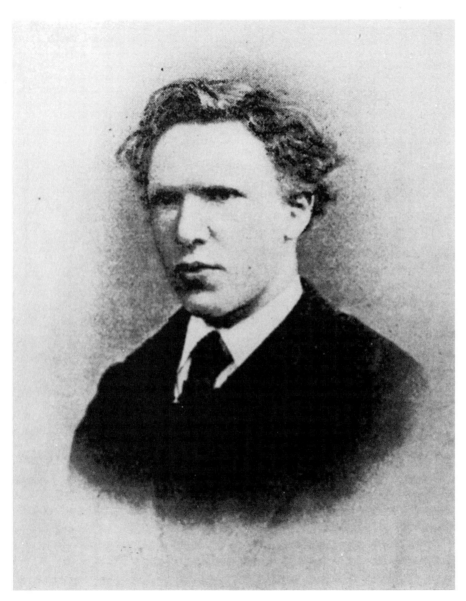

Vincent van Gogh, aged 18, two years before he went to work in London. *Vincent van Gogh Foundation/National Museum Vincent van Gogh, Amsterdam*

can't live in London without one,' he said), a stiff collar and carried a rolled umbrella. The walk took him three quarters of an hour, and occasionally he would stop to make a sketch of something that caught his eye. His mother wrote: 'Now and then Vincent sends home a little drawing from his house and the street and from the interior of his room so that we can imagine how it looks. It is so well drawn.' Theo's wife, Johanna, later described Vincent's stay with the Loyers as 'perhaps the happiest year in his life'.

Lonely and away from home, Vincent fell in love with his landlady's daughter. His feelings seemed to be intensified by the close relationship between the widowed Mrs Loyer and her daughter. 'I am happier than I have ever been,' he wrote to one of his sisters, 'I never saw or dreamed of anything like the love between her and her mother.'

These last two sentences suggested to me that Vincent was perceiving love in terms of family closeness, both in the form of his landlady Ursula Loyer and her daughter Eugénie, and in his intense wish to have them loved for him by his family. As Vincent's sister Elisabeth once noted, he was 'a stranger to his family'. And Vincent wrote: 'My youth was gloomy and cold and sterile . . .'

I could not find anywhere in Vincent's letters a naturally affectionate reference to his mother. During his early years he had been deprived of all the elements of mother-love. The deficiency in this relationship created an impairment which impeded the boy's development into a stable character. Indeed, he felt inferior, lonely, unloved and hypersensitive. The threat of not being loved caused him great anxiety, while rejection resulted in depression that continued into adulthood. Moreover, as Albert Lubin pointed out in one of the most perceptive character studies ever written about Vincent, *Stranger on the Earth*, 'the combination of low self-esteem and high expectation is most apt to produce adults who are highly susceptible to depressed states.'

Not a single drawing or painting from Vincent's adult years bears the family name. He signed his work 'Vincent', he said, because foreigners couldn't pronounce 'Van Gogh'. But he tended to associate the family name with hyprocrisy, narrow-mindedness, coldness and mercenary values. 'Are you a Van Gogh, too?' he once asked his brother. 'I have always looked upon you as Theo.'

It was only because of Theo's financial support that Vincent was able to devote his life to painting. But Theo was, in fact, much more than Vincent's mentor. He served as father, mother, mirror-image, family, audience, patient, and psychotherapist. He became Vincent's connection with the world of human beings.

Bearing all this in mind, it seemed to me essential to investigate the background to Vincent's first assertion of love. The girl, whom previous biographers had referred to as Ursula, rejected his advances and proposals of marriage, and turned him into a religious fanatic. His fanaticism set him on the path that would lead towards total devotion to art. Even seven years after her refusal, Vincent still could not erase from his mind the suffering he felt she had caused him.

I was determined to find out more about this relationship. I also wanted to find out whether the house he had lived in was still standing. Did its present occupants know he had lived there? There was plenty to do in London.

My only lead was Paul Chalcroft, the postman whose name had been given to me by Lily Couvée-Jampoller of the Van Gogh Museum. She had told me he had been doing research on the London period of Vincent's life.

I had lived in London myself for five years in the Sixties and knew the city well. I stayed with my old friends Jim and Nel Mailer at their home in Paddington.

Shortly after I arrived on September 17, I telephoned Chalcroft. It was a long and unexpectedly animated conversation. It revealed all of the man's warmth, enthusiasm and energy. Some of what he told me I already knew, but there were other things that made me want to investigate further. I arranged to meet him when he came off duty at Victoria sorting office.

I got to Victoria early and had to wait a few minutes. When Paul finally emerged from behind a pile of mailbags, I saw a man with a friendly face, penetrating eyes and a sensitive mouth. With his deep forehead, cropped hair and goatee beard, he had the ingenuous air of an English Rousseau. Sitting down on a pile of mailbags, we talked. Or rather, he talked. In ten minutes I had 20 pages of notes.

Paul's working life was no different from that of any other London postman. His shift at Victoria was from 6 a.m. to 2 p.m., and after work every day he cycled over the Thames to his home in Camberwell, south of the river. But after hours he became a dedicated and prolific painter, obsessed with Vincent van Gogh. Every day he transformed his kitchen table into an easel and painted for hours.

'I produce about 200 canvases a year,' he said, 'mostly copied from Van Gogh postcards.' He gave away most to friends and sold others for a few pounds each. And his fanaticism didn't stop with painting. During the long Post Office strike of 1971, he decided to use his spare time to find out as much as he could about the Loyer family, whom Vincent lived with when he was in London.

Like me, Chalcroft had noticed that none of the books mentioned Vincent's London address. He decided first of all to find out what it was, and thought he could do that by searching for the so-called Ursula Loyer.

Since Vincent was 20 in 1873, he assumed the girl would probably have been somewhere between 17 and 28, and had been born, therefore, between 1845 and 1857. Chalcroft went to the national archives in Somerset House and began looking through every birth certificate from 1845 onwards. His search was slow and painstaking: for days on end he would pore over roll after roll of microfilm. Not until he reached the files for 1854 did he discover the only Loyer born in that region of England—on April 10, 1854, a girl named Eugénie Loyer at 2 Somerset Place, Stockwell. The father was Jean-Baptiste Loyer, described as a professor of languages; the mother, Sarah Ursula Loyer.

'I was certain that this must be the girl, but although the age was right (she would have been 19 in 1873), the name was Eugénie and not Ursula, as the books on Van Gogh all said.'

Nevertheless, Eugénie's mother's second name was Ursula. Had historians muddled the names of mother and daughter? Had Vincent's mother confused the names? Or perhaps it was the landlady and not her daughter with whom Vincent had fallen in love.

Chalcroft knew that Eugénie had said she was secretly engaged when Vincent proposed to her in 1874, but he didn't know if she ever married. He went back to Somerset House to find out. This time it took him months of searching through microfilm records to find what he was looking for. The man she married—on her birthday, April 10, 1878, four years after she rejected Vincent—was Samuel Plowman, a 26-year-old engineer. The couple were married at Lambeth Parish Church, and their address was given as Hackford Road, Lambeth, South London. Chalcroft showed me a copy of the marriage certificate. He also showed me a birth certificate: six months after Eugénie married Samuel Plowman, she had a son, Frank Eugene, born October 18, 1878. It looked as if they had married because of Eugénie's pregnancy, which probably raised a few eyebrows behind the lace curtains of Lambeth.

Chalcroft had struck gold with this birth certificate, because now the address shown included house numbers as well as street names. The father's address was given as 17 Hackford Road and the baby was born at 87.

'I thought it strange at first,' said Paul. 'But then it occurred to me that Eugénie's mother could have lived at 87 and Eugénie returned there briefly to have her child.'

If this supposition was correct—and Mrs Loyer had lived at 87 Hackford Road in 1878—then Chalcroft might well have found the address he was looking for. But unless he could establish that she lived there in 1873, when Vincent boarded with her, then the whole thing would be so much conjecture.

Paul had to wait till January 2, 1972, before the final piece of the jigsaw fell into place. On this date detailed information became available of a census held 100 years earlier in 1871, two years before Vincent van Gogh moved to London. This would say exactly who was living at 87 Hackford Road.

'I went to the Public Record Office on the 1st of January and asked to see the census return for 87 Hackford Road,' he said. 'You can imagine I was feeling a bit anxious . . . These records were stored on microfilm, and when the relevant frame came into view I saw that there were only three occupants. Head of the household was Mrs Sarah Ursula Loyer, a widow aged 46; the other occupants were her daughter, Eugénie Loyer, aged 16, and a boarder named Eleanor Tapp.'

As far as Paul was concerned his search was over. He had satisfied his curiosity and that was enough. He didn't even make his discovery known to anyone but a few friends. This wasn't enough for me: I wanted to keep looking. With Paul's blessing I took up where he left off.

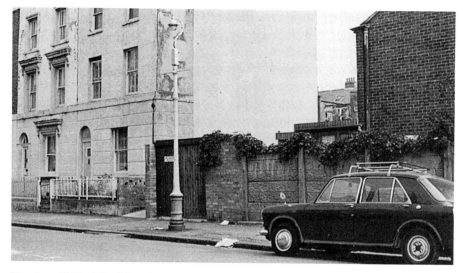

Number 87 Hackford Road, London, as it was in 1972. *Photo: the author*

Paul told me that the house at 87 Hackford Road was still standing. He had passed it several times but had never liked to knock at the door. I suggested we go along together and talk to the present occupants.

'What, right now?'

'If not now, when?' My boldness shocked him but he was ready to come with me.

The house at 87 Hackford Road is as anonymous as scores of other three-storey Georgian terraced houses in South London. It stands at the end of a row and appeared narrowly to have escaped demolition in the 1960s, when the old houses on one side had made way for a housing development. The name on the door was Smith. There was no one in.

As I was taking photographs of the house from the other side of the road, I could see neighbours peeking out from behind curtains. I couldn't resist asking a passer-by if he had heard of a painter called Vincent van Gogh who was said to have lived in the street.

'Van 'oo d'ye sy?'

'Van Gogh,' I repeated.

'Van Goff? Van Goff. Let me see now. A Dutchman, eh? No, mate. Van Nobody like that livin' 'ere. You sure he's Dutch, then? Not Pakistani?'

'No. This was 100 years ago,' I said. 'He was a Dutchman.'

'I'm not that bleedin' old. You from the police or somethin'?'

'No, I'm a journalist,' I replied.

'Oh, one of them,' he nodded. 'Best of luck, mate. Hope you find 'im. Bye bye.'

As Paul and I walked down Hackford Road, we spoke of a walk Vincent had made that ended in this same street. It had begun in Ramsgate, 70 miles away on the coast. He had come to see Eugénie Loyer at number 87 after her disastrous rejection of him. We picked out the trees and houses Vincent might have seen when he walked here 100 years before.

The next time we rang the doorbell, the door was opened by Mr Smith, a man in his forties. We introduced ourselves and Paul quickly came to the point of our visit.

'The painter Vincent van Gogh lived in this house.'

There was a brief pause, then Mr Smith exclaimed, 'Well I'll be blowed!' He was almost shaking with excitement, and it was a few moments before he invited us into the house. He introduced us to his wife Marjorie and son Mark, and immediately told them the news.

'Well I never,' said Marjorie. 'Vincent van Goff. I wonder which room he slept in. Our son Mark is an artist. He's involved in astrology, you know, and makes all his paintings in his room upstairs. When we came here, it was known as the lodger's room. My goodness, to think he lived here. Imagine, he'd have come down these stairs for his breakfast and sat here under this roof. Looked out of that window . . .'

Although the interior of 87 Hackford Road had been modernised, structurally the house had not altered significantly since it was built in 1824. The old brass light switches, immaculately polished, were still being used, but the Smiths assured me there were no traces around of Vincent or earlier occupants. Mrs Smith did mention that the original Victorian outside toilet was still in the garden closet. On my way into the garden to have a look, I trampled on and overturned the cat's litter tray on the kitchen floor. 'Don't worry,' said Mr Smith, 'I'm a sanitary engineer with Lambeth Borough Council. I'm used to it.'

The Smiths' cat had adopted the old toilet-seat lid as his territory and grudgingly sprang off as I approached to lift the lid. There it was. An object which had had a unique view of Vincent van Gogh. The porcelain was inscribed 'The Sirex. Improved Outlet. County Council Pattern'.

Since I was trying to keep the discovery of 87 Hackford Road secret for the moment, I asked them to keep it to themselves. They were happy to co-operate and liked the idea of being part of a secret, even if temporarily.

I took photographs of the house and of the Smiths together with Chalcroft outside, and then walked back with Paul to his home nearby. Over a cup of tea, he showed me another document, a copy of the death certificate of Frank Plowman, Eugénie's son. It gave me my best lead for finding descendants.

The death certificate told me that Frank Plowman had died in September 1966 at the age of 87, and was buried at Biggin Hill cemetery, south of London. But most interesting was the signature in the bottom right-hand corner. It was Kathleen E. Maynard, whom I assumed to be Frank Plowman's closest relative. Married daughter, perhaps. Did that 'E' stand for Eugénie? Biggin Hill, 1966. Perhaps Kathleen Maynard lived there? There was only one way to find out.

But it was already 6.30 p.m. I was still at Paul's house. I decided to save my next task—calling every Maynard in South London—till the next day.

I drove to The French House, in Dean Street, my local when I lived in Soho in the 1960s, and, over a champagne, courtesy of patron Gaston Berlemont, told my friends Jim and Nel everything I'd done that day. When I told them about my plan to call all the Maynards in South London, they looked at me a little strangely. They gently pointed out that there might be hundreds of them. It hadn't occurred to me, but I was determined anyway.

After dinner I combed the London telephone directory for Maynards before realising that Biggin Hill was outside the Greater London area. The telephone operator checked it for me and said there were over 20 registered in the Biggin Hill area, but no Kathleen E. That didn't worry me too much, as I expected that she would be listed under her husband's name anyway. Rather than ask an already harassed operator to give me all the names and numbers, I went to the Post Office the next day and copied down the numbers myself.

I spent that evening on the telephone upstairs in The French House, introducing myself into different Maynard homes. I tried to keep my story as simple as possible.

First Maynard on the list was Albert. Mrs Albert answered. My introduction ran roughly: 'Good evening, Mrs Maynard. I'm sorry to trouble you. My name is Ken Wilkie. I am working for a Dutch magazine called *Holland Herald* and am in London to research an article about the life of Vincent van Gogh, the painter. In connection with this, I am trying to trace a Kathleen Maynard who I think may have lived in the Biggin Hill area in 1966. . . .'

That was as far as I got.

'Oh, goodness me! And you think she may be living here! No, she's not living here. My name's Jemima and my husband, he's Albert. I don't think that there were any Kathleens in the family either. But I'll ask him. Can you hold the line a minute?'

Although Jemima held her hand over the receiver, I could hear most of what she was saying to her husband—mingled with bits of *Coronation Street* on the television.

'Albert!' she shouted.

'What is it, then?' he growled back.

'There's a man on the phone, a painter called Henry Holland or something. He's looking for a Kathleen Maynard . . .'

'I don't know no Kathleen Maynard. Tell 'im to piss off. . . .'

''Em, hello . . . Mr . . . em . . . Holland, was it?'

'Wilkie.'

'Of course, Mr Wilkie. I'm very bad on names. No, Albert says there's definitely no Kathleen Maynards in our family. I'm ever so sorry. I do hope you find her.'

Not every Maynard was so helpful, or even superficially polite. A few inquiries got no further than: 'You're wastin' your time here, mate. Nighty night.'

After scoring the tenth Maynard off my list, I sensed a general nervousness amongst the Maynards I had spoken to. I understood why when Maynard No. 11, Mrs Norman B., answered the phone.

After I had made my short announcement, she asked me to hold the line and I heard her, in a shaky voice, telling her husband: 'Norm, there's a man on the phone asking for a girl called Kathleen. You don't think it could be that "Beast of Biggin Hill" we were reading about in the paper the other day? They say he always phones before he strikes . . . He assaults housewives sexually and he escaped a few days ago from the institution . . . Oh dear . . .'

Norman Maynard took the phone from his wife and said: 'Now look here, I don't care who you say you are, we've had calls from the likes of you before. Now – – – – off before I call the police.' The line went dead.

Something had obviously gone wrong with what I thought was my natural inquisitive innocence. I tried to pick my words to sound as unmenacing as possible. Still, no luck.

Maynard No. 12: '. . . That's a Scottish accent. You're no Dutchman. You can't fool me. I was in Holland during the war.'

Maynard No. 13: '. . . Do I sound like Kathleen Maynard?' This voice was gruff and unmistakably male.

Another Maynard, a spinster, I think, replied: 'I'm sorry I can't help you, but it sounds so exciting what you're doing. Why don't you come round for tea and tell me more about it . . . ?'

After the 15th futile call, I began to feel the irony of the situation. Here I was trying to find a descendant of the woman who rejected Vincent, so I had to be prepared to take a few rejections myself. But I was becoming despondent. I also had in the back of my mind the fact that I had other places to go to in England—not to mention France, Belgium and Holland. My patience hadn't quite given out, but time was against me. A week of my three-week schedule was already up.

It was 10.30 p.m. Both my ears had telephone tingle. I had a quick drink downstairs and back to the phone. I kept trying to convince myself that I was on the right line. I felt I had to follow this lead to its logical conclusion, even if it was a dead end. I kept thinking of the possibilities. If Kathleen Maynard, whoever she was, was related to Eugénie Loyer—perhaps a granddaughter—she might, just might, have photographs of her grandmother. And in that way the world would see for the first time what Vincent's first love looked like.

On the other hand, just because Kathleen Maynard had signed the death certificate in Biggin Hill, it didn't mean she lived there. She could be living anywhere in Britain—or Australia. As the hopelessness threatened to overwhelm me, I dismissed that possibility from my mind and plodded on. Finally, near the end of the Maynard file, and near closing time, it happened. A break.

At Maynard No. 19, Mrs Dorothy, the phone was answered by a pleasant-sounding woman. I gave the usual introduction, my tone so unbeastlike by this time I could have been the new vicar calling up his parishioners.

'Kathleen Maynard? No, not living here,' she said politely.

'You don't have any relations in the family called Kathleen, do you?' I asked.

'Oh yes, as a matter of fact I do,' said Dorothy. 'I have a distant cousin, Kath. She lived in Biggin Hill for many years till her father died. Then she moved away. That was a few years ago now.'

'Did you know her father's name?' I asked.

'No, I can't recall his name.'

'Do you know where she moved to?' I asked again, with clenched teeth. I was fully expecting her to say New Zealand or the Bahamas.

'Yes, down Devon way, I think. A village somewhere in the south of Devon.' Not as far as I had feared.

'Do you have her address?'

'No. I'm afraid not.'

'Was she married?'

'Oh yes, for many years.'

'Do you know her husband's name?'

'Yes. Mort. That's short for Mortimer.'

'Did they have a family?'

'Yes, a married daughter, Anne.'

'Do you have Anne's address?'

'Oh, I'm not sure. I may just still have it. Could you hold the line a minute?'

The minutes seemed like hours as Dorothy Maynard looked for her old address book. There were beads of cold perspiration on my forehead and my hands felt clammy.

'Hello! Are you still there?'

'Yes, yes!'

'Anne and her husband moved down to Devon near her mother. I've

45

got her address.' She gave me the name—Anne Shaw—and an address near Totnes.

'And her telephone number?' I was getting lazy.

She read it out to me.

I never did meet Dorothy Maynard, but at that point I could have given her a big hug. Though I was still not sure I had the right Kathleen Maynard, when I heard that this Kathleen's father had died in Biggin Hill a few years before, I was more than optimistic.

It was well after closing time when I phoned Anne Shaw at her home in South Devon, but she was still up. After apologising for my lateness, I explained who I was and why I was phoning her. She sounded suspicious at first. When I had gained her confidence a little, I began to ask a few personal questions.

'Is your mother Kathleen E. Maynard?' I asked.

'Yes, she is,' replied Anne.

'Does the "E" stand for Eugénie?' I couldn't resist jumping the gun and looked heavenwards while awaiting the reply.

'Yes. Yes, it does. How did you know that?'

'Was your grandfather a man named Frank Plowman who died in Biggin Hill in 1966?'

'Yes. Listen, just how do you know all this about our family? And what does this all mean?'

I explained that I had conclusive evidence that there was a connection between her ancestors and Vincent van Gogh. I kept the specifics for Mrs Maynard.

There was a pause before she spoke again. 'If you will hold the line a second I'll fetch a little silver snuff box I have on the mantelpiece. It belonged to my great-great-grandfather and it has an inscription on it.'

She brought the box to the telephone and slowly began to read.

'To . . . Monsr. Jean . . .'

'. . .—Baptiste Loyer?' I interrupted.

'Yes. You know that too . . . "as a token of regard on his leaving Stockwell Grammar School July 1859".'

I now knew beyond any doubt that this was the right family. I told Anne that I was very anxious to talk to her mother. As Mrs Maynard didn't have a phone, I arranged to telephone her at her daughter's home first thing the following day. Next morning at 9 a.m. I talked to Kathleen Maynard, Eugénie Loyer's granddaughter. She sounded a little nervous, but even more curious. I did my best to contain my own curiosity for a moment and reassured her that there was nothing sordid or scandalous about my call, that I did not belong to the muckraking breed of journalist. She confirmed that her name was Kathleen Eugénie Maynard, and that she had buried her father at Biggin Hill in 1966, and that her grandmother was Eugénie Loyer. I took a deep breath and said:

'Did you know that Vincent van Gogh, the painter, lodged with your great-grandmother, Mrs Sarah Ursula Loyer, at 87 Hackford Road in South London?'

I heard her catch her breath.

'No, no. I didn't know anything about that. Good heavens!' replied Mrs Maynard.

'And did you know that Vincent fell in love with your grandmother when she was in her late teens?'

'You must be kidding . . .'

'And that she rejected him, and this rejection set him on the path to religious fanaticism.'

She was breathless. 'Oh, this is all too much. I knew absolutely none of this. I remember seeing the film with Kirk Douglas in it and I remember the episode with the girl in London. But to think that was Granny . . . Oh, it's really all a bit much to take in . . . How did you find all this out?'

'It's a long story, Mrs Maynard, but I'll be glad to tell you. I wonder, do you by any chance have any photographs of your grandmother Eugénie?'

'As a matter of fact, I think I may well have. My father's hobby was photography and he took a lot of photographs of the family around the turn of the century. I think there are quite a few in the attic, but I'll have to look them out, of course, and there's so much rubbish up there . . .'

By this time I was so excited I was fumbling for words. I asked Mrs Maynard if I could visit her that day and look through whatever photos she had.

'It's a long way from London, you know,' she said. 'The other side of England. But you're very welcome to come and have a look.'

I was all for taking off the next minute, but Mrs Maynard asked if she could have a day to sift through her 'rubbish'. She asked if I would phone her back at her daughter's that evening, and by then she would have a clearer idea of what was in the attic. I agreed, preparing myself for a day of suspense. I knew I was going to have trouble keeping my mind off the contents of Mrs Maynard's attic.

I still had other places to go for my assignment, and thought that a visit to one of them would force me not to think about Devon all day. I chose Welwyn, 30 miles north of London, where Vincent's sister Anna had worked as a teacher. Vincent had walked all the way from London to visit her there.

Anna had lived in a house called Rose Cottage, which still stands today. Its occupant was an elderly lady by the name of Freda Davis. She lived there alone and took a keen interest in the house's history. She often saw Vincent's ghost at nights, and said he was 'always making a consoling gesture as if to pass on the same consolation he himself had received under this roof from his sister Anna when he was grieving over Eugénie. Everyone comes here for consolation.'

Much as I tried to concentrate on Mrs Davis' strange tales, as I sat in the dark drawing room my mind kept drifting off down to Devon. Mrs Davis showed me a little butter dish that she said Vincent's sister had received from Holland as a birthday present. After taking photographs of her and Rose Cottage, I politely took my leave and drove up the Thames to Isleworth, the village where Vincent worked as a kind of curate with the Rev. Thomas Slade-Jones. I photographed the house where he lived and the church where he preached. All part of the assignment, but my heart wasn't in it.

That evening I called Mrs Maynard at the appointed hour.

'Well, I had a look through the attic and I've found a few pictures of Grandma, one when she was quite young. And there are a lot of other photographs Dad made of her and the family. But I shouldn't think you'll be interested in these. A lot of them are on old glass negatives.'

I told Mrs Maynard that any photographs of Eugénie and her family and of Hackford Road were of great interest. I arranged to visit her the next day. I can't describe how excited I was, knowing that the next day I would be looking at a previously unknown photograph of the girl who had changed Vincent's life.

That evening I telephoned my editor, Vernon Leonard, at his home in

The Rev. Thomas Slade-Jones, minister at Isleworth. *Vincent van Gogh Foundation/National Museum Vincent van Gogh, Amsterdam*

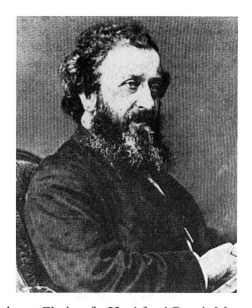

Chislehurst. I wanted to explain about Chalcroft, Hackford Road, Mrs Maynard, and my proposed journey to Devon. I also wanted to share some of my excitement. But his reaction surprised me. He said that in view of the little time left and the large areas yet to cover on the Continent, I was crazy to go all the way down to Devon. He suggested I ask Mrs Maynard to send a photograph of herself and one of her grandmother to the office. I told him I felt Mrs Maynard might not know the significance of what she had and that I was absolutely convinced a visit would be worth it. It was the end of a logical trail. He reminded me that my deadline for research was absolute, that I still had many places to visit, and that I was expected back in the office on the appointed Monday morning, October 2nd. But since a condition of the assignment was that I use the allotted time as I thought fit, Leonard reluctantly agreed.

Early next morning I drove out of London, bound for South Devon. I followed the main road west through the counties of Hampshire and Somerset and at Exeter branched south to Newton Abbot. Bypassing Dartmoor, I followed the little country roads through South Devon. The hedgerows and trees were mellowing into harlequin tones of autumn. My excitement seemed to heighten my perception of the landscape.

One of the narrow roads wound into the village of Stoke Gabriel, a community of cottages clustered around a motionless mill-pond. I followed a lane that climbed and twisted round the church and past a corner telephone-box partly covered in ivy. The Maynards lived in a bungalow on the outskirts of the village, with a long front lawn and vegetable garden. An unlikely place to be tracking down Van Gogh, I thought as I walked up the pansy-lined garden path. Kathleen Maynard and her husband Mort greeted me at the door.

'You must be hungry after that long journey,' said Mrs Maynard. Over tea and sandwiches, I told her in more detail about the assignment and the events that had led me into her living room . . . about the relationship between her grandmother Eugénie and Vincent. How this woman affected him so deeply that he is said to have walked the 70 miles from Ramsgate, where he was teaching, to London—only to catch a glimpse of her. How, if she had accepted his proposal of marriage, he might have become a part of London middle-class society instead of immersing himself in the Bible, devoting himself to his fellow men and finally his painting.

As we talked, I could see out of the corner of my eye two long wooden boxes, like sections of an old library index file, sitting on the sideboard. Protruding from them were bits of grease-proof paper that were used to protect glass negatives. And beside the wooden boxes was an old cardboard box.

'Well, you must be very curious to see Eugénie,' said Mrs. Maynard. She walked over to the sideboard and brought the boxes to the table.

'I spent all day in the attic yesterday,' she said, 'and have brought down everything in the way of photographs that was up there. The wooden boxes are full of glass negatives. Most of them were taken by Dad and some I think by Grandfather. I honestly didn't know what to do with them all when Dad died. He was one of these people who kept everything, and I supose that's one of the things I've inherited from him . . .'

Mrs Maynard dipped first into the old cardboard box on which was written in art deco typography: 'COOKEEN—For Light As A Feather Cakes And Pastries—Ideal For Frying And Every Cooking Purpose'.

She brought out a slightly faded sepia photograph. 'That's Granny before she was married. She was running a school.' And there she was. A

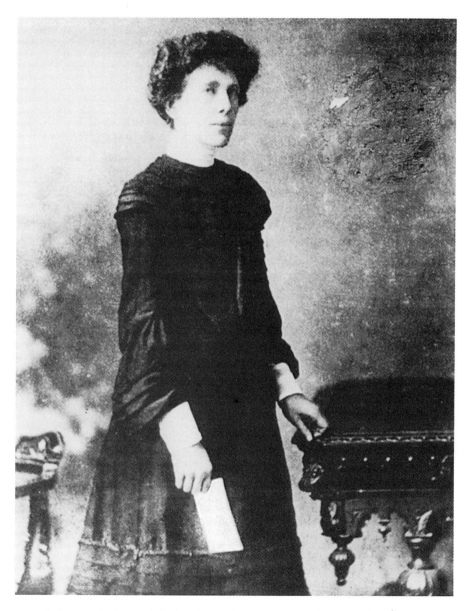

Eugénie Loyer, the landlady's daughter, whose rejection of Vincent in London was a significant turning point in the painter's life. *Collection Mrs Kathleen Maynard*

51

Sarah Ursula Loyer, Eugénie's mother and Vincent's landlady. This photograph of her was taken in about 1850. *Collection Mrs Kathleen Maynard*

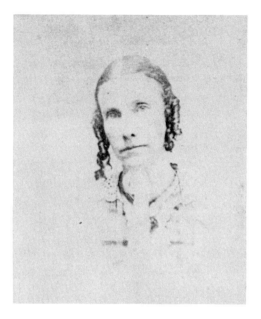

studio portrait of Eugénie Loyer, standing at a table with a letter in her hand. 'Eugénie had a shock of red hair,' said Mrs Maynard. 'Didn't Van Gogh also have reddish hair?'

In the same box was a small photographic portrait of Eugénie's mother, Sarah Ursula Loyer, with her hair in ringlets hanging over a *broderie anglaise* collar and check dress. It was taken in the late 1840s when she was in her early 30s.

To show Eugénie later in life, with her husband and family, Mrs Maynard went to the boxes of glass negatives. We had to hold them up to the light to see them. Eugénie was there—sipping tea in the garden with husband and family, at the beach with the family, and with her pupils. Most of these fragile negatives had been taken by Mrs Maynard's father, Frank Plowman, and Eugénie's daughters, Kathleen, Eugénie (called Dolly), Irene and Enid, were in most of them. 'Aunt Enid is living in Wimbledon,' said Mrs Maynard. And I have two cousins, Molly and Joan, living in Leigh-on-Sea and Worcester Park. (Next stop Aunt Enid, I thought. I hoped she would be able to tell me about her mother.)

We looked through the negatives and prints one after the other. I kept aside the pictures I found particularly interesting—mainly those of Eugénie and her family.

Mrs Maynard had made a preliminary sift through the contents of the cardboard box of prints and had already picked Eugénie out of the assortment. She was about to put the box away when I asked her if I could have a look through it myself. As I had come all this way, I was eager to see everything.

'Go ahead,' she said. 'But I don't think you'll find anything else of particular interest. These are mainly snapshots.'

Snapshots there were, piles of them—the family on holiday; Mrs Maynard as a little girl picking daisies in a Biggin Hill meadow.

There were old business cards of Eugénie's husband, Samuel Plowman, who was a house-decorator, electrical and gas engineer, roof/drain/

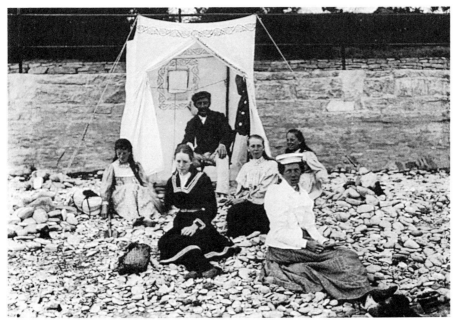

Eugénie and her husband Samuel Plowman, with their daughters, on a seaside holiday. First publication of a photograph taken by their son Frank. *Collection Mrs Kathleen Maynard*

sanitary repair man, and built cars to customers' specifications. Like his father, Frank was also an electrician, mechanic and engineer, as well as being a photographer and inventor. In the cardboard box there were photos of his unique self-made electric power station, with solid slate central panels, which he had built underneath his hand-built house in Biggin Hill. Mrs Maynard, who was her father's right-hand woman in the power station, told me the system worked flawlessly until a stray German bomb, meant for the Biggin Hill air base during the Battle of Britain, put Frank's power-house out of action.

But what I saw next, lying in the very bottom of the box, went beyond the realms of fascination.

It was a little drawing, unsigned and stained with what looked like tea

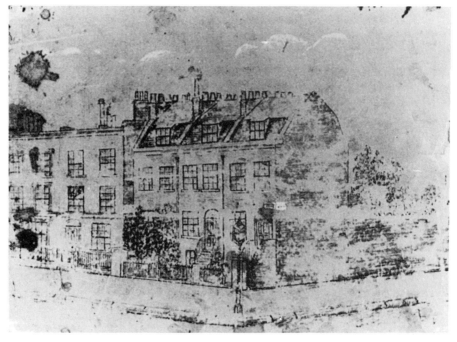

Vincent's drawing of 87 Hackford Road, found by the author in a cardboard box in Mrs Maynard's attic in Devon. The three end houses drawn by Vincent have since been demolished. *Collection Mrs Kathleen Maynard, on loan to Vincent van Gogh Foundation/National Museum Vincent van Gogh, Amsterdam*

or coffee. It was soiled with age and a little frayed at the edges.

I felt a troop of caterpillars run up my spine as I realised what I was looking at. It was a row of houses that included 87 Hackford Road—drawn from the same angle that I had photographed it a couple of days before.

'Do you know what this is?' I asked Mrs Maynard.

'That drawing? No, I don't know where it's meant to be exactly. I remember Dad saying something about it once but I can't remember what. It's been up in the attic for as long as I can remember.'

'That's 87 Hackford Road,' I said. There was a long silence. I looked at the drawing but said nothing. I didn't have to be an art expert to see that this drawing could be 100 years old. From his mother's letters, I knew Vincent had the habit of drawing the houses where he lived, and he had written to Theo that he had taken up drawing, 'but it did not amount to much'. What could have been more characteristic of the love-sick Vincent than to give his beloved Eugénie a drawing of their home in Hackford Road?

'I think that Vincent probably drew this for your grandmother Eugénie,' I said as casually as possible, hoping Mrs Maynard wouldn't faint. There was another long silence. I thought I might faint myself.

'I . . . I suppose he could have,' she said. Her hand made for the teapot.

Like cats around a goldfish bowl, we pored over the little drawing. 'We'd better be careful—it's not used to all this attention,' I said. We laughed nervously.

One thing struck me as odd. Today 87 Hackford Road is a corner house. In the drawing it was the fourth house from the corner. Then I remembered that there were now new houses adjacent to it. With the aid of one of Frank Plowman's old bakelite-framed magnifying glasses, I saw that the artist had written the name Hackford Road on the drawing. 'Christ, he's even written in the street name,' I said.

Another nameplate said Russell Street. From a map of London I had with me in the car, I saw that Russell Street no longer exists. But, uncannily, there was a very old map of South London also in the cardboard box. And this map showed that Russell Street had originally been adjacent to Hackford Road.

Eagerly I scoured the drawing for traces of Van Gogh, although I knew that at the age of 20 he had not begun to develop any distinctive style. The cardboard on which the drawing was made appeared to have been prepared and heightened here and there with white.

I asked Mrs Maynard if I could take the drawing back to Amsterdam with me, where I would have it examined by an art expert. She agreed and also lent me the photos and negatives I required.

Over a glass of sherry, we indulged in a little speculation. Mrs Maynard racked her memory for stories related to the drawing but could not come

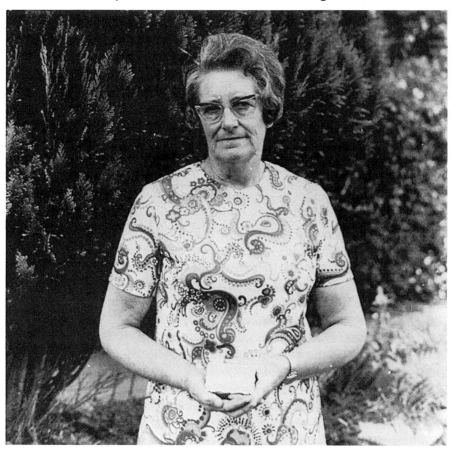

Mrs Kathleen Eugénie Maynard in 1972, with the silver snuff-box that belonged to her great-grandfather, Jean-Baptiste Loyer. *Photo: the author*

up with anything. It all seemed too incredible to be true and we tried not to jump to conclusions. Mrs Maynard agreed not to discuss the story with anyone except her daughter Anne.

As the light was already fading, we went into the garden where I took some photographs of Mrs Maynard with the silver snuff box that had been presented to her great-grandfather Jean-Baptiste Loyer in 1859.

It was nearly 7 p.m. when I left Stoke Gabriel to drive back to London—the little drawing, the photographs and the glass negatives all hidden away. In our enthusiasm and excitement, neither the Maynards nor I had thought about anything as official as a receipt. We had a mutual trust that meant more than slips of paper.

The seven-hour drive back to London passed in a blur of excitement. No matter how sceptical I tried to be, I couldn't suppress the overwhelming feeling that Vincent had made this drawing. Occasionally I stopped the car and looked at it again, almost disbelieving the way I had come across it. Had I found Vincent's drawing of the house where, according to his sister Anna, he had spent the happiest time of his life? But there was a world of difference between personal conviction and an expert's testimony.

I still had a long way to go on the Van Gogh trail, too—drawing or no drawing. I couldn't let these finds take up much more of my time. My fear was that meanwhile I might lose the drawing. I suppose some people would have gone straight to a bank with the goods I was carrying. I didn't. Of course, I wanted to show it to Dr Tralbaut if I met up with him in Provence. But the truth is that I just didn't want to part with it, the little treasure I thought it might be. It didn't look as if it belonged in a bank. And I had worked in a bank myself once. . . .

Before I left England, there was one person I had to look up—Eugénie's only surviving daughter, Enid Dove-Meadows. Having arrived back in London about 3 a.m., I was up first thing next morning and on the road to Wimbledon.

Fortunately, Enid was at home. She was a spry old lady of 84, with a direct manner and a buoyant sense of humour. She could hardly believe it when I told her the story. When shown the photographs I had of her mother, she exclaimed, 'Oh yes, that's her all right, who could forget a face like that? I don't think age improved her, do you?

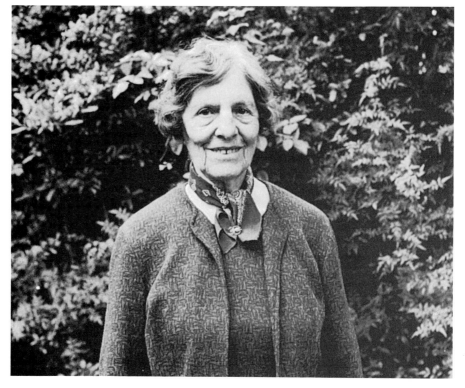

Enid Dove-Meadows, aged 84, at her home in Wimbledon in 1972. *Photo: the author*

'I knew nothing at all about Mother's affair with Van Gogh. Good gracious, it's hard to imagine. Mother was certainly not the sort of person to divulge secrets—least of all to her own family.' I asked Enid about her mother's character. Though she had no photos or drawings, she had a vivid memory and a sharp wit.

'Even by Victorian schoolmistress standards Mother was a severe woman,' she said. 'She was extremely strict—but you wouldn't say unkind. There was certainly no playing around with her, although it's possible that Vincent found it otherwise. She would not express her feelings very often and it was often difficult to guess what she was thinking. But when she did let go, she would fairly explode.

'Grandma [Mrs Sarah Ursula Loyer, Vincent's landlady] was more lenient. She was a kindly old soul and had more warmth about her altogether than Mother. I could imagine that she would have been a very hospitable landlady to Vincent.'

Enid recalled how on Saturday nights, when her mother and father went to the theatre, Grandma Loyer and her grandchildren would gather round the fire and tell stories to each other. 'Grandma always insisted on the maid being there too,' recalled Enid. 'She was a Welsh lass. But when Mother returned from the theatre and caught us all still up she would order the maid from the room and scold us for disobedience. Grandma would protest, but Eugénie ruled the roost. And she could henpeck Father from morning to night, too. He was rather passive. My goodness, I wonder what Mother would have thought of my great love in life today—dog racing? I work at the stadium nearby on the odd evening. The more I think about it, perhaps it's just as well for Vincent that she didn't agree to marry him. Don't you think?'

It was difficult to envisage the compassionate Vincent van Gogh bringing up a family with the haughty woman Eugénie appeared to have been. But the Eugénie that Vincent loved at 20 had probably not yet developed the strict moral standards of later life, as recalled by her daughter.

Eugénie's rejection of Vincent caused him intense suffering that was rooted in the melancholic atmosphere and emotional deprivation of his childhood. It precipitated a prolonged state of depression and a four-month gap in his published correspondence. It is presumed he did write during this time but for some reason these letters have not come to light.

The Eugénie experience, he wrote later, caused him 'years of humiliation'. It made him hypersensitive to the pain of others and intolerant of materialistic values. He diverted his anger from Eugénie to the art business. The assiduous young salesman now began telling customers at the Goupil gallery what he really thought about some of the paintings for sale, and didn't care if they didn't buy. The management transferred him to their Paris office but he couldn't keep his mind off Eugénie and, after two months, went back to London and took a room (in a house now demolished, at 395 Kennington New Road) near the Loyers. After what appeared to be a final refusal from Eugénie, he returned to his

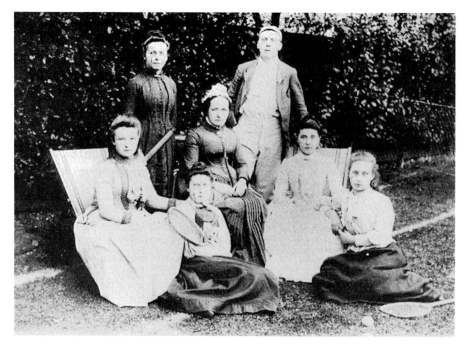

First published picture of the Slade-Jones family with whom Vincent stayed while he was working as a curate in Isleworth in 1876. He filled Mrs Slade-Jones' autograph book with verses from Longfellow and transcriptions from the Bible. *Vincent van Gogh Foundation/National Museum Vincent van Gogh, Amsterdam*

parents, who had moved to Etten in the south of Holland. He was fired from Goupil's.

But still he couldn't forget Eugénie and was soon back in England—at 11 Spencer Square, Ramsgate, on the Kent coast, where he had found a job as an unpaid teacher across the square at 6 Royal Road. Then, after a few months, the unsettled Vincent left his job in Ramsgate and went to Isleworth, the village I had already visited.

In a letter to Theo from Isleworth, Vincent writes: 'Your brother has preached for the first time, last Sunday, in God's dwelling, of which is written, "In this place, I will give peace."' The sermon was delivered at Richmond Methodist Church on November 5th, 1876. Vincent then writes out the 3,500-word delivery in full for Theo. It was based on Psalm 119:19, 'I am a stranger on the earth', and contains the significant passage: 'Sorrow is better than joy—and even in mirth the heart is sad—and it is better to go to the house of mourning than to the house of feasts, for by the sadness of the countenance the heart is made better.'

The letter goes on to reveal the sensitivity of Vincent's visual awareness at this stage, coupled with the emotional revelation of his new role:

> It was a clear autumn day and a beautiful walk from here to Richmond along the Thames, in which the great chestnut trees with their load of yellow leaves and the clear blue sky were mirrored. Through the tops of the trees one could see that part of Richmond which lies on the hill: the houses with their red roofs, uncurtained windows and green gardens; and the grey spire high above them; and below, the long grey bridge with the tall poplars on either side, over which the people passed like little black figures.
>
> When I was standing in the pulpit, I felt like somebody who, emerging from a dark cave underground, comes back to the friendly daylight.

Apart from preaching and teaching, his job also entailed collecting school fees from parents in the slums of London's East End. Here Vincent came face-to-face with human suffering that increased his desire only to help his fellow men and not to take their money. He made one last pilgrimage to the Maison Loyer at 87 Hackford Road, on the day after Mrs Loyer's birthday. Whether he saw Eugénie then is not known, but he finally left England and crossed the North Sea for the last time.

*   *   *

My next pilgrimage to 87 Hackford Road was on a sultry summer evening in 1989. I framed the house in my lens as I had done for the first time in 1972. The angle was the same as that from which Vincent had drawn the house for Eugénie in 1874. The pillar box was still in the foreground, and the 'Children Crossing' sign outside the school over the road.

There was now a blue plaque on the front of the house which had been

61

recently painted. The surrounding area appeared to be undergoing change. To reach Hackford Road from the railway station I had walked along Mandela Street and through Max Roach Park. Judging by the renovations taking place in Hackford Road itself, it looked as if the street was being fortified for an invasion of yuppies.

After all these years, did the Smiths still live there? I rang the doorbell. Mrs Smith opened the front door.

'Just a routine check, ma'am,' I said. She looked at me quizzically for a moment.

'Ken!' she exclaimed. 'Come in.'

There was new paint inside the house as well, and the brass light switches, still in use, were so highly polished that I could see my distorted image in them as I passed into the living room. Arthur Smith was reclining in his easy chair as I had first found him. Over a cup of tea we discussed the ill-fated affair between Vincent and Eugénie, that had taken place in the house. I asked Arthur if the blue plaque on their outside wall, stating, 'Vincent van Gogh lived here', had affected their lives. He laughed with a tone of irony.

'Lambeth Council are very keen to point out our house as a local attraction, but they don't come up with a penny for its upkeep,' he said. 'I'm 68 now and on a relatively low pension. Marjorie still cleans the school across the road twice a day.

'Photographers are always asking me to move my car away from the front door. Journalists come and interview us and never send us a copy of their magazine. We've had film crews in the house from Japan and America. The Americans carried on like they owned the place. The film crew from Thailand were the only really polite ones. And what do we get out of it, Ken? Nothing. What I'm thinking of doing now is going to Sotheby's and auctioning that blue plaque. And the house, too, if I can get the right price.'

On the Smiths' wall were three paintings by Paul Chalcroft, all copied off postcards at his kitchen tale. One was a Vincent self-portrait in which Chalcroft had given him cross-eyes.

I looked out of the window down the long, narrow back garden. It was nearly dusk and the light was blue. Across the garden from the Vincent van Gogh-sat-here outside toilet, I saw a cluster of sweet peas. It brought to mind a letter written to Theo in April 1874, when Vincent's passion for Eugénie was blossoming: 'I am very busy gardening and have sown a little garden full of poppies, sweet peas and mignonette. Now we must wait and see what comes of it.'

I explained to the Smiths that two days earlier I had uncovered a document, dated 11 November, 1956, in the archives of the Van Gogh Museum in Amsterdam, which identified their house as being Vincent's lodgings in London. Until now everyone, myself included, had assumed that postman Paul Chalcroft had been the first person to trace the Loyer residence to 87 Hackford Road. In fact, the address had been there in the London file of the Van Gogh Archives for 33 years, for anyone to see. The document, in Dutch, stated that in the Surrey directory of 1882 there was listed under 'Private Schools' the name of Mrs Sarah Ursula Loyer, 87 Hackford Road, North Brixton (this is Lambeth, near Clapham). This anonymous researcher had also traced the father of Mrs Loyer's husband, Jean-Baptiste. From the directory of Surrey 1860 he or she found listed 'Loyer, Geo., Esq., 2 Brunswick Place, Brixton Hill, London SW. The 'Esquire' indicated that the gentleman was rather well-to-do, noted the researcher, who went on to pinpoint the locations of Goupil and Company from 1873 to 1875 when the gallery moved from Southampton Street to 25 Bedford Street.

No one at the Van Gogh Museum knows who this researcher was. Although deserving of credit, his or her findings in no way detract from Paul Chalcroft's archive work which led him independently to 87 Hackford Road in 1972, when his path met mine in my search for Eugénie Loyer. On the other hand, the two cases prove that archive research can be futile unless someone applies it to human elements in the real world. After all, the Van Gogh drawing was found during a search for a photograph of a girl who lived in 87 Hackford Road in 1873—not because of a piece of paper in an archive.

Throughout my researches, industrial disputes have played a key role. It was because of the postal strike that Chalcroft had time off to trace 87 Hackford Road. And here was I, in the heat of summer 1989, criss-crossing England—London-Devon-London-Isleworth-London-Ramsgate-London-Worcester Park-London-Leigh-on-Sea-London—during an intermittent rail strike. In the few days at my disposal, I had to plan the

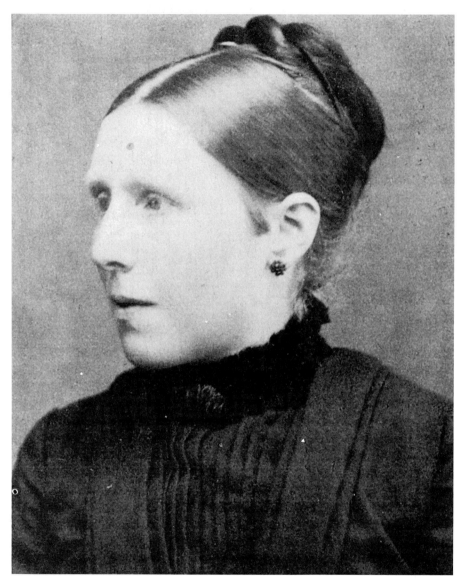

Anna van Gogh (1855–1930), Vincent's sister, who taught French at a boarding school in Welwyn. *Vincent van Gogh Foundation/National Museum Vincent van Gogh, Amsterdam*

long-distance journeys on railway-working days and the shorter trips by
foot, bus (if I was lucky), borrowed car and bike. It would have been an
easier task in 1873.

I eventually found myself heading south-west again from Paddington.
The train was dominated by senior citizens, chatting and nibbling at
cheese-and-pickle sandwiches.

On my knee I had a notebookful of excerpts taken from Van Gogh
family correspondence, released by the family some years after the death
of the Engineer in 1978. While these letters are hardly going to change the
course of art history, they nevertheless give us a little more insight into the
relationship between Vincent and Eugénie and take us a step nearer to
clarifying why Eugénie was referred to as Ursula.

The clue can be found in the correspondence between Vincent's sister
Anna and brother Theo. On January 6, 1874, she wrote to Theo from
Leeuwarden, in the northern Dutch province of Friesland (in English):

On Monday morning at breakfast I found a letter from London
which contained a letter from Vincent and one from Ursula Loyer,
both were very kind and amiable. She asks me to write her and
Vincent wished very much we should be friends. I'll tell what he
writes about her. 'Ursula Loyer is a girl with whom I've agreed that
we will have a brother and sister relationship. You should also
consider her as a sister and write to her, and I think you'll soon
discover her qualities. I say no more . . .' Then there follows a
description of Christmas and New Year and then still the following
phrase: '. . . Old girl, you mustn't think there is more behind it than
what I have written to you; but please don't mention anything about
it to the family, I must do that myself. Only once again, love that girl
for my sake . . .' I suppose there will be a love between these two, as
between Agnes and David Copperfield. Although I must say, that I
believe there is more than a brother's love between them: I send you
here Ursula's letter and so you can judge for yourself. I hope you will
send it back very soon with a long epistle of yourself . . .

So much for Vincent's request that she should keep the information to
herself. Anna then apologises to Theo for not writing in Dutch as she is

practising her written English. She concludes this letter by asking Theo to find out more about their cousin in The Hague, Annet Haanebeek, so that she can inform Vincent. Although Vincent never mentioned Annet in any of his letters, Anna infers that he has more than a passing interest in this cousin whom he had seen several times in The Hague before coming to London. It may, however, have been concern over Annet's health as she died a year later. Vincent's sister Anna seemed to be someone who thrived on gossip.

The odd thing about this letter is that, according to Anna, Vincent refers to Eugénie as 'Ursula', which was Eugénie's mother's middle name. None of Eugénie's granddaughters remembers their grandmother ever being referred to as Ursula, or even having a middle name at all. (I would later see Eugénie's birth certificate and burial notice which finally laid that matter at rest.)

The next letter from Anna to Theo, however, corrects Vincent's mistake, or her own:

> I got a very kind letter from Eugénie, she seems to be a natural and amiable girl. Vincent wrote to me that she was engaged, with a good-natured youth, who would know to appreciate her. I am very curious to know more about him and Annet. We two are just old people who try to know all about persons who are in love . . . He seems to be always in good spirits. In the last letter he writes me: 'I fear that all the sunshine I enjoy from there could be very soon rain—but I will only enjoy as long as possible the sunshine, and have my umbrella in the neighbourhood for the rain that could come . . .'

As we know, his feelings for Eugénie deepened and it was a storm of despair that filled him when she rejected him and he could not persuade her to accept his love or change her mind.

But why the first reference to Ursula? My theory is that it was probably Anna who made the mistake. This theory is based on personal experience: I also made a mistake concerning Eugénie. In 1972, when I was identifying the mass of family photographs from Mrs Maynard's collection, I mistook one of the photographs of Mrs Sarah Ursula Loyer (as a young woman) for that of her daughter Eugénie. I have Vanda Foster, Keeper of the

Gallery of English Costume in Manchester, to thank for drawing my attention to this in a letter to *The Sunday Times*. She noted that the *broderie anglaise* collar and check dress, and the ringlets in her hair, were a feature of the 1840s and early 1850s. When I took this up again with Eugénie's descendants, we came to the conclusion that this particular photograph was of Mrs Sarah Ursula Loyer, who was born in 1816.

When I arrived at the Maynards' in Stoke Gabriel, I found that they had uncovered another store of glass negatives taken by Mrs Maynard's father, Frank Plowman (Eugénie's son). Very soon the living room table, chairs and floor were covered in family albums, envelopes, marriage and death certificates . . . The old cardboard Cookeen box was given an airing, too, with most of its original contents. The drawing was no longer there, as it is now on permanent loan to the Van Gogh Museum.

'Here's a book I came across recently,' said Mrs Maynard. 'It's called *The Boat and the Caravan—A family tour through Egypt and Syria*. It's inscribed to Eugénie from her mother in August 1868, when she was 14—for doing well at school.' Mrs Maynard dipped into another box. 'Here's a drawing of two stags. It's dated August 1874. You see it's signed by Samuel Plowman, my grandfather. He was an engineer but could also draw very well. It's hard to know whether he knew Eugénie at that time or not. She did tell Vincent that she was engaged to another man but we don't know if that was Grandad or not. She may have been engaged more than once. They weren't married until 1878, so it would have been a long engagement.'

Outside the bees were buzzing around the lupins and the ducks in the back garden quacked away at the gate leading into the vegetable garden.

From the most recently released Van Gogh family correspondence, I was able to tell the Maynards some new facts about Vincent's life with the Loyers.

From Vincent's correspondence with Theo from Hackford Road, we knew that he went home to Helvoirt in Holland at the end of June 1874 and brought his sister Anna back with him to London in mid-July. Although Vincent wrote to Theo on August 10 that he went walking every evening with Anna, it was not known that they were in fact both lodging at the Loyers'. But a letter from Van Gogh senior to Theo on 15 August, 1874, confirms that, from mid-July to mid-August, both Vincent and

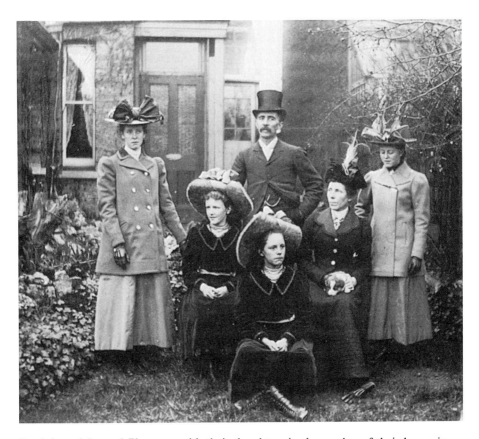

Eugénie and Samuel Plowman with their daughters in the garden of their house in Gap Road, Wimbledon. First publication of a photograph taken by their son Frank. *Collection Mrs Kathleen Maynard*

Anna were staying at Hackford Road. Telling Theo about Anna and Vincent's new lodging at Ivy Cottage, 395 Kennington New Road, their father wrote: 'It appears that at the Loyers' it was not all that it might have been and I'm glad about it; because I didn't particularly trust it there . . .'

This letter also contained an enclosure from Mother Van Gogh:

Dear Theo, We were pleased as ever with your nice letter. Marvellous that you have found good lodgings with good board. I'm always afraid that Vincent, especially when Anna is gone again, doesn't take enough care of himself. He was so skinny, they don't write about how they arrange their meals, only that they have had a delicious breakfast with fried bacon, who fries the bacon we don't know either, how strange it will be for them to part . . . Vincent will not have had an easy time with the Loyers—I'm glad he's no longer there, there were too many secrets and not a family like normal people but certainly if he has been disappointed and his illusions have not come true—real life *is* different from what one can imagine . . .

Mrs Maynard inherited a Van Gogh drawing because her father, who was Eugénie's only son, was a hoarder.

Eugénie's namesake daughter, called Dolly to avoid confusion with her mother, had a son, Ivan, now in New Zealand, and two daughters, Joan de la Chaumette-Rogers, now 75, and Molly Woods, 76.

At her home in Worcester Park, Mrs Rogers recalled with some regret that before the war her mother left behind the family collections of dolls, eggs, butterflies and photographs during one of their many removals. 'We left everything behind in that house. It was a detached bungalow near the station in Norsey Road, Billericay, called Saint Theresa. I often wonder what other things were left in that house.'

However, Mrs Rogers had inherited an interesting portrait of her late mother. Dating from the turn of the century, it was hand-coloured and showed her red hair. Dolly was the only offspring of Eugénie to inherit her red hair. After photographing this portrait, I left for my next stop that day: Mrs Rogers' sister, Molly Woods, who lives at Leigh-on-Sea. I had to take full advantage of British Rail services on the days when they were operating.

I was visiting Mrs Woods to renew acquaintance with two paintings and a gold locket which she had inherited from her mother. The locket contained in one half a miniaturised portrait of the picture of Eugénie I had found at Mrs Maynard's. This one, however, was coloured to show her red hair. In the other half was the man Eugénie had married, Samuel

69

Plowman. On the outside was an elaborate monogram, E, L, and P, presumably representing the initials of Eugénie Loyer Plowman. We had published these photographs in *Holland Herald* in 1973, together with two more of Mrs Woods' heirlooms, a rather fine oil painting of Eugénie's father, Jean-Baptiste Loyer, and a chipped and charred painting of Mrs Sarah Ursula Loyer in later life. 'This painting was hanging for years above Mother's fireplace,' said Mrs Woods, 'and unfortunately has suffered severely from coal fire smoke.'

I took photographs of this material and of a drawing of horses by Samuel Plowman.

Mrs Woods told me that some years before, while compiling a family genealogy, she had been sent a document of a census of Lambeth in which Vincent van Gogh was registered as a 'student lodger' with the Loyer household. 'Unfortunately I can't find this document. It did strike me at the time as interesting.'

But Mrs Woods' research into her family's genealogy did prove one thing conclusively: Eugénie Loyer had no second name of Ursula. She had no other name at all except Eugénie. Both her birth certificate and burial certificate proved this, which means that either Vincent or Anna mistakenly referred to Eugénie as Ursula in that first letter.

As Vincent, at 20, was so overwhelmed by the relationship between Eugénie and her mother, it is probably not so strange if he did make this mistake. And perhaps it was significant, bearing in mind the importance he obviously attached then to family acceptance, and the fact that a warm maternal relationship was foreign to him.

3   The Christ of the Coalmine

It was September 23rd, 1972. I had used up more than half my research time, and I had many places to visit before I returned to Amsterdam. There was no time to delve further into Vincent's life in London. Belgium and France lay ahead, and already it was going to be a race to meet the deadline. I decided to save time by travelling as much as I could during the night.

Driving to the coast, I took the night ferry to Belgium, my new-found material in a hard cardboard envelope which I kept with me at all times.

The boat docked at Zeebrugge before dawn, and I headed south in the darkness to the Belgian 'Black Country', wondering if there was anyone in the mines who could cast light on Vincent.

On the boat to Belgium I had traced Vincent's movements after he left England, in a state of depression. Before becoming a missionary to the poor miners of Belgium, he had a spell as bookseller's clerk in Dordrecht, and as a student of theology in Amsterdam. These were brief periods and well documented by his friends at that time.

In Dordrecht he shared a room with a young teacher named Görlitz who told of his already eccentric behaviour: 'Vincent said lengthy prayers and ate sparingly like a penitent friar. In the evenings, he changed into a blue peasant's smock and spent the night translating the Bible into four parallel columns of French, German, English and Dutch—while also writing sermons. On Sundays he attended three or four religious services.' He also recalled that even when Vincent did not have enough money to buy himself half an ounce of tobacco, he would spend his last coppers to buy bread for a hungry dog.

Vincent resolved to become a minister like his father and left Dordrecht for Amsterdam to study theology under a young professor of classics called Mendes da Costa. They became friends and Da Costa left a poignant description of Vincent in his days as a Greek and Latin scholar: 'I can still see him stepping across the square from the Nieuwe Herengracht bridge, without an overcoat as additional chastisement, his books under his right arm, pressed firmly against his body, and his left hand clasping a bunch of snowdrops to his breast, his head thrust forward a little to the right, and on his face . . . a pervading expression of indescribable sadness and despair. . . . And when he had come upstairs, there would sound again that singular, profoundly melancholy deep voice: "Don't be mad at me, Mendes, I have brought you some little flowers again because you are so good to me. . . ."'

Vincent had great difficulty in coping with formal studies. 'Mendes,' he would say, 'do you seriously believe that such horrors as Latin and Greek are indispensable to a man who wants to do what I want to do—give peace to poor creatures and reconcile them to their existence here on earth?'

The teacher knew in his heart that Vincent was right and wasn't surprised when, in July 1878, Van Gogh gave up his studies and took a three-month crash course at a school for missionaries in Belgium. Because of his erratic behaviour, he failed the course; but in the end he was given a trial term as an evangelist in a poor village called Petit Wasmes in the French-speaking Belgian 'Black Country', the Borinage. There people worked in satanic mines under a yellow-grey sky perpetually foul with fumes and smoke.

It was in this miserable mining land that Vincent reached extremes of self-sacrifice for his fellow creatures. Apart from the restrictions of time, I felt I had more chance of finding human links in a small community like Petit Wasmes, where the pattern of life has more continuity from generation to generation, than in the cities of Amsterdam and Dordrecht. Perhaps the deeds of this extraordinary missionary had not passed totally beyond the reach of human memory.

I had a few basic facts to go on. Vincent had lived with Jean-Baptiste Denis, a baker, and his wife Esther, in their home at 22 rue de Wilson. Vincent would go from there down the 2,000-foot shaft of the notorious Marcasse mine to preach the word of God to the miners—women and children among them—literally on their own level.

In spite of my tiredness—I had slept little on the boat—I felt elated as I drove south in the clear morning light. My trip was turning up far more than I had ever expected: memories, photographs, the drawing. . . . Some of that self-importance I had felt when driving to see Baroness Bonger returned. Even if I didn't take it too seriously, I didn't fight it too hard—it kept me awake and alert for the hour's drive from Zeebrugge to Petit Wasmes.

The Borinage lived up to Vincent's descriptions. The landscape was dreary, barren and forbidding. Dead trees, blackened by smoke, stood like permanent scars on the earth's face. The only living vegetation seemed to be thorn hedges. Slag heaps littered the scene. Everywhere the countryside was gashed by abandoned mines. Not even the friendly sunshine could change the impression that this was indeed the 'Black Country'.

The first people were already on the streets when I arrived. Hob-nailed boots clattered on the cobblestones, drowning what little conversation there was between the miners on their way to work. The people were squat and strong, but their faces looked thin and unhealthy. The women especially looked emaciated and faded before their time. They reminded me of the little gnarled, heavy-boned figures in Breughel's paintings. Their postures were twisted by long hard work under the earth. The French these Belgians spoke was a thick patois that sounded as if their throats were clogged with coal dust.

I went into a baker's shop and bought two croissants. I asked the elderly shopkeeper if she knew of the old baker called Jean-Baptiste Denis, who had lived at 22 rue de Wilson many years before.

She thought for a few moments before answering. 'Denis . . . Denis . . . oh, yes, when I was a little girl I used to buy bread for the family from him. He was a little old man with a long white beard and always used to give me a cake on Saturdays. He died a long time ago. My father worked for him when he was a boy. But Papa, too, has been dead for many years.'

She didn't know any legends about a Dutch missionary who stayed in Petit Wasmes in the 1870s, but she directed me to rue de Wilson.

'You see that mine shaft and slag heap over there? Well, rue de Wilson is up that hill.' Her voice became quieter. 'That mine is called the Marcasse. It's closed now. And a good thing too. There were so many disasters. Two

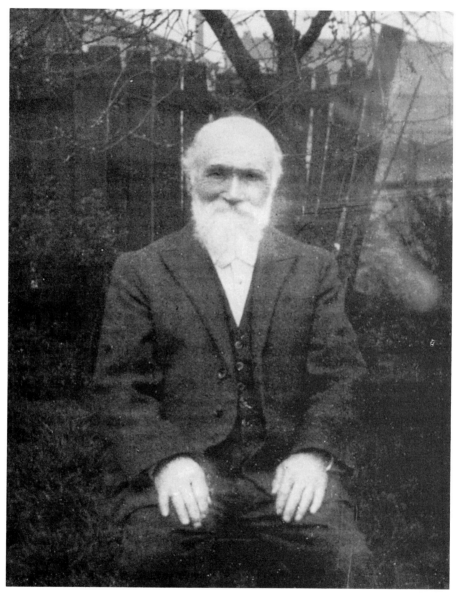

Jean-Baptiste Denis, the baker with whom Vincent lodged in the mining village of Petit Wasmes in the Belgian Borinage. *Collection Jean Richez*

of my uncles died in the Marcasse. I am sure that there is hardly a family in Petit Wasmes who hasn't lost a relative there.'

Number 22 rue de Wilson was at the end of a row of nearly identical two-storey houses. It looked spotlessly clean. The windows were gleaming in the early morning sun, as if the occupants had made sure that the cleanliness of their home compensated for the grime of the pit.

I knocked twice and the door opened abruptly. A tall man with a strong proud chin and straight silver hair stood in the doorway. I explained my mission—in French this time. Kathleen Maynard was already a memory on the other side of the North Sea. I told the man I was looking for descendants of Jean-Baptiste Denis, the baker who had once lived at this address.

'You need look no further,' said the man in a thick accent. 'My name is Jean Richez. I am the nephew of Jean-Baptiste Denis. I was named after him. Come in. You have come far from England. Sit down.'

What luck, I thought to myself. The door opened into a spacious tiled room that served as both kitchen and living room. It did not look as if it had changed much since Vincent's day. Some bread and cheese lay on the scrubbed wooden table in the middle of the room. A wooden rocking-chair stood beside the open hearth.

Richez offered me a glass of dark Belgian beer and we sat down at the table. After a few slow sips, he began to tell me about his uncle the baker.

'Uncle Jean died in 1934. He was 84, and till the day he died he made the best *baguettes* in the Borinage. As far back as I can remember, I spent my holidays in this house with Uncle Jean and Aunt Esther.'

'And did they ever say anything about the painter Van Gogh?'

'Oh yes. They often talked to me about their strange lodger Monsieur Van Gogh. He seemed to be a very unusual man. They told me that he insisted on sleeping like a beast in a little hut—like the one you see out there.'

I looked out of the window. A tumble-down shack stood at the end of the narrow garden that tapered away into the mine-ravaged land beyond. Not far off were the black pyramids of waste that towered over Pit Number 7, the Marcasse that Vincent knew so well.

'When Aunt Esther asked Monsieur Van Gogh why he insisted on sacrificing his room upstairs in favour of that hovel outside, he replied:

"Esther, one should do like the good God. From time to time one should go and live among His own. . . ." Aunt Esther reprimanded Monsieur Van Gogh for rushing out every morning to visit the poor, without spending time to wash or do up his laces. To this, Monsieur Van Gogh's reply was: "Esther, don't worry about such details, they don't matter in Heaven. . . ." '

Having arrived at the stage where he had no shirt or socks, Vincent is said to have made shirts out of sacking.

'Monsieur Van Gogh would quite often hold improvised services for the miners—in a hut, in the street, or actually down the mine shaft—dressed in nothing but an old sack. Aunt Esther used to say she wished there had been more men around like Monsieur Van Gogh. She told me he often did the washing to help some of the local women. My wife is certain that no man before or since has done that here in the Borinage.'

I asked Richez if Vincent had left behind any drawings of Borinage life. 'Uncle Jean told me that when he was baking bread for the following day, Monsieur Van Gogh would sit and quietly draw him at work. Unfortunately, I have no idea what happened to these drawings. Knowing Aunt Esther, she probably threw them out. She left nothing lying around the house. She was so tidy she used to make the sun wipe its shoes before it was allowed to shine through the windows in the morning. No, there is no attic here and there are certainly no drawings or paintings in this house . . . if that is why you are looking around the walls!' Without even being aware of it, I was doing just that, but the only piece of art was a little wooden statue of the Virgin Mary hanging in a corner of the kitchen. Richez did have a little photo of Jean-Baptiste Denis and his wife which I photographed outside with my own camera.

As Richez reminisced, it became apparent that Vincent's charity was not confined to mankind in these dark religious days.

'Aunt Esther said she remembered how Monsieur Van Gogh would pick up caterpillars and put them back on branches. He would even put cheese and milk outside for the mice. This was while he was living on bread and water himself, mind you. People treated him like a madman in the village, but they loved him just the same, so my aunt used to say.'

While Vincent was in the Borinage, there was a series of fire-damp explosions. Richez remembered his uncle telling him that the Dutchman worked frantically for days and nights on end to help the injured miners—tearing his remaining linen into bandages and steeping them in olive oil and wax to treat the miners' burns.

'Aunt Esther said she used to hear Monsieur Van Gogh crying all night in his hut outside. He made a very deep impression on her. None of the miners who knew him ever forgot Vincent. They called him the Christ of the Coalmine.'

Noticing how I kept looking out of the window that framed the pithead of the Marcasse mine, Richez remarked: 'You seem interested. I'll take you to it.' We finished our beer and walked out into the dreary cobbled street leading to the mine. It had developed into a grey, lightless day. Apparently the sun had given up. Did it feel out of place here?

Richez walked erect, with hands clasped behind his back. He never smiled and rarely altered his fixed, stern expression.

'After the last disaster in 1960, the Marcasse was closed,' he said,

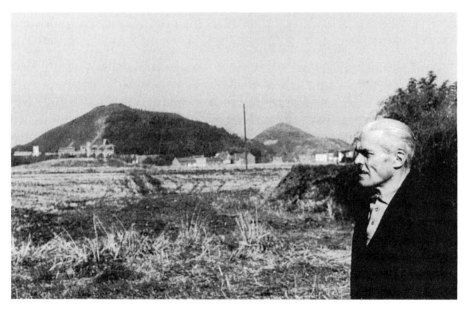

Jean Richez and the now disused Marcasse mine (Pit no.7). *Photo: the author*

pointing to the shaft. 'You see it is filled with concrete. If the mining company hadn't closed it, I'm sure the miners would have done it themselves. It was a killer.'

Richez stared thoughtfully at the ground. He told me that two of his own family had died in the Marcasse and he himself had narrowly escaped with his life before he was pensioned off.

Under the rusty girders there were still stables with straw waiting for the pit ponies. Among the rubble lay a rusty miner's helmet, half buried in the black earth, an eerie reminder of the men, women and children who never came up. The word Marcasse is still met with disquieting looks from the local people. 'The mine is closed,' said Richez, 'but its memory will always remain in the minds of the people of Petit Wasmes.'

Richez didn't talk much at the head of the Marcasse mine shaft. There was no need. The long heavy silences said it all.

I felt that so much of Vincent's life must have been dominated by darkness. Indeed, it was this darkness that he went down the mine to find. Through religion he tried to bring light into the lives of these poor miners. Instead, he plunged himself into a deeper darkness of disillusionment. The only light that fired him in the Borinage was the eerie pale reflection on the miners' faces as they sweated in the labyrinths of the Marcasse. It was this light that he would recreate in his first masterpiece, painted a few years later, *The Potato Eaters*.

Coming out of the minehead, both Richez and I remained silent. I imagined Vincent's reaction to the suffering he must have seen in that awful place. We walked back to Richez's house, where I said goodbye to him and his wife. They stood outside watching me as I drove off. Something in their stance suggested indomitable pride, a refusal to give in to the forbidding land where they made their home. From there I drove to the nearby village of Cuesmes, where Vincent lived after leaving Petit Wasmes. He had walked there, half-starved, and lodged with a miner called Decrucq and his family. As in Petit Wasmes, Vincent discovered that men, women and children were working like slaves 12 hours a day. He was furious when he found out how the mine bosses operated. Out of every 100 francs of net receipts, they paid only 60.9 in wages and turned over 39.1 to the shareholders.

Vincent took on the capitalist machine single-handed. He went to the mine bosses and demanded a fairer share for workers. In return he received insults and the threat of being shut up in an asylum.

Vincent now abandoned all hope of following his father's footsteps through religion and was on the point of following his mother's—into art. For even in the most unlikely situations in the Borinage, he would always find time to draw the miners plodding wearily to and from the pit. He actually wrote to Theo at this time that his devotion to Rembrandt was as sincere as his devotion to Christ. Drawing, he said, liberated him. And he had begun to make copies after Millet, the French painter of labourers.

I had no better luck in Cuesmes than Vincent. An old miner, sitting on his doorstep, directed me to the Decrucq cottage. It was a roofless ruin, listing to one side, and sinking into a marsh. Ghosts would have been all that I could possibly find there.

Not surprisingly, there were no hotels in Cuesmes, so I decided to spend the night in my sleeping bag, parked near the ruined miner's cottage where Vincent had stayed for a few nights. Where did he go next? I traced his movements in my mind as darkness set in. From the Borinage he went to the art academy in Brussels, but very soon found it too expensive and returned to his parents' home at Etten.

This was in April 1881. The spring began peacefully enough till Vincent's cousin Kee Vos and her little son came to stay with the Van Goghs for the summer. Kee Vos's husband had just died and Vincent felt a sympathy for her that developed into a deep passion—a feeling that had been smouldering in him since his unsuccessful love affair with Eugénie Loyer in London.

Till now, he admitted to Theo, he had been living in the emotional wake of Eugénie's refusal. And his cousin Kee seemed to appeal to his combination of sexual need and human compassion. But when he declared his love, she, too, firmly rejected him. She was still in mourning and left immediately for Amsterdam. Vincent was in torment. He bombarded her with letters which she apparently refused to read. Theo even gave him money to go to Amsterdam to meet her, but she refused to see him. 'Kee left the house as soon as she heard you were at the front door,' said his uncle at the doorstep of Keizersgracht 453. Vincent was admitted to the parlour and was convinced Kee was still in the house. There followed the scene, borrowed from one of Multatuli's characters,

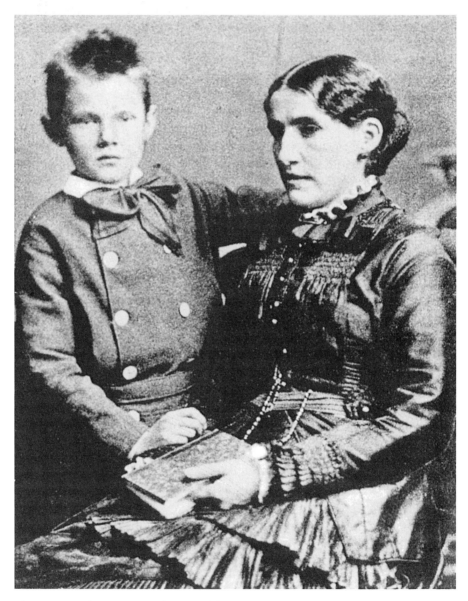

Vincent's cousin Kee Vos-Stricker and her son. *Vincent van Gogh Foundation/National Museum Vincent van Gogh, Amsterdam*

where Vincent held his hand above the flame of an oil lamp, insisting he would keep it there for as long as he could not see Kee. But Pastor Stricker blew the lamp out and told his eccentric nephew to leave the house.

On Christmas Day, 1881, things came to a head at Etten when Vincent and his father had a violent quarrel, mainly over Vincent's refusal to attend church. The minister told his son to get out within the hour and Vincent took the train to The Hague to take lessons with the painter Anton Mauve. While there, his thoughts turned away from religion. He wrote to Theo: 'I am a man and a man with passions, I must go to a woman, otherwise I shall freeze or turn to stone. . . .'

The woman he found was a prostitute called Clasina Maria Hoornik, and not long after meeting her, he set up home with her and her daughter Maria. He spent several weeks in hospital being treated for gonorrhoea and meanwhile Clasina bore another child, Willem, several months after they had begun living with each other. When Vincent began to talk of marrying her, his father contemplated having his son confined in a mental asylum. Instead, the family threatened to withdraw Vincent's allowance unless he left her: he was faced with the choice between losing Clasina and losing his sole means of support. Unwillingly, he chose the former.

I had a vague feeling that there was still something to be learned about Vincent's Hague period. I remembered noticing, back in the Van Gogh Museum archives in Amsterdam, that parts of some letters from this period were missing and there were deletions in others.

Was someone hiding these letters from public view? If they were, why? What possible motive could there be for censoring the letters of a painter? Government documents, certainly—but an artist long dead? It seemed absurd, yet there it was. . . . Clasina of course must have died years ago—but what became of her baby, Willem? I calculated that if he were still alive he would be about 90—no older than Piet van Hoorn, who had collected birds' nests for Vincent in Nuenen. Was Willem still alive? Did he know of his background? I wanted to find answers to these questions.

To do so I would need time—time for research in archives, time to follow God knew how many blind alleys. Getting my map and flashlight out of the car, I assessed my position. I was sitting in a marsh in the south of Belgium. In a week I had to be back in Amsterdam with the makings of a story in my notebook. I still had Arles, Saint-Rémy, Paris and Auvers-sur-Oise to visit. I also wanted to talk to Dr Tralbaut, in the south of France. I would have to cover over 800 miles as the crow flies—not allowing for diversions of any kind. I got out of my sleeping bag and paced around like a caged wolf. 'How the hell am I going to do this?' I muttered aloud. My head was spinning with road maps, drawings, photographs. After a few minutes the spinning stopped and one thing became quite clear to me: I could no longer follow Vincent's movements step by step or even year by year. I would have to decide to see some places, and skip others. The idea infuriated me, but I no longer had any choice. That deadline seemed closer every time I looked at it.

So what came next? From The Hague Vincent went to the isolated province of Drenthe, in the north-east of Holland, where he spent a few lonely months. Then he returned again to his parents who had moved to Nuenen in the south of the country.

Old Piet van Hoorn, the centenarian who knew Vincent, had already talked to me about the painter's stay at Nuenen. Of course, what he had told me about Vincent had much more significance now that I had been following his life so closely.

A series of unfortunate events occurred in Nuenen. Margot Begemann, the Van Gogh family's next-door neighbour, who was ten years older than Vincent, was one of the few women to have fallen deeply in love with him. But her father and sisters tried to turn her against him, which drove her into a nervous collapse. Vincent was actually considering marriage until Margot tried to poison herself with strychnine. Vincent rushed her to hospital where she was saved and sent to a sanatorium in Utrecht.

In early 1885, Vincent spent a lot of time at the home of a peasant family, the De Groots, who posed for *The Potato Eaters* and many other studies. Unfortunately, the unmarried daughter, Gordina, became pregnant while he worked there, and Vincent, of course, was an easy target for suspicion. The local Catholic priest even issued an edict forbidding Catholics to pose for him, thus cutting off his chief source of models. Vincent vehemently denied the accusation and Gordina herself claimed the father of her child was one of her nephews. Nevertheless all this only increased his conviction that he was misunderstood and

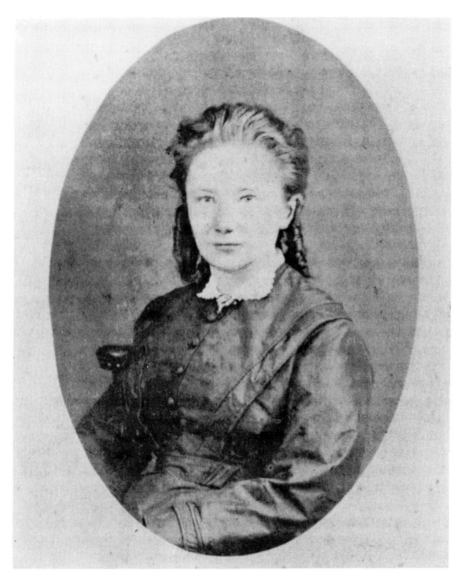

Margot Begemann, one of the very few women who seem to have fallen in love with Vincent. *Vincent van Gogh Foundation/National Museum Vincent van Gogh, Amsterdam*

victimised. He packed his bag and left Holland for good. He went to nearby Antwerp in Belgium and became a pupil at the art academy there for a while. His professor thought his drawing inadequate, however, and demoted him to a preparatory class. He studied Rubens and learned to brighten his palette.

While all this was interesting from the point of view of Vincent's artistic development, I didn't think there would be much of personal interest during his short stay in Antwerp. The Paris period I had learned about from Baroness Bonger. Perhaps I should head directly for Arles. Digging out a letter I had received from Dr Tralbaut, I saw that he was going to be in Provence only briefly. If I delayed my trip there I might miss him. That clinched it.

I packed up my things and drove off—after the shortest night's sleep I had ever had. As I sped along the dark, narrow roads that led out of the Borinage, making south for the French border and the *autopaysage* to Arles, I realised that something about this assignment had caught me and held me fast. It was more than an assignment now. I didn't know exactly *what* it was, but I did know that I would not be satisfied with the limitations of my deadline. I would return one day to the places and mysteries that time was now forcing me to skip.

4　Mistral

The countryside was dark and silent as I drove along the cobbled backroads leading to the highway that would take me south over the French border. Already I had doubts about the wisdom of driving alone and at night—some 500 miles lay between me and Provence. I'd had little sleep the night before but I pushed on. Through the Marne and Haut Marne, past Reims and into Burgundy. Past Dijon I joined the *autoroute*, which made the driving faster but more monotonous. When my eyelids threatened to clamp shut, I pulled over and slept for a few minutes.

Always, while awake, my thoughts jumped back and forth between the sequence of Vincent's life, the events of the last few days, my deadline, my plans for the rest of the trip. At moments it all turned into a jumble. I was following Vincent through books, visiting places where he had lived, talking to people about him. What had I done, what had I read, whom had I talked to? Who was it who was going to Provence, me or Vincent? He had fled there after his tempestuous stay in Paris, and in a letter to Theo he wrote: 'I need to take myself off somewhere down south, to get away from the sight of so many painters that disgust me as men.' As I recalled these words by the roadside, I laughed aloud. What would the painters have said about Vincent? But at least he had his convictions to propel him south. All I had was a deadline, a scribbled-up notebook, and a tiny drawing. I looked at the drawing again and again, sometimes holding it on my lap as I drove. It seemed to bring me closer both to Vincent and to the reality of my assignment. Was it really a Van Gogh? The question didn't seem to matter so much any more.

Just past Avignon, dawn began to break over the Alpilles mountains. Slowly the darkness gave way to a soft purple, bathing in radiance the lush cornfields of Provence. My eyes felt as if they were being unscreened after the bleakness of the Borinage.

At Tarascon I left the highway at last. It was a relief to take a country road again. Stopping the car, I walked up a hill to stretch my legs and breathe the crisp morning air.

Physical exertion made me realise that I had barely moved a muscle for hours. My eyes ached, my legs were stiff and tight, my throat was dry and my stomach empty. At least I was able to quench my thirst with bunches of succulent black grapes and to wash my face in the morning dew.

With my face still moist, I sat down to watch the sunrise. The same dew in which I had washed my face hung like teardrops from the sombre green branches of the cypress trees. They twisted as if in agony out of the fields, clutching and leaping at the empty sky. Symbols of death, Vincent had called them. In this dazzling display of copper, bronze and gold I could see why. Their beauty was almost unbearable. Suddenly I was aware of real tears welling up behind my eyes.

This was more than I could cope with. I arose abruptly, as if to shake myself soundly. 'Come on, you're just tired.' I spoke the words aloud. The sun was now cradled in a saddle of the Alpilles and the day was beginning. With parcel in hand, and the last remnants of dew drying in my beard, I stumbled down the hill towards my car. I wanted to find Tralbaut.

The author's address was in Mausanne, a village not far from Arles. The drive there was an uninterrupted spectacle. Every turn held another field, another stand of cypress trees. My vision was affected as much by Vincent's intense interpretations of these views as by the scenes themselves. I found at times that I was confusing what he had seen with what I was seeing myself.

The drive took about an hour and a half, and led me to a tiny village of small houses well spread out over a large, hilly area. A villager pointed me in the direction of Dr Tralbaut's house on the side of one of the hills. Getting there meant taking my car up narrow roads little wider than the breadth of the car itself.

By mid-morning I reached the house. No one at home. I walked up the hill to a point from which I could see the Crau valley, where Vincent painted for days on end in the burning heat. The sun had turned lemon-yellow as it eased up into the sky and filled the air with a blinding light.

The glowing cornfields below were being whipped by the prevailing wind the Arlesians call the Mistral. I remembered Vincent's descriptions of painting in that wind—of how difficult it was to keep the Mistral from blowing away his easel and canvas. In the distance, near a cluster of olive trees, a stooped figure with a straw hat was climbing a hill path to Tralbaut's home. I walked back down the hill towards him and recognised him from a photograph I had seen at the Van Gogh Museum: it was Van Gogh's biographer himself.

As we approached each other, Tralbaut called out: 'You must be Ken Wilkie. I had a premonition you would arrive today.' He greeted me warmly and we walked to his house.

Tralbaut's home was spacious and simply decorated. Surprisingly (for an art historian), the walls hadn't a single picture on them. The main feature was a crammed bookshelf. I had never seen so many books in a house before.

Over a bottle of Provençal wine, we talked of my travels and discoveries. He was enthralled by the drawing.

'Scholars spend lifetimes hoping they will discover an unknown drawing by a major artist. Of course, I'm not saying that what you have *is* by Van Gogh. I would have to make a detailed study to be sure. But it looks to me that it may well be. That is judging purely by the style—not even taking into account the circumstances in which you found it. The trees are the point of departure. I would like to see a microphoto of the trees. Then I would be sure.

'Even if the drawing proves not to be a Van Gogh, you have made an important discovery in the photographs of Eugénie. Your postman friend, Mr Chalcroft, is to be congratulated for his research. Strange, isn't it, the way people get drawn into learning about Van Gogh. . . .'

Tralbaut told me that he had felt he himself was predestined to be a Van Gogh scholar. He was born in 1902 on a boat called the *Theo* as it was passing Vincent's resting place in Auvers-sur-Oise. He talked of the years he had spent researching Vincent's life and work—of the trials and frustrations, the joy and satisfaction.

Now Tralbaut was living in semi-retirement in the land that Vincent had loved so much. Even at the age of 70, however, he couldn't leave Vincent completely: he was in the process of finishing a book on the influence of Japanese prints and paintings on Vincent's art. And much of his time was taken up with the Van Gogh scholars and enthusiasts who came down to Provence to visit him. A team led by the Swedish director Mai Zetterling, who were making a film about Vincent near Arles, had just been to see him.

'And last week,' said Tralbaut, 'I had a visit from an Englishman called Alfred Schermuly. Schermuly had been in a mental hospital as a result of war injuries. But in the hospital he read my book, became absorbed in Vincent's life, and began to paint. He is now a full-time painter and lives with his wife and family again. He had made the pilgrimage to Provence to absorb the atmosphere here. Just as you have.'

The afternoon was wearing on, as was our bottle of wine. I sensed that Tralbaut was looking forward to an afternoon nap, and decided it was time to leave. First, of course, I wanted to get from him any possible leads in France. I explained that I was trying to find people with a significant living link to Vincent, and asked whether there would be any in Provence.

Tralbaut took the question seriously, but assured me that there weren't. 'As you know, Van Gogh had few contacts here, since the townspeople mostly thought he was out of his mind. The daughter of the postman Roulin, Vincent's only friend, died in Marseilles some years ago. But if you go to the asylum at Saint-Rémy, I can give you the name of a café in the village that used to be frequented by an old man called Poulet, whose grandfather was Vincent's warder in the asylum. I'm not sure if he's still alive, but if you find him he may have something to tell you.'

Tralbaut also mentioned that if and when I visited Auvers-sur-Oise, where Vincent died, I should try and trace the descendants of a certain Madame Liberge, concerning the relationship between Vincent and his doctor's daughter, Marguerite Gachet. I wrote down the names.

Tralbaut walked me out into the blazing afternoon sun. 'Do keep me informed of what you are doing. I know you will find new things, because you search with the dedication that one needs for a subject like Van Gogh. His greatness inspires greatness in oneself. Good luck.' We shook hands and I started walking back down the hill, not feeling particularly great at all. My eyes seemed to be filling with pools of sunlight.

'Where to now?' I thought as I walked down the dusty track. Arles being the most written-about period of Vincent's life—when his mental

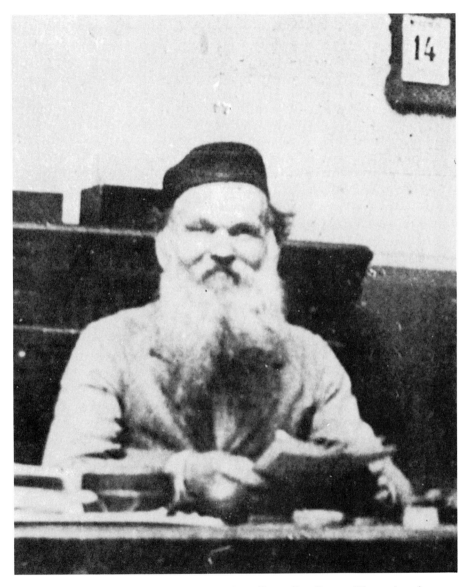

Roulin the postman. A post official with the railway, Roulin was Vincent's only friend in Arles. *Vincent van Gogh Foundation/National Museum Vincent van Gogh, Amsterdam*

illness broke at the height of his creativity—I was hardly treading virgin ground. I laughed at a mental image of dozens of Vincent researchers covering every square inch of Provence with notebooks and magnifying glasses. 'And they've probably all walked down this same hillside.' Oh well, all I could do was keep my eyes and ears open, and not get discouraged. And, as always, remember the deadline, a mere seven days away. I swallowed my panic as it rose in my throat.

I decided to pay a visit to the team of people making the film that Tralbaut had told me about. After asking around a bit, I traced them to an old farmhouse in the valley of the Crau, and introduced myself to Mai Zetterling, the leader of the group. She introduced me in turn to

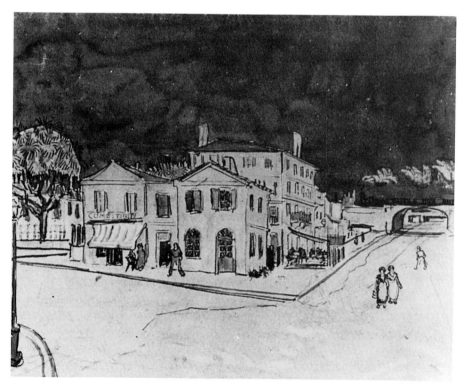

Vincent's painting of the Yellow House in Arles, May 1888. *Vincent van Gogh Foundation/National Museum Vincent van Gogh, Amsterdam*

cameraman John Bulmer and actor Michael Gough. They had rented the farmhouse for five months with the purpose of exploring the genius and suffering of Van Gogh during his stay in Arles. Michael Gough was living the part of Vincent. Like Vincent, he was starving himself of luxury and even necessities.

'At one point I wasn't speaking to anyone and I'd live on nothing but coffee and brandy for three days, then go out in the boiling heat to work to see what it does. It had an extraordinary effect. Enough to make anyone go mad. . . .'

Gough admitted that he had grown to love Vincent. 'In a way the film has turned out to be not really about Van Gogh at all, so much as the action of creation. That, and the attitude of society to the artist and the effect of the artist on society. I found the more I looked into the area of Van Gogh's madness, it seemed to me that so often the way we treat the Van Goghs of this world—the people who are not of the establishment and are unorthodox in their attitudes—is a bit like baiting a bull. You bait him until he charges, then you say: Kill him!'

As Gough talked I detected something akin to the look of mild fanaticism I had first seen on the American I had knocked over on my bicycle earlier in the year, and in the postman Paul Chalcroft. I began to wonder if I was looking that way myself.

I left the group as they were preparing to get back to shooting. They were hardly a living link with Vincent, but in Michael Gough I had found a different kind of link: a testament to the profound effect that Vincent has on people today. How many artists, however great, have the same kind of effect?

After leaving the film group, I went into Arles, which is built around a Roman amphitheatre on the River Rhône and has a labyrinth of narrow winding cobblestone streets. I headed first for the Place Lamartine. Vincent had rented a yellow-painted house there for a while with Paul Gauguin. The Yellow House, as he called it, had gone, but the house behind it, called the Hotel Terminus Van Gogh, was still standing. The building can be seen in Vincent's painting of the Yellow House.

I took a room at the hotel as I hadn't slept in a bed for several nights. Climbing the staircase, I noticed, framed on the wall, a little photograph of a destroyed building with a woman running from it. I recognised that it was the Yellow House. Looking closely, I saw that the hotel was in the picture, too.

When I went back downstairs, I asked about the picture. The hotel-keeper told me that it had been taken by a war correspondent after the Yellow House was bombed by the Nazis in 1944. In the early Fifties the reporter had come back as a guest and given her the photograph. I took the little print outside and photographed it in the Place Lamartine.

That evening, after a light dinner, I strolled around the square. Opposite the hotel in the Place Lamartine is a place overlooking the Rhône where, during the day, the old Arlesians play bowls in the shade of the chestnut trees. This was where Vincent painted his first *Starry Night*. I stopped at a café nearby and had a few glasses of pernod, the drink most similar to absinthe, which Vincent had drunk here. Absinthe is no longer legal. Made with the herb wormwood, it proved to affect the sight and

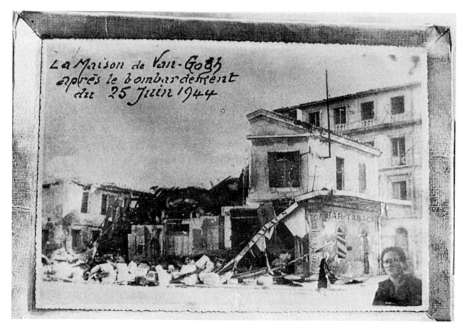

The Yellow House directly after it was bombed on 25 June, 1944. *Author's collection (photographer unknown)*

contribute to insanity. The authorities banned it in the Thirties when they became worried by a proliferation of blind madmen. Considering the amounts Vincent is reported to have drunk, it probably had some effect on him. By my fourth glass of the weaker drink, I was feeling rather peculiar myself.

Easing myself to an unsteady upright position, I made my way across the square. On the other side is the site of the Café Alcazar, the scene of the painting *Night Café*, in which Vincent intended to show 'a place where people could go mad or commit a crime'. Nearby was the brothel where he and Paul Gauguin used to go for what Gauguin called 'nocturnal promenades for reasons of hygiene'. But there's not much to look at any more: both the Alcazar and the Maison du Tolerance have made way for a supermarket. I tried to imagine what they might have looked like by remembering Vincent's pictures.

Feeling the need to rest my feet again, I walked over and sat on a wall by the banks of the Rhône. From there I looked across the Place Lamartine towards the site of the Yellow House, that ill-fated house in which Vincent had dreams of establishing a kind of commune where 'a community of painters' could pool their resources and live and work together under the same roof.

All his life he seemed to be seeking that type of haven, where love or the spirit of good fellowship formed a protection against the indifference and hostility of the world. In Arles he had found a seemingly ideal situation for his artistic family—yellow, the colour of the house, was for Vincent the colour of friendship—but his dream was to end in disaster. The only artist he managed to coax to Arles was Gauguin, and their relationship ended in anything but happiness.

Sitting on the wall, I thought about their brief time together. Gauguin, originally a well-paid stockbroker, had packed his wife and family off to Denmark and chosen to devote his life to painting. A Frenchman with Créole blood, he was worldly, lucid, cool and quick-witted. Vincent was the opposite—intense, explosive and had difficulty in expressing his thoughts verbally. He also idealised Gauguin. The two painted together in the blinding heat during the day and became intoxicated by absinthe and tobacco at night. It wasn't long before their nerves and tempers began to fray. Gauguin didn't share Vincent's belief in universal goodness, and thought his paintings naïve. He often teased Vincent, and the two were frequently at loggerheads. The tensions culminated in a series of dramatic confrontations in the autumn of 1888.

In his memoirs, written 15 years after Vincent's death, Gauguin described how one evening, when the two were drinking at a pavement café, Vincent suddenly threw a glass of absinthe at his head.

The sequel to this incident, according to Gauguin, took place on Christmas Eve in the Place Lamartine. 'In the evening I had a snack for supper and felt the need to go out alone to take the air that was laden with the scent of oleanders in bloom. I had crossed almost the whole of the square when I heard behind me a light step. It was rapid and abrupt and I knew it well. I turned round, just as Vincent was coming at me with a razor in his hand. I must have looked at him then with a very commanding eye, for he stopped, lowered his head, and turned round and ran back towards the Yellow House.'

The third act of the melodrama was even more bizarre. This time the police were called in and the local press reported the event, telling how (on the same night as the attack on Gauguin) Vincent had appeared at a brothel near the Yellow House and given a parcel containing the lower half of his ear to a woman called Rachel, saying: 'Guard this object carefully.' The girl fainted when she saw the piece of ear and, according to the local newspaper report, the police found Vincent back in his bed the next morning, unconscious. He was taken to the hospital in Arles, accompanied by his friend Roulin.

Reviewing these events in my head, I got up and walked round the square again, tracing as best I could Vincent's footsteps when he crept up behind Gauguin with the razor in his hand. With my head cocked and eyes on the ground, I held the imaginary blade in my hand. What was going through Vincent's mind as he walked those silent steps? I had nearly reached the other side of the square, where Gauguin said he turned round and found Vincent following him, when I heard a shuffling noise behind me. I swivelled round abruptly—to find an old woman in a shawl staring at me. I don't know which of us was more surprised. I murmured a few words in French and walked back towards the hotel. I slept very soundly that night.

Next morning I visited the hospital in Arles and photographed the quadrangle at the same angle from which Vincent had painted it after his recovery.

The interior had changed beyond recognition. In one neglected room, however, in a part of the building scheduled for renovation, I found one of the original hospital beds, a strange contraption fastened to the walls and floor, presumably to discourage bizarre bed collectors or patients who showed signs of developing an unnatural attachment to their bed.

Felix Rey was the doctor who treated Vincent's mutilated ear in Arles. In gratitude, he painted Rey's portrait in January 1889. Vincent had cut off the lower quarter of his left ear. Oddly, in the portrait of Dr Rey, he painted the upper three-quarters of his left ear crimson and the lower quarter normal skin-colour. It's the only example of humour I have been able to find in Van Gogh's art.

Dr Rey allowed Vincent to return to the Yellow House, but he suffered from chronic insomnia which he told Theo he cured by placing a strong dose of camphor in his pillow and mattress. He also described how during his illness his mind went back to his birthplace at Zundert, and how he saw again 'every path, every plant in the garden, the views of the fields outside, the neighbours, the graveyard (where his namesake brother was buried), the church, our kitchen garden at the back—down to a magpie's nest in a tall acacia in the graveyard . . . There is no one left who remembers all this but mother and me.' The last statement is a clear fantasy of unique communion with his mother.

After asking a few passers-by whether they might know of a relative, a friend, a postman, whose ancestors knew Van Gogh or had some connection with him, I began to sense that they were looking at me as if *I* were some kind of oddity. Asking about a painter who sliced off his left lobe and went into a mental hospital? Dead for 80 years? Perhaps they had heard about me from the old woman I had met in the square the night before. I felt rather isolated.

I sat alone in a café and had lunch—an omelette and some red wine. I shuddered to think of Vernon Leonard, who was probably looking at his calendar back in Amsterdam, waiting to see whether I would meet my deadline. What would he say about the two days I had spent here without finding a Van Gogh painting? I wasn't even sure what I would say myself. Was I wasting time? Was I going crazy? Something was overpowering the

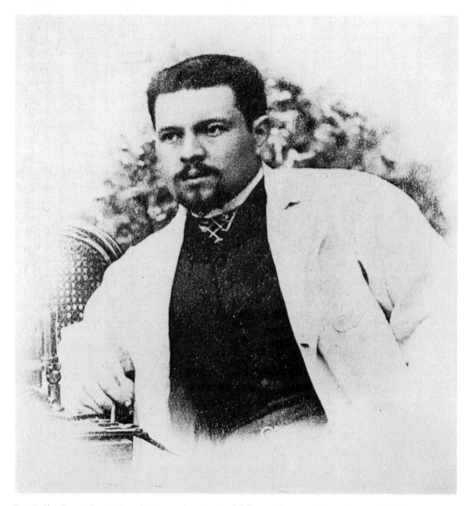

Dr Felix Rey, the Arles doctor who treated Vincent's ear. *Vincent van Gogh Foundation/National Museum Vincent van Gogh, Amsterdam*

journalist in me. I was now looking for something more than 'the story'.

I spent a long afternoon walking through the fields that surround the town. I absorbed the power of the sun, drank in the mad colours of the sky, the green fields, the riots of flowers. I found myself peering through the camera into the hearts of sunflowers, going down on my knees to get

96

close to the corn, the vines, the twisting olive trees. The sombre cypress trees seemed always present. I thought of how Vincent must have identified with them. They appeared as incongruous to me in the Provençal landscape as Vincent must have felt in the community of Arles.

As evening fell my thoughts returned to the question of where to go next. For once there weren't too many choices—Vincent's next stop was only 20 miles away.

After his ear had healed, he started to paint feverishly again. His sense of the universal rhythm of nature returned and he was painting up to 37 canvases without a pause. After his breakdown, however, he had a lot of trouble with the Arlesians. They continually pestered and taunted him, and finally drummed up a petition asking the mayor to lock him up. The police closed the Yellow House. In its brochure for Arles, the city's tourist office apologises for the way the community treated Van Gogh. 'We hope to make up for it by being more hospitable to you.'

Vincent now found himself friendless. Gauguin had gone. Roulin had moved to Marseilles. In March 1889, realising he had experienced three crises in four months, Vincent committed himself to the Saint-Paul-de-Mausole asylum in the hill village of Saint-Rémy-de-Provence.

It was obvious that I should go there too. Tralbaut had told me of someone there who might have something to tell me, and I wanted to see the place where Vincent had spent over a year struggling with his madness. I decided to sleep out in the hills near Arles, and drive on the next morning to Saint-Rémy. I stopped in a café for a pernod, and, as the sky darkened to dusk, headed for the countryside.

The night sky was brilliant, shimmering and sparkling with stars. Lying in my sleeping bag, with the envelope under my head, I thought about the *Starry Night* that Vincent painted in Saint-Rémy, with its sleeping houses, the black flames of cypresses surging into a deep blue sky with whirlpools of yellow stars and the radiations of an orange moon. The painting seems an attempt to liberate himself from overpowering emotions. In the depths of his loneliness, he animated the heavens with dynamic and furious motion.

Creeping back to the car, I got out a torch and my copy of Tralbaut's book, and crawled back into my sleeping bag. There was a quotation from a letter that I wanted to re-read. Writing to Theo, Vincent said:

Looking at the stars always makes me dream, as simply as I dream over the black dots representing towns and villages on a map. Why, I ask myself, shouldn't the shining dots of the sky be as accessible as the black dots on a map of France? Just as we take the train to Tarascon or Rouen, we take death to reach a star. . . .

I lay back in my sleeping bag and thought of Vincent's sense of isolation, of his fear of his illness. He wrote to a critic that the emotions aroused by looking at the cypress trees were strong enough to incapacitate him for weeks. The intensity of his response to nature made him, he said, a coward.

Lying alone under the sky, I wondered whether I could ever sympathise completely with Vincent's mental state. The rational side of me said that I didn't want to: who wanted to experience his suffering? But another side told me that Vincent's nephew, the Engineer, was right: there is something of Vincent in all of us. Lying under the night sky he had fought to capture on his canvases, I felt that solitude he spoke of so often. It chilled me. I had to struggle against the influence of something stronger than myself, something that would take my will away as he said his was taken. I convinced myself that I was exhausted—I still hadn't slept much since I'd been travelling—and needed a hot meal. In the morning I would be all right. Finally, my head full of reassurances, sleep came. It was just after midnight.

About three hours later, I woke up again. The full moon was staring me in the face. The stars were dancing in the deep blue of the sky. In the distance I heard howling. Just a dog, I thought. Nothing to worry about. But I didn't sleep. I felt that I was being watched by the inhabitants of the night sky, and I couldn't get them out of my mind. Finally I abandoned yet again all hope of a night's sleep. I re-read Tralbaut, I walked around, I scribbled in my notebook. When sunlight came I welcomed it as an old friend. I washed my face in the dew, as the early morning mist slowly lost its grip on the vines and evaporated into a purple haze.

After sitting a few moments to watch the play of light on the cornfields, I packed up and got into my car. Next stop, the asylum.

5   In the Asylum

The asylum began life as an Augustinian monastery, and was converted to its present use in the 1880s. It seemed a friendly enough place as I approached it with camera, notebook and envelope tucked under my arm. Friendly by the standards of a nineteenth-century prison, anyway. I still remembered Vincent's descriptions of his fellow inmates shrieking and crying. I hoped not to hear too much of that.

The whole compound is surrounded by a high wall, and can be entered only through an iron gate. I was surprised to find the gate unlocked. Strolling down the shady drive that led to a side entrance, I kept looking behind me—something I never used to do—till I bumped into a massive metal door. I pulled the bell. After a minute or so, the metal latch of the rusty old peephole opened. For a few seconds I had the uncomfortable feeling that 'they can see you but you can't see them'. I smiled, trying to look as innocent and sane as possible.

The door creaked open, and a little nun stood in the doorway. She was frail but had eyes like a weasel. She introduced herself as Sister Marie-Florentine.

'Good morning, my son. Have you come to join us?' Her beady eyes beckoned a positive reply.

'Well, not quite yet,' I replied. There was something ominous in the way she asked the question. 'I'm under a different kind of order. I am writing about Vincent van Gogh. I believe he lived here in 1889, sister?'

'Yes, he did, my son.' I didn't like the way she called me 'son'.

'I was wondering if I could take a few photographs from the window of his room—if it still exists?'

'Of course, my son. I will take you to his room. Come this way.' She spoke as if Vincent was still living there and was waiting for me. 'This part of the hospital has not been in use for many years.'

On our way down the dark stone-walled corridor Sister Marie-Florentine asked me twice if I knew that Nostradamus was born in Saint-Rémy. Twice I told her that I didn't know but would bear the fact in mind for future reference. Perhaps she was a relative.

Near the end of the corridor we stopped at a door. Sister Marie-Florentine brandished an arsenal of keys which looked like it weighed slightly less than I do, and suddenly the door swung open.

I don't know what the inmates' cells looked like when Vincent lived at

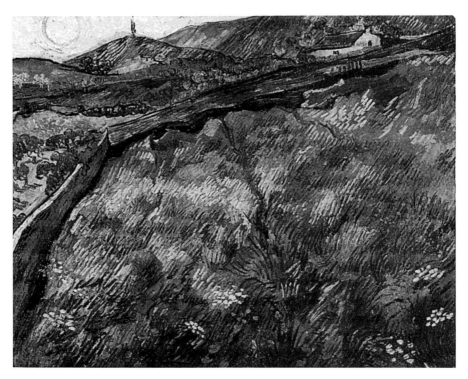

'Field of spring wheat at sunrise', Saint-Rémy, March–April 1890, oil on canvas. This was one of the studies Vincent made of the view from his room in the asylum. *National Museum Kröller-Müller, Otterlo*

the asylum in 1889, but I can't believe they were quite as comfortable as the cells that visitors are shown today. That's to be expected, I thought. You don't want people thinking you used to run a chamber of horrors. But when I stepped to the window to take a picture, I was even more surprised. The view from that window was definitely not the one Vincent painted. After humming and hawing for a few moments, I pointed this out to Sister Marie-Florentine. Her smile turned immediately sour.

'Non! Non, monsieur!' I had suddenly changed from her son to 'monsieur'. 'Vincent van Gogh slept here. He had his fits here!' She was obviously under orders to tell this to visitors. I showed her a reproduction of one of Vincent's views from his window, reproduced in Tralbaut's book. But she was adamant.

'You are mistaken, monsieur. Monsieur van Gogh lived in this room.'

Well, not much point in arguing, I thought. I dutifully clicked off a few frames and changed the subject.

At Theo's request, Vincent was permitted to paint in the grounds of the asylum. In one of the works he did here—a *Pieta* copied from a work by Eugene Delacroix—Vincent gave Christ his own features and Mary the features of Sister Epiphany, the mother superior of the cloister. I had seen mention of Sister Epiphany in Vincent's letters and wondered whether she was still remembered.

Apparently she was. When I showed a photograph of her to the nun, she clasped her hands, trembled slightly and began to mutter to herself. When she had stopped mumbling, I asked her about Sister Epiphany.

'She was a living saint,' said Sister Marie-Florentine. 'So good. So kind. Everyone loved her and treasures her memory still today.'

'Vincent seemed to have a very high regard for her too,' I said.

'Yes, and Sister Epiphany had a special place in her heart for the painter Van Gogh. On more than one occasion she stopped him from eating his paints. She was very sad when Monsieur van Gogh left here.'

'I would have expected her to be glad he was well enough to leave,' I said.

'Ah yes,' replied the sister, with a glint in her eye. 'But he was a very special case. You must agree. People respected him here and left him alone to work. Here he found peace. And we of the Saint-Paul-de-Mausole asylum are proud we had him. You see these flower pots?' she

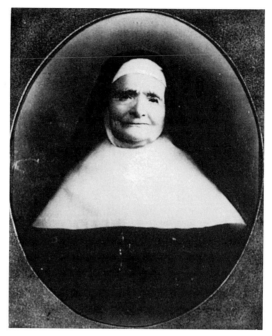

Sister Epiphany (Madame Deschanel), Mother Superior of the cloister at the time of Vincent's confinement. *Vincent van Gogh Foundation/National Museum Vincent van Gogh, Amsterdam*

said, complacently pointing to a bath full of earth in the corridor. 'Well, that was the bath where Vincent spent hours as part of his hydropathic treatment.'

'With water and not earth in it?' I cracked a sickly smile that felt quite out of place in the cell.

'Water, naturally,' replied the nun. Her eyes narrowed suspiciously. No more jokes in here, I thought.

'What was his diagnosis?'

'Either epilepsy or schizophrenia. He was originally diagnosed as an epileptic, but today people are not sure.'

From my reading I knew this to be the case. I made a note for future reference to delve further into Vincent's illness.

While we were talking, I continued to think about which room Vincent had really stayed in. I glanced occasionally out of the window, gauging distances and looking at the trees in the courtyard. Finally I decided that it was upstairs, one flight up. I raised the subject again with Sister Marie-Florentine.

'You know, I think that the room Van Gogh stayed in might be upstairs. If I could have a look . . .'

'Monsieur, you think incorrectly,' she cut in. 'If you do not believe that this is Van Gogh's room then that is your affair. Everyone is entitled to his own belief. But that means there is no longer any reason for you to be here.' She rattled her chain of keys.

'Just a quick look?' I said, raising my eyebrows like a little boy trying to persuade his mother to take him into a toy shop.

'Non! Non! Non!'

'You know I've come all the way from . . .'

'Non! Let me show you out.' Sister Marie-Florentine took me by the arm and walked me back down the corridor. We stopped at the door.

'Goodbye, sister.'

'Goodbye, my son.' She said with a smile as sweet as a razor.

To hell with this, I thought as I trudged down the drive. Looking back, I could see the sun reflecting off the nun's glasses behind the peephole. I wondered how long I would keep sane in there.

In the olive grove at the back of the asylum wall, I photographed the trees at close range. Vincent had painted and drawn them often, seeming to find in their twisted forms a mirror of his own torment.

The mid-morning sun was now climbing to its peak in the blue expanse of sky, and the air was hot. I trudged up a hill overlooking the back garden of the asylum and dropped wearily to the ground. The sun was making me sweat, but Sister Marie-Florentine's obstinacy had made me fume. How does she know? What's she so worried about? I stared angrily into space.

Suddenly I realised that the garden below me was the one that Vincent had painted from his window. Click. A crazy idea came to me . . . If Sister Marie-Florentine wouldn't show me the upstairs of the asylum, I was going to go there myself. I would get my picture yet, in spite of her and her chain of keys.

Studying the angle of the painting that Vincent made from his window,

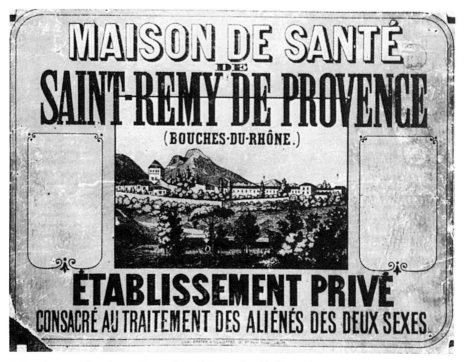

Advertisement for the asylum, viewed from the Alpilles. *Vincent van Gogh Foundation/National Museum Vincent van Gogh, Amsterdam*

I deduced that his room was probably one floor up from Sister Marie-Florentine's shrine of reflection. I even made a guess as to which room was likely to have been his. Now all I had to do was find a way of getting in there.

I figured that if I climbed the telegraph pole at the foot of the asylum wall, I could crawl along the top of the wall and enter Vincent's wing through a broken, barless window I had noticed. And providing it wasn't Sister Marie-Florentine's private toilet, I would be all right. So up the pole I went together with drawing, camera, and notebook.

When I was about six feet off the ground, a Dobermann Pinscher and a ferocious mongrel bounded, fangs bared, at the spot where I had been standing seconds before. My eyes bulged in disbelief. Surely they could see that I was trying to get in, not out. Surely they didn't think that I was an inmate. Surely . . . I didn't wait to find out what they thought. Pulling myself up as fast as I could, I finally made it to the top of the garden wall. They were still down there, snarling and clawing at the base of the pole.

Crawling along the garden wall like an intrepid old cat, I suddenly felt rather absurd. Perhaps the Arlesian sun really had begun to affect my head. I mean, who in his right mind would risk encountering Sister Marie-Florentine again after her lunch of gruel and newts? And who would believe me if I told them what I was trying to do—that armed with a drawing I suspected was a Van Gogh, and looking like he must have on one of his bad days, I was trying to break into his asylum cell? Could I blame them if they tried to keep me in?

Anyway, there was no turning back now. Apart from any doubts I had, it was physically impossible for me to turn round on top of the wall. After ten minutes of crawling, I reached the broken window and looked inside. The room was empty. I stuck my hand through the window, raised the rusty latch, and crawled in.

The walls of the room were damp and peeling. The whole place smelled like mouldy mustard. As there were no bars, I supposed it had been a warder's rest room. Easing the door slowly open, I tiptoed down the damp corridor past a beautiful wooden statue of the Virgin Mary. She seemed to be looking down accusingly at me. As a rat scurried away into a cell on my right, I wished I had never gone so far.

The old wing was falling apart, but it was unmistakably the same place that Vincent had painted and described in his letters. The faint sound of my footsteps echoed the steps of the unhappy souls who had walked here in days gone by. Vincent wrote in one of his letters that the more time one spent with them, the less one thought of them as mad. I nosed into the empty cells, one by one. Each was exactly like the one before, except for the view. Which was, of course, all I was interested in.

Finally I found the view Vincent had painted, with the garden (now overgrown) and the Alpilles sloping away in the background. The hunter and his prey, the fisherman and his catch. This was what I'd been looking for. Yet . . . somehow I didn't feel quite the thrill I ought to have felt. Before I had been like a child in front of a toy store. Now I was actually inside the store, but had discovered the toys weren't nearly as much fun to

105

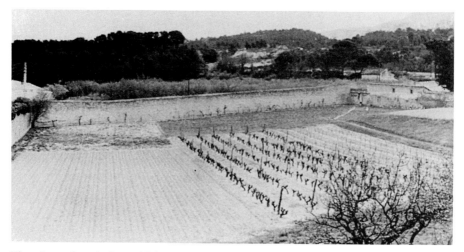

View from the window of Vincent's room in the asylum of Saint-Paul-de-Mausole, Saint-Rémy, in 1972. *Photo: the author*

play with as they were to look at. At least I could record the great discovery on film. I made several exposures to be sure of getting the right one, and that was it.

The room had only a bed and a chair and was somewhat more basic than the one shown to tourists. I felt the dampness creep into my bones. This place was enough to turn anyone into a depressive. There was only one thing I wanted to do now: get out quickly. I crept along the corridor and down the stairs, hoping to get out by the door this time. Damn! It was padlocked. The only thing I could do was climb back along the wall. I tiptoed upstairs again and, as I was making for the room with the broken window and my freedom, I heard an ominous jangling of keys.

I didn't have to think twice about who was on the end of the key ring. I tried one cell door. Locked. Another. Locked. Two more. Locked. Locked. Hell! The jangling was coming closer and any moment I expected Dracula's answer to Audrey Hepburn to appear around the corner. There was only one refuge in sight: a huge statue of the Virgin Mary which stood between me and the direction from which the jangling was coming. I crouched behind the statue and waited.

Along she came, padding softly down the hall. Suddenly her footsteps stopped. She was right in front of the statue. I thought the game was up. What should I do? Pray? Then I heard her mumbling a prayer herself. Of course! She couldn't pass without paying her respects. The prayer went on . . . and on. For what felt like half an hour I was bent double at the feet of Holy Mary. But it couldn't go on for ever. I prayed she would stop praying. And it worked: Sister Marie-Florentine rose and went on her way. I suppressed a snort of laughter. As soon as she was out of sight, I darted back to the room with the broken window. I reached the window and began to crawl back along the wall. All went well until I reached the telegraph pole. The dogs were still at its base, gnashing their teeth in anticipation.

What now? All I could do was sit there. It was too far to jump and only a lunatic would feed himself to these two man-eaters. I waited. They waited. I like dogs so I tried talking to them, but they weren't having any. Ten minutes passed. Fifteen minutes. Half an hour. The wall was narrow and uncomfortable. I sat in every possible position and finally ended up lying on my stomach. Was this a Sister Marie-Florentine torture? Had she noticed me all along and just let me think I'd got away? I imagined how Vincent would have painted her, and then worked her into a Hieronymus Bosch torture scene.

About 40 minutes passed before a hunch-backed man came by. He looked up at me and waved his walking stick.

'What are you doing up there?'

I tried to explain, but when it became complicated, he interrupted.

'I'm the caretaker of this asylum,' he said. 'No one is allowed to leave the hospital without the authorisation of the Mother Superior or the doctor-in-charge. Climb down and come with me!'

'I'd have done that long ago if it weren't for these dogs.'

'Yes, I bet you would. And it's just for the likes of you that we keep them here!' But he obliged me by whistling to the dogs, who abandoned their duties and wagged over to the caretaker's side. I clutched the drawing and camera to my sides and slithered down the pole. It felt good to touch earth again.

Unfortunately I made some sort of sudden movement, for the dogs began their barking and took a few steps in my direction. I was getting ready to shin up the pole again when the caretaker called them off.

'Boris! Vincent!'

I couldn't believe my ears. 'Did I hear you say *Vincent?*' One of the dogs looked up at me with his head cocked.

'Yes, Vincent,' replied the caretaker indignantly. 'Come on now, don't keep me waiting.'

I didn't know whether to laugh or cry. Perhaps laughing would be less suspicious.

We walked towards a modern building adjacent to the old asylum. On the way I tried to explain myself, but he just nodded and agreed with everything I said. He clearly thought I was a lunatic and felt he had to humour me. In the end I got tired of repeating myself and shut up. We entered the hospital and stood at the registration desk.

'I found this man escaping over the wall,' said the caretaker proudly.

'That's a lie,' I retorted. 'I'm a visitor. I didn't escape. I broke in . . . I mean . . . I just wanted to photograph Vincent van Gogh's cell. You see, I'm. . . .' Sometimes words fail you when you need them most. A doctor was called in. I introduced myself.

'Now, Monsieur Wilkie,' he said in a sickeningly sympathetic voice, 'you tell me all about it. You can say anything you like to me. Don't worry. . . .'

I asked him to *please* check the hospital register, which would prove I was not an inmate. This was done and at least that was settled. But the doctor seemed to feel that he had some sort of grip on me.

'Now if you feel you need to come here for whatever reason,' he said, 'we would prefer if you would approach us through the official channels. You will find that Monsieur Van Gogh did so through his brother.'

What bureaucratic lunacy, I thought. Calmly I informed the doctor that I was not ready to come into his cosy little establishment and didn't expect to be ready for some time; that I was a serious journalist and resented his implication that I was mad. I told him to watch what his dogs got their teeth into, because what they were offering to administer was anything but tender loving care. My voice rose slightly as I neared the end of my little speech. Time to leave. Get out of this cuckoo's nest fast.

I said goodbye and headed into Saint-Rémy. My hands shook slightly and I was still angry. What was going on? Maybe there was something about the atmosphere of Provence that affected the brain. I needed a drink.

I went to the café where Tralbaut had suggested I might find old Poulet, whose grandfather was Vincent's warder in the asylum. While ordering a pernod, I asked the proprietor if a Monsieur Poulet frequented the place.

'Old Poulet? Oui, Monsieur, he's due any minute.'

I sat down at a table near the bar and a few minutes later the café owner nodded to me as an old man with white hair and cheeks like fresh apples came shuffling up to the bar. He ordered his usual, which was a St Raphael. I went up and explained what I was doing and asked him if he would join me. He did so gladly. I got straight to the point.

'Did your grandfather have any connection with Van Gogh?'

'Oh yes,' said the old man. 'My grandfather was a warder at the asylum, you see, and he used to take Van Gogh out into the country around Saint-Rémy. They went on long walks and Van Gogh would take his paints and easel with him.'

I asked Poulet what Vincent told his grandfather about himself.

'Ah, monsieur,' he replied, 'alas, nothing. My grandfather said that Van Gogh would not utter a word to him—either in or out of the asylum. But he would paint quietly. He said that Monsieur Van Gogh lived in his own world but seemed to know what he was doing.

'Very occasionally he would become violent. On one occasion, for no reason, he kicked my grandfather's backside as they were going up the asylum stairs. He didn't tell me much else, my grandfather, apart from one story about Van Gogh's paintings that you may be interested in.'

'Go on.'

'Well, Monsieur Van Gogh left behind him at the asylum a case of canvases and my grandfather saw what happened to them,' said Poulet. 'The son of Monsieur Van Gogh's doctor, Dr Peyron, found the case and showed the canvases to his friend, a boy called Henri Vanel. The boys decided to use them as targets for their bows and arrows. They stood the paintings up on the steps of the asylum and shot holes in them till they were in tatters. Only much later, when the painter Van Gogh became so famous, did they realise what they had destroyed . . .'

6 Yellow Flowers

After a few drinks with old Poulet, I left the café and went for a walk. I was slowly calming down from my encounter with Sister Marie-Florentine, the doctor, and the asylum guard dogs. I still had the ability to think about where I was and what I was doing.

The picture was not entirely rosy. It was now Thursday afternoon. I was 900 miles from Amsterdam. I had to be back there by 9 a.m. on Monday, and between now and then I wanted to visit Auvers-sur-Oise, where Vincent had spent his last three months. Tralbaut had told me of someone to look up there, and it did seem a logical place to end my trip. Worse still, I also wanted to visit Vincent's and Theo's apartment in Paris. Thinking about the layout of the article, I knew a photo of the apartment would go well with Baroness Bonger's description of Vincent's life there.

But how was I going to do it? The nights of sleep I'd been missing were starting to catch up with me, I had hundreds of miles to drive and I was nearing the end of my money. More than anything I wanted to be in Amsterdam—a hot bath, a good meal, and then 15 or 20 hours' sleep. But that would have to wait. I got into my car and started driving. I tried not to think of anything except getting to Paris.

I arrived there in the early morning and headed for Montmartre, the hilly district in the northern part of the city where Vincent and Theo had lived. I hoped to get a room near rue Lepic, their street.

No luck. The hotels were either full or no one answered the door. Well, at least the cafés are open, I thought. I decided to walk down to 62 Boulevard de Clichy, to see what was left of the Café-Brasserie du Tambourin, where Vincent used to carouse with *Les Impressionistes du Petit Boulevard*—men like Toulouse-Lautrec, Anquetin, Emile Bernard, Gauguin and Emile Zola.

Disappointment awaited me. The site was occupied by a sex club and a plastic and chrome café-restaurant called The Two Notes. No one in

110

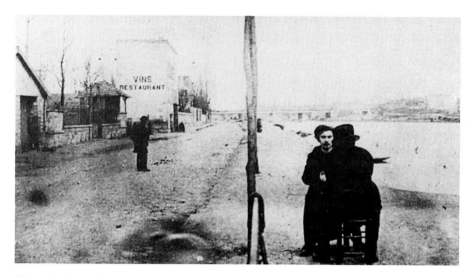

Vincent's backview as he sits in conversation with his friend Emile Bernard at Asnières in 1886. This is the only photograph known to have been taken of Vincent after the age of 18. He had a contempt for photography, feeling it lacked depth. (Automatic shutter release by Emile Bernard). *Vincent van Gogh Foundation/National Museum Vincent van Gogh, Amsterdam*

either establishment knew of a Café Tambourin. In The Two Notes I had a look in the back yard and could see that the building had been totally rebuilt. Nothing to look for here.

In a café in rue des Abbesses, I referred back to the notes made during my talk with Baroness Bonger.

At the time when her husband, Andries, was living with Theo and Vincent in their third-floor flat at 54 rue Lepic, Theo was involved in a relationship with an apparently rather disturbed girl referred to by all three as 'S'. It was not a satisfactory relationship, and Vincent felt that, though his brother must part company with the girl, he ought not to be harsh about it in case it drove her to suicide or madness. He came up with the extraordinary proposal that if Theo and 'S' agreed, he would be prepared to make an 'amicable arrangement' by taking 'S' off Theo's hands and, if necessary, agreeing to a *mariage de raison* with her.

Bonger, who was living with Vincent and 'S' while Theo was away, told

Theo that he agreed with Vincent's reasoning, apart from the offer of marriage which he found 'impractical'. He accused Theo of having handled the woman insensitively.

There follows a gap of a year in the brothers' correspondence during the time they lived together, between summer 1886 and summer 1887, after which there is no further mention of 'S' in any letter. In the meantime, Vincent had developed a tempestuous relationship with an Italian, Agostina Segatori, who ran Café Tambourin. Van Gogh's young painter friend Emile Bernard wrote later that Vincent had an arrangement with La Segatori (was this the same person as 'S'?) whereby he ate at Le Tambourin in return for a few paintings a week. The walls were lined with Van Gogh's work but when the café went bankrupt there was a punch-up between Vincent and the management over the paintings. In an unpublished manuscript of Bernard, who made his first sale at Le Tambourin, he stated that Vincent removed all his paintings from the café by wheelbarrow. Although the relationship was over, Vincent wrote that he still felt affection for Segatori and hoped she did for him. He described her as being ill following either an abortion or a miscarriage.

What happened to La Segatori? I wondered. Within an hour, I was combing the *Archives de Paris*, with a list of 14 names and facts to check, including the address of Cormon's studio where Vincent studied for four months and met many contemporaries.

But Segatori seemed to have disappeared with her café in 1888. Scouring one huge register after another, I concluded that she was lost without trace. And, actually, I was glad because one condition of research in this airless archive was to have the *Conservateur des Archives de Paris* hanging over my shoulder like an overfed vulture. Madame Felkay's breath, filtered through a mouthful of teeth like a battered old piano keyboard, had the fragrance of decaying cabbage as it was wafted in my direction with every turn of a massive page in the old register.

In the late afternoon, I staggered out of the Archives and, drunk with fresh air, reeled back up to Montmartre.

Feeling I had done enough research for one day, I walked up the rue des Abbesses looking into one café after another. My precious envelope was by now covered with wine and coffee stains, but the contents were protected by stiff cardboard and waterproof wrapping.

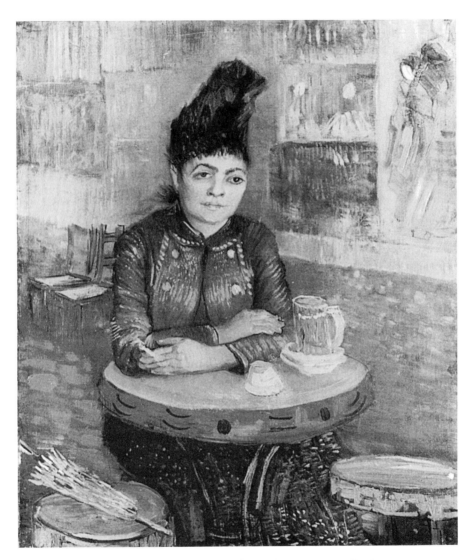

Vincent's portrait of Agostina Segatori, Paris, 1888. *Vincent van Gogh Foundation/National Museum Vincent van Gogh, Amsterdam*

In the second café I stopped at, I met up with a French boy, a Breton named Daniel Marais who had lived in Amsterdam, and an Irishman of about my own age, Gerald O'Keefe. O'Keefe tried to convince me that apart from being a flautist of some note he was the John Millington Synge of the Seventies. His first novel had been burning inside him for 15 years and he was waiting for a W. B. Yeats to come along and discover him. Seeing how full he was of the blarney—not to mention the wine—I told him jokingly that I thought he belonged in one of Samuel Beckett's dustbins—a reference to Beckett's play *Endgame*. The remark was intended as a compliment, but he didn't see it that way.

'I'll stick you in the bloody dustbin,' he said, with all his formidable Irish charm. He lurched across the table and would have pounded me into it, if Daniel had not separated us.

We ended up in the streets around Les Halles, drinking bowls of onion soup between bottles of wine. It was a wild night.

I woke up the next morning with an aching head and a dim memory of all the silly things I had said, but after several coffees and croissants in a pavement café I felt more than ready to launch out on my quest for Van Gogh again.

I went first to the Banque Nationale des Pays Bas to arrange for a little money to be transferred from my account in Amsterdam. Coincidentally, this was the bank—indeed the same building—where Vincent received his allowances from Theo when Theo was out of the country. As it would take a couple of hours for the transaction to be completed, I used the time to visit 54 rue Lepic.

The baker across the road from number 54 told me that the one-time Van Gogh flat was now occupied by a certain Madame Moreau.

'There she is crossing the road. You'll just catch her,' said the baker. 'If you're lucky . . .'

Madame Moreau was a stalky middle-aged woman with a square chin and thick biceps. She reminded me of the strong-armed aunt of a cowboy cartoon character, Desperate Dan. She was at the door of 54 when I nipped across the road and asked her: 'Excuse me, madame, my name is Ken Wilkie. I am a . . .'

I didn't get further than the word 'journalist' when she flashed an icy glare over her shoulder and stopped me dead.

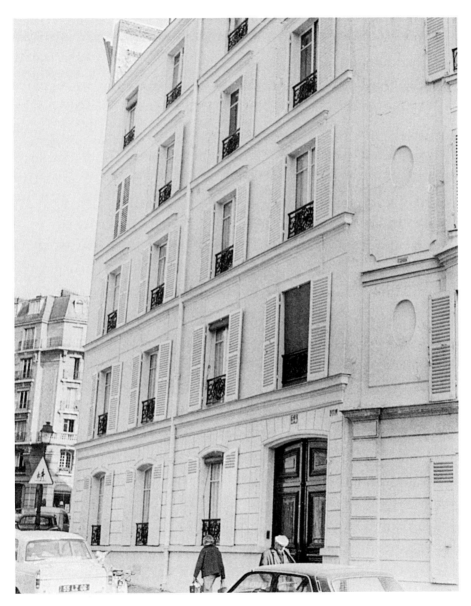

Number 54 rue Lepic. The flat shared by Theo and Vincent was on the third floor. *Photo: the author*

'Don't say it!' she said. 'I know what you're after. You want to see the inside of my house, don't you? Well, it's my house now, and I don't *care* who lived in it 100 years ago. It's *mine* and I'm sick to death of the likes of *you* pestering me day and night. Even the plaque on the wall outside has been stolen twice in the last five years. Did you know that?'

'I have no intention of disturbing you, madame . . .' I began. But she stomped up the wooden stairs with her shopping.

Madame Moreau, I thought, was probably no more quarrelsome than Vincent was under that same roof during the night-long arguments with his brother. But the present inhabitant's anger had nothing to do with art or literature. Her patience had been strained over the years by tourists following their guidebooks of Montmartre, and all wanting to see inside her home. But I had approached her politely and without presumption.

I decided to wait a little, let her cool off, and then try again. Perhaps I had just caught her on a bad morning. I climbed to the third floor and pressed the bell. Silence. Then . . .

'I see you. You can't fool me!' She was looking through a peephole. Her voice came like a horn from the other side of the door.

'I am truly *sorry* to trouble you, madame, but could I just take one photograph of your home. Just one and I'll be gone. Gone forever,' I said. Baroness Bonger had described Vincent's life with her husband, the girl called 'S' and Theo in this flat, and I was longing to see the place as it was today. But the reality of Madame Moreau looked like being more than I could deal with. I wondered if I was handling her properly. Should I resort to deception and disguise as a plumber, perhaps? Or should I take the cow by the horns? There are limits to everyone's tolerance, as Theo found out under this very roof. I certainly wasn't going to grovel to her.

'I've had enough Americans knocking at my door,' she yelled next.

'I'm Scottish. Not American,' I replied, hoping to appeal to the traditional French regard for the Scots.

'Scottish? Where's your kilt, then? At home with your bagpipes, I suppose?'

'In fact, yes. If I come back with my kilt on and serenade you with my bagpipes, will you let me take a photograph?' I asked.

'I didn't know Scotsmen used cameras,' she replied.

'Oh yes. Since 1835,' I informed her.

That did it. She flung the door open, a formidable sight with face beetroot-red. I could see at once that she hadn't changed her mind about letting me in. She let me have it instead. As I turned to run down the stairs, she coshed me over the head with a loaf of French bread—a well-fired loaf, which knocked me off balance. I slithered down the stairs clutching envelope and camera-bag. She heaved down the stairs after me, shouting and waving her rolling-pins of arms like a discus thrower gone wild. 'Get out! Get out!' she yelled after me as I limped down rue Lepic.

So much for Paris. There was nothing to do but collect my money and leave. It upset me to have to go without getting the photograph I wanted, but I had no choice. It was Friday afternoon, and I hoped to be in Amsterdam by Sunday evening, to try and get a good night's sleep.

I drove out of Paris, northward to Pontoise, and followed the River Oise to Auvers where Vincent spent his last months in the care of Dr Gachet.

While in Auvers, Vincent stayed in a little inn belonging to Gustav Ravoux. Now called Café Van Gogh, it is situated directly opposite the Town Hall. As I sat in the café, looking out of the window and collecting my thoughts, I was reminded of Vincent's birthplace in Zundert, which was also opposite a Town Hall. But here it was, in a room upstairs, that Vincent died.

Innkeeper Ravoux's daughter Adeline was often painted by Vincent and, before she died, she described to Dr Tralbaut how she saw Vincent that evening after he had shot himself. I sat in the café and read the passage in my copy of Tralbaut's book.

Monsieur Van Gogh had lunch at midday and went out. Nobody thought anything of it for he came and went all the time and neither my parents nor I noticed anything unusual about his behaviour. But in the evening he didn't return. It was a warm night and, after we had finished the meal, we took the air outside the café. Then we saw Monsieur Vincent staggering along the road in big strides, his head tilted towards his maimed ear. He looked drunk although he never drank at Auvers.

When he came near us, he passed like a shadow, without saying 'Bonsoir' as he always did. My mother said to him: 'Monsieur

Vincent, we were worried at not seeing you. What happened?' He leant for a few moments on the billiard table in order not to lose his balance, and replied in a low voice: 'Oh nothing, I am wounded.'

Monsieur Vincent slowly climbed the 17 steps up to his attic room. When I went to the foot of the stairs, I heard him groan. My father went upstairs then. The door was not locked. He went in and saw Monsieur Vincent lying on the narrow iron bedstead with his face turned to the wall. My father asked him what was the matter. 'I shot myself . . . I only hope I haven't botched it,' replied Monsieur Vincent. Then father saw a trickle of blood coming from Monsieur

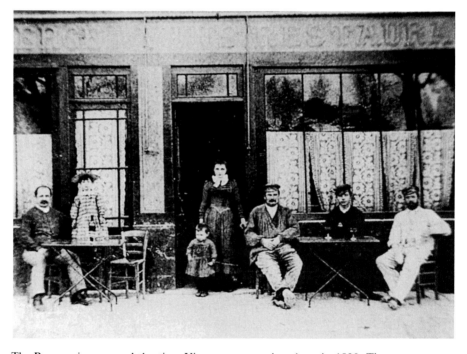

The Ravoux inn around the time Vincent was staying there in 1890. The owner, Gustave Ravoux, is seated far left, and his daughter Adeline is standing in the doorway with her little brother Levert whom Vincent used as a child model. Said Adeline of Van Gogh: 'You soon forgot his lack of charm when you watched him amusing the children.' *Vincent van Gogh Foundation/National Museum Vincent van Gogh, Amsterdam*

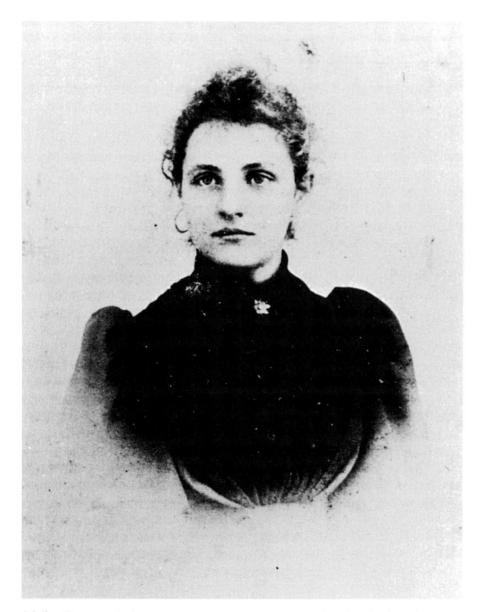

Adeline Ravoux, the innkeeper's daughter who modelled for Van Gogh at Auvers.
Vincent van Gogh Foundation/National Museum Vincent van Gogh, Amsterdam

Vincent's chest. He remembered that he had given the painter his pistol that day. Monsieur Vincent said that he wanted it to scare the crows away from his canvas when he was painting in the fields. The police arrived and demanded to know where the weapon was. But Monsieur Vincent refused to give an explanation. 'I am free to do what I want with my body,' he said. 'Can I have my pipe and tobacco?' I climbed the stairs myself and saw him smoking quietly, staring straight ahead of him.

Was that room still there? Was it open to visitors? I introduced myself to the present owner of the café, who said he'd be happy to show me the room.

'It's remained exactly as it was in 1890,' he said.

We climbed the creaking wooden stairs that Vincent himself had staggered up, clutching his wounded chest. The only furniture in the tiny room was an old iron bed, a tattered straw chair, a chest of drawers, an oil lamp, the painter's easel, and a little calendar for the year 1890.

Here Vincent patiently smoked his pipe, waiting for the end to come, while Theo journeyed from Paris to be with his dying brother.

What happened in Auvers to bring on this final act of self-destruction? I wondered. I pictured the weeping Theo, and Vincent's last words: 'I wish I could die now . . .'

By all accounts it wasn't another attack of insanity that made him shoot himself. When Vincent arrived in Auvers he had written to Theo: 'I feel completely calm and in good condition. Since I gave up drinking, I do better work than before.'

I stood silently for a few minutes in that damp attic room where Vincent had died, and depression began to fill me. Thanking the owner, I walked out of the café into the sun. I passed the low thatched cottages by the placidly flowing river, walked up the well-trodden steps linking streets on different levels, under the flowering chestnuts, along the white dusty roads that cut through the patchwork of tilled soil, and ambled in the luxuriant gardens. Vincent had painted them all. And by the time he had been in Auvers for a month, he had also made portraits, not only of Dr Gachet, but of the doctor's daughter, Marguerite, playing the piano.

In Provence, Dr Tralbaut had told me that back in the Thirties he had

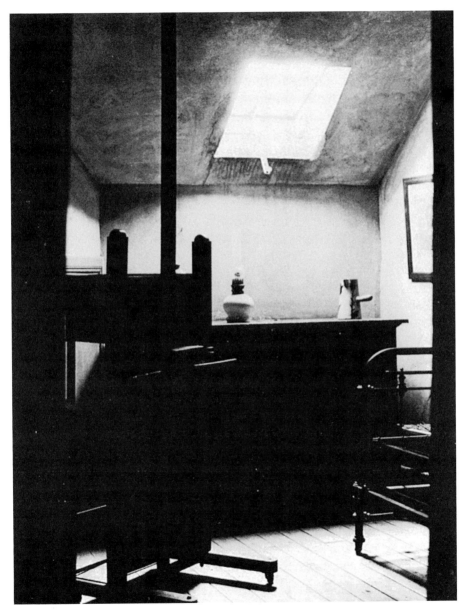

The room in the inn where Vincent died on 29 July, 1890. *Photo: the author*

heard about events leading to Vincent's death that involved Dr Gachet's daughter. This intrigued me. I had found his first love; perhaps Marguerite was his last. But where was the evidence? The only name Tralbaut could give me was a certain Madame Liberge who was said to have information relating to the affair.

I checked with the Town Hall register to see if Madame Liberge had any descendants still living in the region. The clerk showed me that Madame Liberge had died in 1947, but her daughter, Madame Giselle Baize, still lived in the family house in rue Van Gogh—so called, the clerk told me, because Vincent often set up his easel in that road.

Madame Baize had no telephone, so I walked to the outskirts of Auvers and found the house on a bluff of the river Oise.

As I approached, I could see Madame Baize, dressed in a flowery overall, feeding the hens at the door of her house. A woman in her fifties, she had a broad, open Gallic face and greeted me at the door without the slightest hint of suspicion or annoyance. When I explained my reason for calling on her, she took me into her big kitchen and over mugs of *café au lait* she told me her story.

'My mother was Marguerite Gachet's best friend. And she was the only person, as far as I am aware, who knew about the love affair between Vincent van Gogh and Marguerite. Marguerite was a proud girl but suppressed by her father. She confided to my mother that Vincent and she had fallen in love with each other and that Vincent wanted to marry her. But the thorn in the flesh was Marguerite's father, Dr Gachet. Though an advocate of free love in theory, he was strongly against an association between Vincent, who was of course his patient, and his daughter. Gachet forbade Marguerite to see the painter.'

So in Auvers Vincent may well have felt himself losing a last opportunity of founding a family. This may have helped to strain his already fragile emotions to breaking point.

Madame Baize continued: 'After Vincent's suicide, Marguerite's depression became so serious that she practically never went out and withdrew more and more. She was never able to get over the shock of his suicide, my mother said, and she never married. She became reclusive and the only times her eyes are said to have come to life were when Vincent's name was mentioned.'

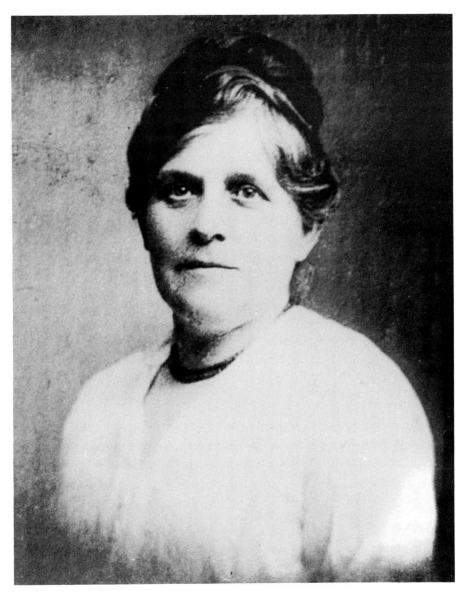

Marguerite Gachet in later life. *Vincent van Gogh Foundation/Museum Vincent van Gogh, Amsterdam*

I asked Madame Baize if she had any photographs of her mother. She had a look upstairs and came down with . . . yes . . . a cardboard box full of old photographs of her family. She picked out the ones of her mother and told me to take the ones I was interested in. I examined the contents of the box thoroughly. There were no drawings . . .

'You may be interested in this photo of my grandfather,' said Madame Baize, pointing to a sepia picture of an aristocratic old country gentleman.

'Why him?' I asked.

'Because he is the only person who knew the truth about where Vincent really shot himself in Auvers,' replied Madame Baize. 'Our family has always wondered about all the books that assume, for some reason— probably the romantic appeal—that Vincent shot himself in the cornfields. These fields frame the cemetery near where he painted the canvas of the wheatfields and crows not long before his death. For some reason the local paper, *L'Echo Pontoisien*, stated vaguely that Van Gogh shot himself in the fields. And all the biographers went along with it. My grandfather said he could not understand why no one ever told the true story. He told me he saw Vincent leave the Ravoux inn that day and walk in the direction of the hamlet of Chaponval (which also happens to be the direction of the Gachets' house). Later he saw Van Gogh enter a small farmyard at rue Bouchet. My grandfather said he heard a shot. He went into the farmyard himself, but there was no one to be seen. No pistol and no blood, just a dung heap. The pistol was never found.'

'Did your grandfather tell this to the police?' I asked.

'No,' said Madame Baize. 'He said he thought it would complicate matters unnecessarily. He felt it wasn't really important where the man shot himself.'

Madame Baize insisted that anyone who knew her grandfather would say he was always to be trusted. 'No one has ever asked me about this before,' she said. 'You may keep these photographs of my mother. They seem to mean a lot to you. As you see, I have others.'

Surprises till the end, I thought. I thanked Madame Baize and walked along rue Van Gogh and up the hill toward the cemetery.

I passed the Gothic church which was one of the last subjects Vincent painted. He painted it without a door and included a woman walking

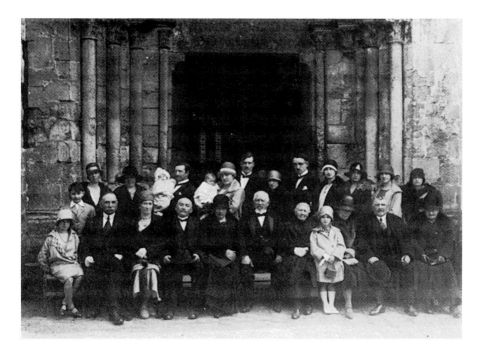

Family group at Auvers with Monsieur Liberge (*centre*). *Author's collection*

away with her back to him. Although dressed in Dutch costume, she appears to represent his thwarted love affairs with Eugénie Loyer, Kee Vos, Clasina Hoornik, Margot Begemann and Marguerite Gachet. The other road on this canvas led to the graveyard. It was this road I was standing on, the road that Vincent's funeral procession took. As I stood there, I read Tralbaut's account of it.

Many of Vincent's old painter friends went to Auvers for the funeral. The best description was given by the painter Emile Bernard, Vincent's friend from Asnières.

> . . . On the walls of the room where his body lay, all his last canvases were nailed, forming something like a halo around him. Over the coffin was draped a simple white sheet and masses of flowers, sunflowers that he loved so much, dahlias, and yellow blossoms

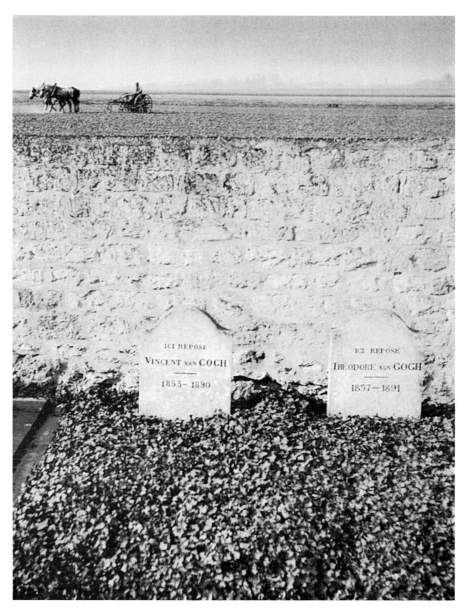

The graves of Vincent and Theo at Auvers. *Photo: Ed van der Elsken, 1952*

everywhere. For that was his favourite colour, symbol of the light of which he dreamt in hearts as well as paintings. Near the coffin lay his easel, folding stool and brushes. His friends carried the coffin to the hearse. Theo sobbed ceaselessly. Outside the sun was scorching. We climbed the hill of Auvers talking of him, of the bold forward thrust he gave to art, of the great projects that always preoccupied him, of the good he had done to each of us. We arrived at the cemetery, a small graveyard dotted with fresh tombstones. It is on a height overlooking the fields ready for reaping, under a wide blue sky which he might have loved still—maybe. And then he was lowered into the grave. He would not have cried at that moment. The day was much too much to his liking to prevent us from thinking that he could still have lived happily . . .

For several weeks Theo was too overcome to acknowledge the letters he had received. He lost his reason shortly after Vincent's death and was admitted to an asylum in Utrecht where he spent his last weeks in a deep melancholy and state of total apathy. He died in the asylum on January 25, 1891, less than six months after Vincent. He was 33.

In 1914, Theo's widow, Johanna van Gogh-Bonger, arranged for his remains to be moved to Auvers-sur-Oise, so that today the bones of the brothers lie side by side with identical tombstones, the simplest in the cemetery. The graves are linked with ivy, the symbol of fidelity. In death, at least, Vincent is not alone.

I stood at the foot of Vincent's grave and recalled Madame Baize telling me that Marguerite Gachet was one of the few friends of Vincent who didn't attend the funeral. Instead, she went the following day and planted two sunflowers by his grave. And till she died in 1949, at the age of 78, she was occasionally seen walking up the hill to the cemetery, a bouquet of yellow flowers in her hand.

7 Back in Amsterdam

It was now Sunday, October 1st, two weeks and six days since I had left Amsterdam. My deadline was a mere 20 hours away. I calculated that if I left Auvers now I could be in Amsterdam by midnight—plenty of time to get a decent night's rest. Fine. I sat in a cornfield and ate French bread and cheese, washed down with the dregs of a bottle of wine brought with me from Paris. The sun was setting and I felt relaxed. No reason, I thought, not to get a half-hour of sleep before I set off on my long drive. I stretched out lazily and with the cawing of crows sounding faintly in my brain, I fell asleep.

When I woke up, it was nine o'clock and pitch-black. I had overslept by two and a half hours. I had at least six ahead of me on the road. My unintended snooze had hardly refreshed me: I felt worse than when I dozed off. I got into the car and drove off, cursing myself.

Most of that drive was a blur. I reacted automatically to road signs and other cars, keeping my eyes ahead of me in a glazed stare. The only thing I remember well is what I had been blessed in avoiding up until then—about ten miles from Amsterdam, I had an accident. Weekend traffic was heavy. There was a hold-up on the motorway and I couldn't brake in time to avoid ploughing into the back of the car in front of me. No one was hurt, but my car got the worst of it. The hood had a strange twist to it and the fan belt was jammed. I called the highway distress service, the *Wegenwacht*, and was towed into town. It was about 4 a.m. on Monday when I flopped into bed. I set my alarm for eight and crashed into deep sleep. For the first time since I had found the drawing, I didn't sleep with it under my head. Eight o'clock seemed to come about ten hours too early. I turned the alarm off and sat up. Every cell in my body told me to go back to sleep but I was determined to keep my 9 a.m. deadline. I would be at my office typewriter by nine if it killed me.

When I arrived at work, on two wheels again, everyone was waiting for me. They had heard about my discoveries and were eager to see what I had. Once again I told the stories of the drawing and Mrs Maynard and Dr Tralbaut and Paris and everything else. I was getting a little blasé about the whole thing, but their interest revived my own. I found myself reliving certain parts of the story as I told them.

Our discussions were interrupted in mid-morning by a telephone call from London. It was Vernon Leonard, the editor who had so wanted me back in the office first thing that morning. He was surprised to hear I had made it. When I told him what I'd found in Devon he answered abruptly.

'Yes, I've heard all about it. But it doesn't mean anything till I've got a letter of authentication on my desk. I leave that to you, it's your story. But I don't want you wasting your time in museums, hear? You've got a story to write, and you're a slow writer. You know how long it takes you to get copy out. The research is complete now, it's just a matter of writing it up.'

But despite his advice, I couldn't help paying one more visit—to the Van Gogh Museum, where my travels had begun. The people there had helped me so much, and now I wanted to share my excitement with them. After the telephone conversation with Vernon, I managed to extricate myself from the rest of the staff and drive over to the museum. Amsterdam was at its autumnal best—the air rich with enveloping light.

Once at the museum I went straight to Emile Meijer, whose last words to me before I left had been: 'You never know what you'll come back with.' What would he think of my loot? I was a little nervous as I knocked at his door.

When I entered, he rose from his chair and greeted me warmly. I don't think he had expected to see me again. He asked me how things had gone, and whether I'd seen Tralbaut, and whether Chalcroft had anything interesting to tell me, and half a dozen other rapid-fire questions. We both sat down and I began to tell him what I'd done. He was interested to hear about it all, but when I showed him the photos of Eugénie and the drawing, he nearly fell off his seat.

'This is incredible,' he said, 'I'm flabbergasted.' He pulled a book off his shelf to compare the drawing of 87 Hackford Road with other drawings done by Vincent during his stay in London. Magnifying glass in hand, he looked first at the drawing, then at the book. Back and forth, book to drawing, his head moved rapidly but carefully. Finally, after a few very long minutes, he lifted his head.

'Yes, I'm sure this drawing was done by the same artist.'

A small tidal wave of optimism momentarily engulfed me. It was quelled rapidly when I reminded myself that the drawing had to be officially authenticated. I asked Meijer about the procedure to follow.

'. . . Mm . . . That's a difficult one,' he said, looking silently out of the window for a long time. 'In your case, I suggest Dr Hans Jaffé. He is Professor of Art History at the University of Amsterdam.'

'Shall I just write to him?' I asked.

'No, you must approach the Institute of Surveys and ask them if they will appoint Jaffé to give an official assessment,' advised Meijer. 'Why don't we go upstairs and see Dr Van Gogh? I think he's in his office, and I'm sure he would like to hear about what you've done.'

I agreed, of course. Seeing him would close up the fragile chain of links in Vincent the elder's life: the day before I had stood in front of the Engineer's father's grave in Auvers.

The distinguished-looking old man was sitting at his desk in the office specially reserved for his use. Whatever he was doing, he gladly dropped it to talk to us. Once again I described what I had done and where I had been. And once again my audience was appreciative. Van Gogh was particularly intrigued by the fact that biographers had till now referred to Vincent's London love as Ursula and not Eugénie. 'I think when my mother heard about Vincent's affair from Theo she probably confused the names of Eugénie and her mother. It simply proves that there is always more to learn about Van Gogh's life.'

He asked if he could see the drawing, which Emile Meijer had left downstairs in his office. As we walked down to see it, we were joined by Lily Couvée-Jampoller and Loedje van Leeuwen. Apparently word had quickly got around the small museum staff that I had brought back something interesting, and they all wanted to see it. Once again I was telling the story of Paul Chalcroft, Mrs Maynard, and the boxes full of photographs. I began sounding to myself like a broken record—but at the same time I was refining my story-telling abilities. In the back of my mind was the story I would soon have to write up for the magazine.

Before I left, Meijer and I took the drawing round the corner to the restoration department of the Stedelijk Museum in Paulus Potterstraat. The drawing was covered in coffee or tea stains and we wanted to ask the chief restorer what he thought the chances were of having it cleaned up. He picked the drawing up and examined it closely.

'Looks like a silverpoint to me,' he said. 'The cardboard has been prepared with chalk, and that makes cleaning difficult. But it might be worth a try. By the way, who made the drawing?'

'We think probably Van Gogh.'

The restorer stiffened visibly. He put the drawing back down on the table, took off his glasses and wiped them with a large handkerchief produced from his breast pocket. Then he picked up the drawing again, looked at it for a minute, and spoke.

'No, I wouldn't try to clean it. The stains are not very big, and they don't endanger the drawing. And besides,' he lowered his voice a little, 'it's not worth the risk. Good afternoon. Thank you for showing me the drawing.'

The restorer's reaction to the thought that the drawing in his hands might be a Van Gogh amused and impressed me. After all, I had been using it as a pillow for a couple of weeks.

Leaving Dr Meijer, I went next to the office of the Institute of Surveys and filed my request. A few days later I was informed that I could take the drawing to Dr Jaffé at the university.

Jaffé was an amiable little man, scurrying about his room like a busy hamster. I told him of the events that had led me into Mrs Maynard's living room in Stoke Gabriel and about the uncovering of the photographs of Eugénie Loyer and her family. Then about the drawing. He listened intently but without expression.

When I had finished, he began to examine details of the drawing with a magnifying glass and, like Emile Meijer, compared the sketch with others done by Vincent during his stay in London. 'Very interesting and a fascinating story. But that's all I can say at the moment.'

'How long before you can give me an official verdict?'

'Well, as usual I'm up to my ears in work. It might take a few weeks. But I'll try to have a decision for you as soon as possible,' said the professor, giving me a wink as I left. What did that mean? Had Jaffé made up his mind already? Or did he just have a nervous twitch?

During the next days things were relatively quiet. I spent nearly all my time sorting through my notes and trying to figure out what form the article should take. Finally I began writing. The basic problem was to adapt my findings to the chronology of Vincent's life. I discussed it with Vernon, who was helpful when you sought his help, and finally decided to weave the people I had met into the story of Vincent's life. Apart from the main article, which totalled nearly 8,000 words, I wrote separate pieces, about 4,000 words in all, on the sketch discovery, the Van Gogh Museum, the reaction of experts, Paul Chalcroft the London postman, the Engineer Dr Vincent van Gogh, the filming in Arles, Dr Tralbaut, and a story about plaques in Paris and London.

The Van Gogh issue was scheduled for February the following year. Volume 8 number 2 was the 75th issue of *Holland Herald*. It turned out that of the 40 editorial pages in the issue, 28 were related to Van Gogh. The main feature on his life occupied 22 pages and the article was illustrated by some of the photos I had taken myself, some of the ones I had found, and others that I had selected from the archives of the Van Gogh Museum.

The piece that had to wait until last before it could be written was the discovery of the sketch. It hinged on whether or not the drawing was authenticated. As the copy deadline approached, I still hadn't received a letter from Jaffé.

Nearly every day I had phoned him to find out if he had finished the examination. Once he had been sick, at other times he had been overwhelmed with work. It was always 'Next week, Mr Wilkie'. Finally I went to see him and he gave me his profuse apologies again. 'I promise to let you have it at the end of the week,' he said. 'Come back on Friday at 4 p.m.'

At 3.55 p.m. I was there, pacing up and down outside Jaffé's door like a father-to-be in an old Hollywood movie, trying in vain to distract myself by thinking about other things and talking to students. Jaffé scurried up the stairs. 'Ah! Hullo,' he said. 'Come in. Come in. Sit down.'

'I've been so busy,' he said yet again. 'I'm so terribly sorry it's taken so long. I really am.'

'That's all right,' I said. Looking through the window at the last of the autumn leaves hanging delicately on the branches outside, I thought of the trees in the drawing outside 87 Hackford Road. I braced myself to pop the question.

'Wh-what conclusion did you come to?'

'See for yourself,' he said, handing me his report.

My eyes raced off the edges of the pages and finally settled on the last paragraph. It read:

On the grounds of topographical evidence, the origin of the drawing, but especially on the grounds of the style in which this drawing has been made, like the two above comparisons, I do not hesitate to accept the drawing shown to me as a work of Vincent van Gogh from his London period 1873–1874.
Amsterdam, Dec. 14th, 1972.   *H. L. C. Jaffé.*

I sat silent for a while with a lump in my throat and then asked him what he had taken into consideration in making his judgement.

'I was quite convinced when I saw the way he drew the top part of the lamp-post,' said the professor. 'There is the same attention to detail shown in other sketches he did in London as a young man. But it is not drawn exactly in the silverpoint technique, as you were told. True, the paper was prepared with chalk, but the drawing has been made with a pencil. If you hold it at a certain angle, you can see the lead shining. Vincent has heightened the drawing with white in some places. I didn't know that he had ever used this technique. It's a truly remarkable find. Congratulations.'

We shook hands and I left. As I walked down the corridor, my mind flashed back to the living room in Devon, to the cardboard box, the speculation and the doubt. I relived those doubts vividly; they had always seemed perpetually at war with the anticipation of success. Try as I had not to believe anything about the drawing, I had never in my heart considered that it could be anything but a Van Gogh.

Now, with the letter of authentication in my hand, all doubts were resolved. Back in the office I showed the letter to my colleague Rick Wilson, who was doing the layout. After congratulatory handshakes I left the letter with him and the other people who had gathered round, and went to phone Mrs Maynard. Her reaction was nearly as ecstatic as mine.

'Oh Ken, how marvellous. It's too good to be true, I'm so excited for you. But what happens now? Should I give the drawing to you, or sell it, or what?' I told her I would investigate the different possibilities that were open to her. But in the meantime, could she possibly keep the good news to herself?

'Oh, of course, Ken. I've still only told one or two people about any of this.'

Next call was to Vernon Leonard in England. I told him of Jaffé's verdict and his response was characteristic:

'Very good, Ken. But now we've got to get that last story done. You know what a slow writer you are. I've given you more time for that article than anyone else would need.' No point in arguing.

Next call was to Meijer. He was delightfully blasé about the whole thing.

'I told you so, didn't I?'

'You did. Perhaps you could tell me what should be done with the drawing now. Mrs Maynard wants to co-operate completely with you, but she doesn't really know how.'

Meijer said that of course he would like the drawing for the museum. If Mrs Maynard wanted to place it on display there, there were various ways of doing it. She could sell it, give it as an outright gift, or give it on loan, for two years, with an option for renewal. Otherwise she could sell it privately or at auction.

The idea of an extended loan seemed best to me. In this way the drawing would still be Mrs Maynard's property but would be on public view alongside Vincent's other works. In the meantime it would increase in value in case Mrs Maynard ever wanted to sell it. When I called her back, she agreed.

The authentication of the drawing was a kind of high point in the excitement generated by my article—at least for me. Word got around and people I didn't know were coming up to me at parties and congratulating me. The magazine had people phoning from many countries wanting to know about it. Things were buzzing for several days.

I, of course, still had the last article to write. This was the article on the discovery of the drawing, and it was by far the hardest to write. It was the only one in which I had to treat myself as a participant in the events I was describing—something which I didn't usually do.

At last everything was written, and only design and production of the magazine remained. We worked hard all through November designing the issue and sent it off to the printers around the beginning of December. Production was complete by Christmas, just in time for the holidays, which in Holland last several days. I had planned to visit Scotland, and was eager to get out.

New Year—called Hogmanay in Scotland—is a festive time. This one lasted for several days—days of going from house to house and friend to friend, singing, dancing, kissing whoever was nearby, and telling stories till we couldn't tell any more. Flutes, fiddles and bagpipes played till dawn. And all the time, malt whisky flowed like Highland rivers in spate.

It was a perfect way of forgetting about Vincent temporarily. Here I could leave behind the Borinage, Paris, Arles and Saint-Rémy. I began to feel my old self returning—a self that seemed to have been taken over by the Dutch painter whose life I had been researching.

On the way back to Amsterdam, I met Vernon Leonard in London and together we went down to see Mrs Maynard in Devon. We invited her, and her husband and daughter, to come over to Amsterdam for a press conference, planned for February 1st, at which she would officially present the drawing to the museum.

The press conference had been Vernon's idea—a good way of promoting *Holland Herald* as well as the museum—but Dr Meijer, the museum director, had been even more enthusiastic about it. He immediately offered the museum as a place to hold it, even though the museum was not yet open to the public. Naturally, he was eager to have the drawing hanging there when it opened.

Everyone seemed to have an excellent reason for wanting a press conference, but it was all going a bit over the top. I had thought I had done my work, now it was time for the next assignment. I was wrong. My work might have been over, but everyone else was just beginning to decide how to make the most of what I'd found. Still, I tried as much as possible to ignore the commotion and get on with my work.

During the weeks prior to the press conference, I worked on new articles, and they took most of my time. But even during that time my mind was occupied, even when I didn't know it, with research on Vincent. Usually, after I've seen an article printed and bound in the magazine, I simply throw away my notes. This one was different. There were questions in those notebooks that continued to perplex me. I couldn't turn my back on them. Journalistic concerns had turned into personal concerns, and I was finding it impossible to extricate myself completely from Vincent's life. Not that I idealised the man. Far from it. I was very aware that the greatness of his art was matched by the seriousness of his personal flaws. His letters, for all their intense sensitivity, are totally devoid of humour.

I began to think about what it was that drew me into his life and, reluctantly looked for parallels. An only child, my boyhood had been rather lonely. My father, who travelled a lot, died when I was 11 and my mother was a victim of recurring bouts of mental depression which required frequent hospitalisation.

My happiest times were spent with friends in the jazz band on hilarious trips to the Highland glens, north of my home town of Dundee. There, when not playing music for the audience of sheep (they're very good listeners) we would explore forests and heather-clad mountains, follow rivers to their source and watch otters play in the pools of fresh melted snow.

In 1962, at the age of 19, I propelled myself south to London where I studied English literature, psychology and the media. Since then, I have moved around the world quite a lot in a variety of capacities but latterly as a writer. Although I have enjoyed writing from as long as I can remember holding a pencil, it took me a long time to settle for journalism where my specialities have become profiles of artists and travel stories, while editing a monthly English-language magazine in Amsterdam.

Vincent, too, was a mover, a searcher. In his short life, he lived in over 20 places, and tried art dealing, teaching and the Church before he discovered his vocation. I felt it could be our mutual restlessness that drew me to him so strongly. In fact, it had been Vincent's letters to Theo, and not his paintings, which initially had interested me back in 1968. I had been struck by their almost mesmeric intensity of feeling. Later, I realised that his deep melancholy was rooted in the birth of his stillborn namesake brother whose shadow he followed as a child and whose grave would reappear again and again to him in hallucinations.

Repeatedly failing to establish lasting relationships with women, I could see him sink into depression following the inevitable rejection, then glorify his sorrow and channel it into first religion, then art, and express it in the most exceptional words and images. In both his letters and his art, Vincent's personality leaps off the page or painting in an amazing symbiosis of nature and human nature, always using his brother Theo, whose birth must have relieved his childhood isolation, as a life-long link with the human world.

Because of my involvement in the article, I had had a greater opportunity than most people to explore Van Gogh's life. I had got a feeling of character from visiting his many homes, from reading and re-reading his letters and biographies, from talking to people who had a connection—if only a slim one—with the man himself.

Discovering a Van Gogh drawing was incredibly exciting but I didn't expect to find another one. In fact, the drawing was not the most important element of my journey. More than anything else, it was the people—the forgotten people with stories to tell—that I wanted to search out. I had found that actual living connection with Van Gogh was still barely within grasp. I wanted to explore that as far as possible. There were questions I still had about several periods of Vincent's life—about his relationship with a prostitute named Clasina in The Hague, about his illness, about his time in Paris. Perhaps there was someone who could tell me something about these things.

As the press conference drew near, my resolve strengthened steadily. The press conference was the culmination of my first journey, but only the beginning of my second.

There were numerous preparations for it. We assembled a press kit consisting of a copy of the magazine, various photographs, and a press release telling how I had discovered the drawing. The museum provided a room and refreshments.

At the *Holland Herald* there was a general mood of excitement. Everyone gave extra time to arranging things, contacting people, making sure that everything was right. The day before the conference itself,

Vernon and I drove out to the airport to pick up the Maynards, who had flown in from London, and that night we had dinner with them as guests of the Amsterdam Hilton.

The conference was scheduled for 10.30 a.m. the next day, and by 10 a.m. the room was packed. Dutch, British, American, German, and Japanese newspapers and magazines were all represented. I was seated at a long table with the Engineer, Dr Meijer, Mr and Mrs Maynard, and Vernon Leonard. I felt as if I was on the panel of a TV game show.

Dr Meijer officiated. He told the story of how I had found the drawing and photographs, sparing no eloquence about either my investigative skills or the importance of the discovery. He then introduced Mrs Maynard, who was nervous but calm. The flashbulbs flashed as she officially handed the drawing to him. In return he gave her a framed reproduction.

A journalist asked: 'What is it worth?' No one really knew, but the Engineer Van Gogh nudged Mrs Maynard's arm with his elbow and said quietly, 'What any fool likes to pay for it.'

I was looking on rather placidly when I became aware of someone nudging me in the ribs. I looked up at Dr Meijer and saw that he was motioning in my direction. He called me up to the rostrum and, after thanking me for what I had done, presented me with another framed reproduction—this one of a Van Gogh self-portrait. I thanked him, a few more flashbulbs flashed, and I sat down. The ceremony was over.

Afterwards other journalists flocked around to ask me questions. The most common was whether I had tried to take advantage of Mrs Maynard. 'Didn't you think of buying the drawing or making some kind of deal?'

'The thought never entered my mind. I followed my instincts all along and played it straight. I never considered trying to rob Mrs Maynard of what was hers.'

After the conference broke up, the Maynards were packed off into a horse-drawn carriage to go on a tour of Amsterdam arranged by Dr Meijer. I said goodbye and prepared to leave myself. On the way out, I bumped into Dr Van Gogh, who was also leaving.

'So, Mr Wilkie, what are you going to work on now?'

'Various things, Dr Van Gogh. My first long assignment is on the artist

M. C. Escher.'

'Ah yes, and anything else?'

'Well, I don't think I'm done with Vincent van Gogh yet.'

'Oh, you have another article planned?'

'No, just some questions raised by my first article which I would like to explore further."

We reached the Engineer's chauffeur-driven car. He pulled his overcoat tight around him to keep out a chilly wind that had blown up.

'It is good you will do more work on Van Gogh. I am always interested in new information about him. Perhaps we will speak again.'

'Yes, I hope so.'

We shook hands and smiled at each other, and he was driven off. Neither of us knew it then, but we would indeed meet again. And next time there would not be so many smiles.

8   Brothers and Doctors

For the few weeks following the press conference my time was completely taken up by various articles for the magazine. The research on M. C. Escher involved some travel around Holland and to Washington D.C., and other short pieces required as much time going from place to place in Amsterdam as sitting in front of the typewriter. Between travelling and typing, I had no space for Vincent.

But I continued to think about him. Every time I sat down in my office at home, I saw a list of the questions I wanted to go into further. In a burst of activity one afternoon I had typed them out neatly and pinned them to the wall. They sat there for days, reminding me of the task I had set myself—and which I was now unable to perform. I would often lie awake thinking about what I wanted to do. Finally I resolved that I would devote weekends to further research. It was the only way.

The first question on my list concerned the change Vincent had gone through between the time he lived in Nuenen, in 1884, and his stay two years later in Paris. Old Piet van Hoorn had described a friendly if eccentric man, while Baroness Bonger had reported her husband's description of someone virtually impossible to live with. They seemed to be talking about two different people. What had caused the change?

The explanation must, I thought, lie mainly in the three months or so that Vincent spent in Antwerp between his time in Nuenen and his time in Paris. Had something happened to him there to cause this fundamental change in his personality?

On my first free weekend, I went to the Van Gogh Museum archives to read through the letters and sift through any documentary evidence I could find. I wanted to assemble in my mind as complete a picture of Vincent's stay in Antwerp as I could.

Vincent had left Nuenen in less than happy circumstances. His father had died in March 1885, and the event had a profound effect on him. He had been touched also by rumour and scandal: Margot Begemann, the girl next door, had fallen in love with him and tried to commit suicide. In August, the local Roman Catholic priests had criticised him severely for getting 'too familiar with people below my rank'; one even went so far as to offer money to prospective models if they would refuse to be painted.

So, late in November 1885, Vincent went to Antwerp. His earliest letters there describe with delight the harbour area, where he spent time watching the bustle of daily life, talking to 'various girls who seemed to take me for a sailor', and observing the light on the docks and buildings. He had his usual money problems—models were expensive and the bill for paints, he said, was like a millstone around his neck—but he worked hard and had the opportunity to examine paintings in churches, galleries and museums. Antwerp is the city of Rubens, and Vincent studied his work closely.

However as the letters continued, Vincent's mood changed. He spoke increasingly of his health, which was not good. He confessed to Theo that he was afraid of dying before his talent was recognised, and that he was afraid of madness. He produced two macabre pictures: one a painting called *Skull with Cigarette*, which shows a skeleton smoking, and another drawing of a hanging skeleton. Moreover, his first self-portraits which date from this period seem to reflect a morbid introspection.

Perhaps Vincent's ill health was connected with this self-awareness. Perhaps the key to the change in his personality was to be found in the illness itself. This was the line I decided to follow.

I soon discovered that I was by no means the first to try to identify Vincent's disease. Among the numerous hypotheses that had been put forward were one or another form of epilepsy, schizophrenia, dementia praecox, meningo-encephalitis luetica, cerebral tumour, hallucinatory psychosis, chronic sunstroke and the influence of yellow, dromamania, turpentine poisoning, and hypertrophy of the creative forces.

What was I going to add to this forbidding array of diagnoses? At least I knew that some of them could have nothing to do with Vincent's behaviour in Antwerp: chronic sunstroke is hardly a danger in Belgium. Nonetheless, the multitude of medical explanations was baffling.

As I sat in the Van Gogh Museum wondering where to go next, I remembered something Dr Tralbaut had told me in Provence. When he was doing some research on Vincent, he had come across the name 'Cavenaile' scrawled on the back of one of his Antwerp sketchbooks of 1885. Tralbaut had noticed what seemed to be consultation hours scrawled with the name. From this he had supposed Cavenaile to be a doctor.

I decided to check out this reference. I asked to see the notebook and it was soon produced. Sure enough, there on the cardboard back was written: 'A. Cavenaile, rue de Hollande 2, consultations: 8 à 9, 1½ à 3.' Tralbaut was surely right in thinking that Cavenaile was some sort of doctor.

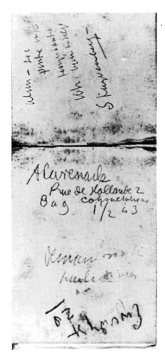

Vincent's notes on the back of one of his Antwerp sketchbooks. These jottings led the author into a search in Belgium and England for a missing Van Gogh painting, a portrait of his doctor, Cavenaile. *Vincent van Gogh Foundation/National Museum Vincent van Gogh, Amsterdam*

I leafed through the rest of the notebook to see whether it might have anything to supplement this rudimentary clue. It did. On one of the pages was written: *'demain midi huile de ricin. Alum 20c pinte ou ½ temps à autre 10h. bain de siege.'* And written at the bottom of the page was the single word 'Stuyvenberg'.

The castor oil must have been for the stomach ailments of which Vincent frequently complained to Theo. But he never mentioned the alum and sitz-bath, which I knew was a kind of bath used in therapeutic treatment. What were they for? And what was Stuyvenberg? I decided to go to Antwerp to find out.

The first weekend I had free was in mid-March, and I set out early on Saturday morning. A friend who had grown up in the city had told me that Stuyvenberg is the name of one of the Antwerp hospitals. It stands at the end of the rue des Images, not far from Vincent's house in what is now called the Lange Beeldekenstraat. With this lead and the name Cavenaile, I thought I was certain to find something—maybe some hospital records, or reports on Vincent's condition.

I arrived in the city at around 10.30 a.m. and went straight to a café for a mid-morning cup of coffee. I sat by myself, studying the street map to work out how to get to the hospital. I was eager to get my fingers into the medical archives. But a phone-call to the Stuyvenberg Hospital revealed that the records of the last century had been destroyed in a fire.

I was heading for my car when it suddenly occurred to me that I was neglecting my customary homage to fellow Scotsman Alexander Graham Bell—why not look up the name Cavenaile in the phone book? It was a long shot, but as I was here . . . I went back into the telephone booth and thumbed through to the C section of the book.

What I saw took me completely by surprise. There was one entry for Cavenaile. The first initial was A., just as on the back of Vincent's notebook. And this A. Cavenaile was a doctor too.

For a moment I did not grasp what I was seeing. Could this be an old phone book? Was the original Dr Cavenaile still alive? A quick calculation made him about 150 years old. Impossible. There was only one thing to do, and I couldn't dial the number fast enough. The phone rang twice. A pause, and then a slow, solemn voice spoke:

'You are speaking with Doctor Amadeus Cavenaile.'

143

It sounded as if he had lived to be 150 after all. I explained who I was and what I was looking for. The slow voice spoke again.

'The Cavenaile you are looking for was my grandfather. My father was a doctor too. I am from a whole dynasty of Antwerp doctors called Cavenaile.'

He paused, then went on.

'I think I may have information that could be of use to you.'

'May—may I come and talk to you?'

'Certainly, if you wish.'

Seconds later I was racing through the cobbled streets of Antwerp to Dr Cavenaile's office. In my excitement I turned the wrong way up a one-way street and drove almost straight into the arms of a traffic policeman. My heart pounded while he wrote out the ticket. I had never been so enthusiastic about a doctor's appointment in my life.

Dr Cavenaile's office was in a solid nineteenth-century red brick house. I rang the bell twice and waited for a few moments until the doctor himself answered the door. He was a short, thick-set man in his late fifties, with straight silver hair, small eyes and a fine hooked nose. He could almost have been a Van Gogh . . .

He led the way to his office, a spacious and rather old-fashioned complex of rooms on the first floor. We went into his consulting room and he motioned me to sit in the patient's chair facing his desk. He went round the desk and sat back in his own creased brown leather chair. Unhooking the stethoscope from around his neck, he started talking.

'My grandfather's name was Hubertus Amadeus Cavenaile. He was born in the town of Oudenaarde, on the river Schelde, about 15 miles from Ghent, in 1841. He established himself in Antwerp in 1883.'

I was trying to be polite, but my mind was on other things. I tried to bring Cavenaile to the point.

'Hmm . . . that would be about two years before Vincent van Gogh was in Antwerp.'

'Two years. He came to see my grandfather several times late in 1885. In fact, he would have sat in the same chair you are in now. I brought that chair with me from his consulting room in rue de Hollande.'

'Then Van Gogh was a patient of your grandfather's?'

'Oh yes. Grandfather never talked about it to anyone outside the

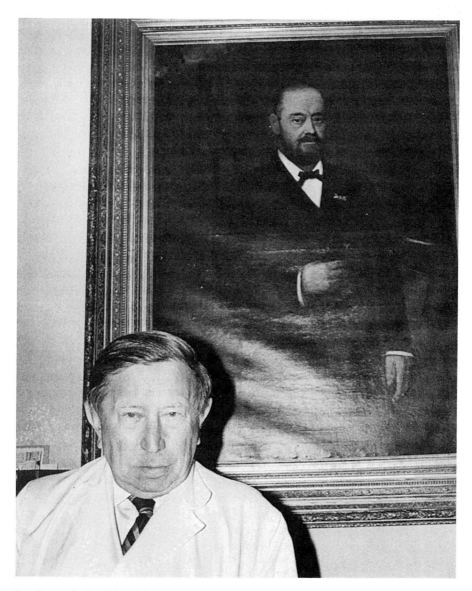

Dr Cavanaile in 1976 with a portrait (not by Van Gogh) of his grandfather, Dr Hubertus Amadeus Cavenaile, who treated Vincent for syphilis in 1885. *Photo: Lia Schelkens*

family. But he did confide in father and me.'

I sat on the edge of my historic seat as Cavenaile began to describe events that had taken place in his grandfather's surgery a century before.

'Van Gogh came to see my grandfather because the dockland was then very near the rue de Hollande. Many of his patients were sailors or dock workers.

'Van Gogh struck my grandfather immediately as a strange and unstable character. He was wearing ragged workman's clothes. He never went into many details, unfortunately. I don't think he regarded them as important.'

'Did your grandfather tell you what he treated Van Gogh for?'

'Yes, he did regard that as important. He said he treated Van Gogh for syphilis. He prescribed a treatment with mercury and sent him to the Stuyvenberg hospital for hip-baths. Van Gogh did not have a bath in his own lodgings. . . .'

I was taken aback by this information. I knew that Vincent had been hospitalised for gonorrhea for three weeks in The Hague in 1882, but syphilis? I did recall Tralbaut making a passing reference to it somewhere in his biography of Van Gogh, but he had offered no proof, and somehow I hadn't given his mention of the disease much thought. I would have to look at Tralbaut's book again.

'Did your grandfather say whether Van Gogh was cured by the treatments?'

'He could not be cured,' replied Cavenaile. 'The treatment was not effective in those times before we knew about penicillin.'

'Would the disease have repercussions on Van Gogh later in life?'

'Without a doubt. If you have syphilis now, without having received treatment early enough, your prospects are grim. At that time they would have been even worse. My grandfather said that Van Gogh pressed him for details about the disease. He seems to have been worried about himself. My grandfather told him that syphilis could affect the brain and even be fatal.'

'Do you think it likely that the disease would have started to affect Van Gogh's brain by the time he was in Arles, in 1888? As you know, he began to have nervous breakdowns of some sort there.'

'In its third, and final, stage it could have been, at the very least, a contributory cause of his ultimate madness, yes. But there may also be other factors that make the matter too complicated to be explained by a single disease.'

After that we changed the subject to the charms of Antwerp, the relative merits of various Belgian beers, and other trivialities. I felt I had found more in Antwerp than I had bargained for.

As I drove back to Amsterdam I thought over what I had learned from Cavenaile. The changes in Vincent's character while in Antwerp seemed to make more sense now. The sudden introspection in the form of those first self-portraits; his preoccupation with death, evident in the macabre skeleton paintings; his fear, expressed to Theo, of going mad or dying before his talent was recognised. These must have had something to do with his discovery that he had syphilis—and that the disease might eventually affect his brain.

What surprised me about Dr Cavenaile's revelation was that Vincent, who always seemed to be so open in his letters to Theo, had never mentioned the nature of his illness to his brother. He talked about his stomach problems, his teeth falling out, his weakness—but never gave any hint of this most serious disease. In fact, on more than one occasion, he begs Theo not to ask for more details about his illness.

As soon as I reached home, I went to the copy of Tralbaut's biography which the Museum had lent me. I knew I had seen a reference to syphilis somewhere. After a few minutes I found it on page 261. And what I found there was more interesting than a mere reference.

Tralbaut writes: 'Moreover, Vincent had caught syphilis, probably at Antwerp, and this certainly contributed to his physical and mental condition. . . .' So Tralbaut did know about it, even though he seemed to place little importance on it.

What intrigued me much more than Tralbaut's words was a hand-written note in the margin of the book. The word 'syphilis' was circled in the text and next to it were the words 'NO! Where does Tralbaut get it from?' And the note was signed: V.W.v.G. Vincent Willem van Gogh. The painter's nephew, the man I knew as Dr Van Gogh and whom others called the Engineer. How could the Engineer be so sure about this? And why was he so agitated by the reference to syphilis?

I took the following Monday off work and went to the Museum to look through the archives. While scouring Vincent's letters for further clues about his disease, I found a passage that might explain why the Engineer was so edgy about the subject. The passage was in letter 489, written to Theo when Vincent was in Arles. In it Vincent reveals that he had received treatment from a Dr Grüby in Paris for an ailment that must have been either gonorrhoea or syphilis. And Theo was receiving the same treatment—for the same ailment.

The letter reads, in part:

What you write about your visits to Grüby has distressed me, but all the same I am relieved that you went. Has it occurred to you that the dazedness—the feeling of extreme lassitude—may have been caused by this weakness of the heart, and that in this case the iodide of potassium would have nothing to do with the collapse? Remember how last winter I was stupefied to the point of being absolutely

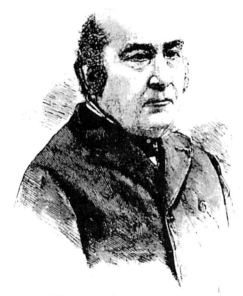

Dr David Grüby, prominent Hungarian-born practitioner of natural medicine. He lived near the Van Gogh brothers in rue Lepic and treated them both for syphilis. *Bibliothèque Interuniversitaire de Médecine, Paris*

incapable of doing anything at all, except a little painting, although I was not taking any iodide of potassium. So if I were you, I should have it out with Rivet (the family doctor) if Grüby (noted practitioner of natural medicine) tells you not to take any. I am sure that in any case you mean to keep on being friends with both.

I often think of Grüby here and now, and I am completely well, but it is having pure air and warmth that makes it possible. In all that racket and bad air of Paris, Rivet takes things as they are; without trying to create a paradise, and without in any way trying to make us perfect. But he forges a cuirass, or rather he hardens one against illness, and keeps up one's morale, I do believe, by making light of the disease one has got. If only you could have one year of life in the country and with nature just now, it would make Grüby's cure much easier. I expect he will make you promise to have nothing to do with women except in case of necessity, but anyhow as little as possible . . .

I believe iodide of potassium purifies the blood and the whole system, or doesn't it? . . . Did you notice Grüby's face when he shuts his mouth tight and says—'No women!' It would make a fine Degas, that. But there is no answering back . . . It will be the same story as mine, get as much of the spring air as possible, go to bed *very early*, because you must have sleep, and as for food, plenty of fresh vegetables, and no *bad wine* or *bad* alcohol. And very little of women, and *lots of patience.*

It doesn't matter if you don't shake it off at once. Grüby will give you a strengthening diet . . . I shall not believe you if in your next letter you tell me there's nothing wrong with you. It is perhaps a more serious change. . .

The vehemence with which the Engineer had insisted that his uncle had not contracted syphilis suddenly made sense. If true it might mean that Theo, the Engineer's father, had also had the disease. And if Vincent's syphilis had contributed to a mental breakdown, then this too must be alarming for the Engineer. Most worrying of all, if Theo had syphilis in 1888, he might have been suffering from it in 1889, when the Engineer was conceived . . .

I knew I was on sensitive ground but I had to ask the Engineer directly about these questions. He was not at his office in the museum that day, but I arranged to see him there a few days later.

On the day of the appointment I was very nervous. At times I seriously considered cancelling the meeting and forgetting the whole thing. Why should I cause him aggravation? But I forced myself to go through with it. To do otherwise would have gone against my resolution.

So, on March 22nd at 10.30 a.m., I found myself standing at the door to the Engineer's office. My mouth was dry and my hand shook a little as I knocked softly. I was called in.

The Engineer was sitting behind his desk, dressed as I had always seen him, in a suit and tie. He greeted me with his customary politeness and asked me to sit down. We chatted a few minutes about trivial matters, and than I came to the point.

My journalistic training had taught me that you stand a better chance of finding out about a person if you refrain from telling him everything you know. It is better simply to raise a question and give him an open platform to talk on. For this reason I had decided not to tell the Engineer what I had found in Antwerp.

'I've been looking into a few questions about Van Gogh's life, and was wondering whether you might be able to help me with one or two of them. Is it true that Vincent contracted syphilis?'

Dr Van Gogh's reaction was one of surprise and suspicion combined. His eyes narrowed and his mouth seemed to set. He paused for several tense moments before answering.

'No, he never had syphilis. Where did you get that idea?'

'I read it somewhere. A biography mentions it. You're absolutely certain . . . ?'

'Of course I am,' he answered rather sharply. 'Surely you have something more substantial to ask about.'

'What was your father suffering from when he lost his reason shortly before his death?'

The Engineer looked me straight in the eye. The politeness was still there—he is a true gentleman, I thought—but the warmth had definitely disappeared. Van Gogh stared at me icily for a few moments, then looked away. A few more moments of silence. I repeated the question, rephrasing it a little to make it slightly less abrupt.

Still looking away, the Engineer made a peculiar gesture. With his arm bent in an awkward, stiff position, he pointed between his legs. He looked rather embarrassed.

'Water,' he said, as if the word were difficult to pronounce. 'He had difficulty passing water.'

When I asked what the cause of the difficulty was, he shook his head. 'I don't know. Don't ask me.'

'Was there any connection between your father's illness and Vincent's?'

Again he gave me that look, unswerving as a laser beam aimed right into my eyes.

'None whatsoever. There is no evidence for that.'

The Engineer was determined not to give me an inch, and there was no point in staying around to get negative answers to all my questions. I thanked him for giving me his time, and left.

Riding my bicycle back to the office, I thought about the stone walls of denial with which Dr Van Gogh had answered my questions. I could understand his reluctance to acknowledge a history of venereal disease in his own family. I could appreciate that his uncle, and his father as well, had been written about ceaselessly by scholars and critics of all kinds. The burden of a famous family is never an easy one to bear.

But Dr Van Gogh's refusal even to consider these things infuriated me. His family fame was a burden, but it was also a serious responsibility. He couldn't, I thought, be selectively interested in new information, listening only to whatever conformed to the view he would like people to have of his family.

I resolved that I was not going to let myself be intimidated by the personalities involved. I would pursue whatever questions interested me about Vincent, regardless of how much his nephew, the Engineer, opposed me.

For me, the discovery that Vincent had syphilis was important in trying to understand more about his life.

*   *   *

In the summer of 1989 I was able to discover more about Theo and the illness that afflicted the Van Gogh brothers. For this research I turned to archives in Paris, London, Amsterdam and Utrecht.

Apart from the attention paid to Theo's life by Jan Hulsker in his book *Lotgenoten*, biographers have always cast Theo in the shadow of his brother. Born four years after him and named after his father, Theo was openly favoured over Vincent by his parents. Much of the parental love for their dead son, Vincent I, was given to Theo, bypassing Vincent II. Theo was certainly not a replacement child and had his own identity from birth. Nevertheless, his life, too, would take on a tragic dimension.

A close bond was formed between the brothers from early childhood. Leaving school at 15, Theo worked in his uncle's art dealing business of Goupil and Company, first in Brussels, then The Hague and finally in Paris. Unlike Vincent, Theo had social graces and was liked by most people. Vincent recognised this and occasionally asked Theo to influence their parents on his behalf.

In 1877, Theo seems to have had a love affair that resulted in a family drama, but no details are known because, true to family form, a relevant passage was withheld by his widow from the first edition of the collected letters and was not replaced by the Engineer in his 1953 edition.

By the time he reached 25, Theo had acquired some authority over his brother and sided with their parents in the controversy over Vincent's attempt to set up a family of his own in The Hague with the prostitute Clasina Hoornik.

Vincent was to become a great psychological burden on Theo. After his first emotional breakdown over Eugénie in London, and the resulting withdrawal into religion, his need for Theo increased. His letters and paintings often seem to be a desperate attempt to communicate with his brother. He was totally dependent on him and very demanding. Like a child, he felt helpless if Theo threatened to withdraw his support, and if he did not receive unconditional support, even when he was not being completely open with his brother, he would attack Theo with verbal venom. He expected the same of everyone and, not surprisingly, no one accepted him. Except Theo.

In 1882, while Vincent was in the throes of his problems with Clasina, Theo had an affair in Paris with a woman called Marie who came from Brittany. She was sick and had to undergo an operation. She was a

Roman Catholic and not accepted by his parents when he told them he planned to marry her. In the end he did not do so. Apart from social pressures, it would have been almost impossible for him to support a family at that time, for he was already financially responsible for most of the Van Gogh family.

When Vincent left Antwerp and moved in with Theo, uninvited, and stayed on for two years, Theo was living with the woman referred to as 'S'. She was on the point of a nervous breakdown and it is hard to imagine that an overdose of Vincent around the house would have done much to help. As the brothers' friend, Andries Bonger, related to his wife, Vincent ground Theo down with his inconsiderate behaviour, until the younger man was forced to move out of rue Lepic for a while.

As early as 1886 Theo was showing signs that he was suffering from a serious illness. In a letter recently made available by the Van Gogh family, Andries Bonger wrote, on December 31st of that year: 'He (Theo) was in a serious nervous condition, so bad that he could not move. To my great surprise I found him yesterday back to his old self; he appeared stiff as if he had had a fall, but further no consequences. Now he must finally take care of his health. It is very necessary.' And on February 18th, 1887, Bonger wrote that if Theo were not so stubborn, he would have gone to Dr Grüby long before.

Vincent never ceased to yearn for closeness with another human being, but closeness to him meant a merger that was almost frightening in its intensity. His fierce determination to achieve his goal was so powerful that the other party felt threatened. He was incapable of achieving intimacy and ultimately reconciled himself to channelling his longings into his art.

Theo remained his only line of communication with the ordinary human world; he was at the receiving end throughout his life and it took its toll. 'Being friends, being brothers, love, that is what opens the prison', Vincent wrote. He talked in terms of 'our art'. But this fantasised relationship could only succeed by mail or brief visits: the two years when they shared a flat in rue Lepic drove Theo to despair. He confided in a letter to his sister Wil that the days of his close friendship with Vincent were over; no one was more glad than Theo when Vincent moved to Provence, although he continued to feel responsible for him.

153

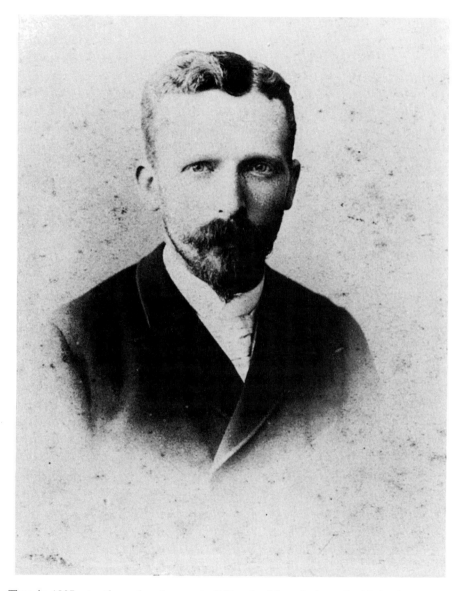

Theo in 1887, at a time when he was in failing health and plagued with business worries. *Vincent van Gogh Foundation/National Museum Vincent van Gogh, Amsterdam*

Theo eventually acquired the wife and child Vincent could not have, and this may have stirred up feelings of jealousy combined with guilt, especially when Theo was in financial difficulties.

A month before Vincent's suicide, Theo wrote his most emotional letter to his brother. His baby Vincent was sick, his apartment in Paris was too small and he had been fighting with his bosses. It was the only letter which he ever began, 'My very dear brother'. He asked Vincent: 'Ought I to live without a thought for the morrow? . . . And when I work all day long, not to earn enough to protect that good Jo from worries over money matters . . . those rats Boussod and Valadon are treating me as though I had just entered their business, and are keeping me on a short allowance.' Thereafter Theo's health continued to deteriorate, despite treatment from the jovial family doctor, Rivet.

In the archives of the Bibliothèque Interuniversitaire de Médecine de Paris, I was able to find out more about the Van Gogh brothers' other doctor, David Grüby. He was a 78-year-old bachelor with ideas ahead of his time. Born in Hungary in 1810 of Jewish parents, he studied in Vienna and moved to Paris in 1841. He had a practice in rue St Lazare and lived up the road from Theo and Vincent at 100 rue Lepic. As indicated in Vincent's letters, Grüby administered natural cures which were frowned on by many orthodox Parisian doctors who, in 1854, attempted in vain to throw him out of France. While he was criticised by many of his colleagues, his patients swore by him. Many of them, like Heine, belonged to the world of letters and the arts. Grüby's patients marvelled at his powers of observation, practicality, and classification. Long before Pasteur, he was studying micro-organisms.

The treatment which Grüby gave Vincent and Theo was a health cure that included abstinence from sexual intercourse and, reluctantly it seemed, iodide of potassium. To find out more about this I contacted Dr Alex Vasse, a general practitioner in Aix-en-Provence. He had just completed research at the Medical Library of Marseilles University, and as a result was able to tell me: 'From the archive material covering 1886 to 1890, it became clear to me that iodide of potassium was specifically used in the treatment of syphilis. Not in the treatment of gonorrhoea.'

It was therefore apparent that the Van Gogh brothers were being treated for syphilis.

In London's Wellcome Institute, which was featured in an excellent BBC 4 radio documentary on the subject of syphilis in the last century as a metaphor for AIDS today, I found a book, published in Paris in 1890, entitled *La Syphilis Aujourdhui et Chez Les Anciens*, sub-titled *Nihil Sub Sole Novum* (Nothing New Under the Sun). Dr F. Buret's opening statement reveals the social attitude to the disease at the time: 'Daughter of prostitution, syphilis was born when commerce, chasing away love, presided over the exchange of kisses.'

He writes that in Paris of the 1880s, decades before penicillin (the present cure) was discovered, the basic treatment for the disease was mercury and iodine, with increasing doses of iodide of potassium as the illness progressed into its third stage.

'In the second stage of syphilis,' he says, 'one of the best preparations is *Le Sirop de Gibert* which includes 0.5 grams of iodide of potassium combined with one centigram of biodure hydrargie.' Another method practised in 1890 was the combination of a dose of iodide of potassium or sodium and massage with Neapolitan ointment.

'In the third stage,' Dr Buret continues, 'larger doses of iodide of potassium are prescribed: one, two, three, and up to six grams per day for periods of two months.'

The most serious of the sexually transmitted diseases then, syphilis could prove fatal. In its third stage, the brain and spinal cord were often affected, which caused insanity (general paralysis of the insane, or GPI) and loss of muscular co-ordination. Indeed, tertiary syphilis may involve any organ and mimic virtually any other chronic disease.

As we know, Vincent suffered from gonorrhoea as well as syphilis, and it seems probable that Theo also suffered from both diseases for he later suffered a stricture which was a narrowing of the urinary passage and a late consequence of infection in the days before antibiotics. And gonorrhoea could also spread to the joints, tendons, muscles, heart and brain.

After Vincent's suicide in July 1890, Theo's health deteriorated even more rapidly, although it should be remembered that he was observed as having paralytic attacks as early as the winter of 1886. He had been ill for a long time and did not have the robust physique of his brother. He began to behave irrationally—for example, he sent a telegram to Gauguin in

Brittany, asking him to travel to the tropics, all expenses paid. He was often found in paralytic states and unable to walk or urinate. Camille Pissarro reported that Theo had wished his beloved wife and child dead, and his successor at the Goupil gallery recorded that he was interned after attacking his wife and baby.

In Autumn 1890 Theo was finally admitted to La Maison Dubois in Faubourg Saint-Denis. After two days, he was taken to the clinic of Dr Blanche at Auteuil. Theo's sister Wil, herself destined to spend the last 39 years of her life in an asylum, was 'deeply grieved but calm and positive', according to Bonger, but Theo's wife, Johanna, was unhappy about the way her husband was being treated and furious at the matter being taken out of her hands by, it seems, her brother who reported event-by-event almost every day to his parents in Amsterdam. I was to discover later that it was they who arranged for Theo's certification.

The family doctor, Rivet, said that Theo's case was 'much worse than Vincent's and that there was no ray of hope'. But which case? Among all the testimonies and accounts, there was no mention of the exact nature of poor Theo's disease, beyond what we read in Vincent's letters. One French doctor, Doiteau, suggested that Theo's mental state was caused by urine poisoning instigated by kidney stones, but this cannot be taken seriously since the brothers were being treated for the same disease, and kidney stones were the least of Vincent's problems; nor was iodide of potassium prescribed for such an ailment.

The last weeks of Theo's life are obscure because of the lack of available information, and I have to conclude that the information has been deliberately concealed. I only knew that Theo was transferred from France to 'an asylum for the insane in Utrecht', on November 18 1890, where he died on January 25 1891, aged 33.

According to a Professor G. Kraus, who is said to have had access to documents from the hospital at Utrecht, the reason for Theo's illness was stated thus: 'Chronic illness, too much exertion and sadness. He had a life full of emotion, worry and exertion.' Hardly a satisfactory explanation for a fatal disease.

The mental hospital in which Theo was confined is now a psychiatric centre called the Willem Arntsz Huis, named after its founder in 1461. I telephoned its director, Dr Hardeman, and asked him if his hospital had

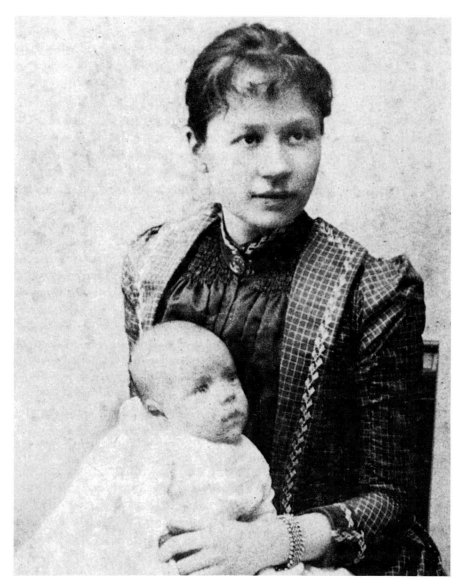

Johanna van Gogh-Bonger, Theo's wife, with their baby Vincent for whom his uncle painted the tender 'Almond tree branch in blossom' while in the asylum. *Vincent van Gogh Foundation/National Museum Vincent van Gogh, Amsterdam*

the medical records of Theodore van Gogh, giving him the dates of Theo's admission and death. Dr Hardeman said he would look into it and ring me back. Two days later he did so, and I realised that he was angry.

'We have the medical records of all our patients for 1890 and 1891,' he said. 'Everything is filed neatly in order—except the file for Theo van Gogh. It has been removed by someone, and it's impossible to say when. But I can tell you that it would certainly not have been by accident. I am very sorry about this, I would have liked to help you. It could have been removed a long time ago. It would have been easier then.'

But Dr Hardeman did come up with another document from a file that had escaped the archive raider, and it gave me a possible lead. It was a hand-written copy of a request by Theo's father-in-law, Henrik Christiaan Bonger, of Weteringschans, Amsterdam, to the Lower Court in Amsterdam, to have Theo certified on the evidence of Dr Frederik van Eeden, the well-known Dutch writer who had a psychotherapeutic out-patient clinic in Amsterdam with a Dr van Renterghem. There was also a copy of the court order of November 17 1890 to admit Theo to the asylum in Utrecht.

At that time, Van Eeden was a progressive young psychoanalyst who worked with hypnosis and corresponded with Freud. Did he keep a record of his medical assignments? I wondered. I had already been to the State Archives in Haarlem where further legal records relating to the declaration of insanity should have been kept. But the Van Gogh file there had been removed as well, much to the astonishment of the archivist. By this time it was less of a surprise to me.

But there was still Van Eeden. I assumed that he must have travelled to Paris to examine Theo before declaring him insane, and I felt that there was a chance he might have recorded the visit. Van Eeden's diaries are published in four great volumes that span most of his writing life. To my horror, I discovered that the only year he did not record the events of each day was 1890—the very year I was concerned with. This was the limit. Beyond the limit. Just why 1890 was missing from the Van Eeden diaries I learned coincidentally a few days later from his granddaughter who works in the bookshop of a friend of mine in Hilversum. 'Grandad didn't keep any diaries that year,' she said, 'because it was the year he fell in love, which interrupted his daily flow of words.'

159

Where next? Through Anton Korteweg, of the Literary Museum in The Hague, I reached the acknowledged expert on Frederick van Eeden, Jan Fontijn, who was putting the finishing touches to a new book to be published in 1990.

Fontijn listened with great interest to my story, but informed me regretfully that there were no medical records he knew of from either Van Eeden or his partner Van Renterghem for the year 1890.

'It's known that Theo's widow, Johanna Van Gogh-Bonger, later became a family friend of the Van Eedens, and often paid social calls to their country house, Walden. All that Frederik ever wrote about Theo, as far as I know, was in his diary on January 26 1891: "Theo van Gogh is dead." That was all.'

The medical records may have been hidden or destroyed but the surviving letters cannot conceal that Theo was stricken with a debilitating venereal disease for which there was no cure in the nineteenth century. Syphilis in Theo's time was subject to taboos similar to those of AIDS when it first came to light. 'If only it had been an ordinary illness that had killed me,' said Oswald in Ibsen's *Ghosts* in the early 1880s. 'A loathsome sore,' said one London theatre critic of the play at the time. Columbus's crew were said to have brought syphilis back from the New World in the 1490s. The Italians named it the 'French disease' . . . The Dutch called it the 'Spanish Pox' . . . and the Russians the 'disease of Polanders'. Like AIDS, it was always blamed on foreigners, people were scared of it. Whereas in the seventeenth and eighteenth centuries it had been treated as a natural disease, albeit not very pleasant, in the second half of the nineteenth century it was used as a moral metaphor, and carried with it shame and feelings of guilt 'unfit to be spoken of in decent society, hospital wards and asylums were filled with patients suffering from syphilis.' Like AIDS it could also be carried by someone who was not chronically suffering from it. Its symptoms were ill-defined and confusing, and only in 1905 was it discovered that the disease was caused by a bacterium.

Apart from the disease itself and all Theo's woes, it seems very likely that he was also racked with guilt about his illness, which would account for what an expert in the upper echelons of the Dutch museum world told me: that Theo committed suicide in the asylum in Utrecht.

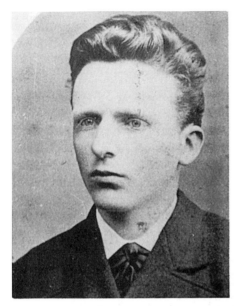 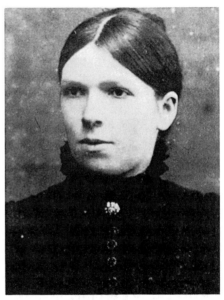

(*Left*) Cor van Gogh (1867–1900), youngest of the family. After his marriage collapsed, Cor enlisted as a volunteer in the Boer army in South Africa. The Red Cross recorded that he committed suicide. He was 33. (*Right*) Wilhelmien van Gogh (1862–1941). Of all the brothers and sisters, Wil was the closest to both Vincent and Theo. *Vincent van Gogh Foundation/National Museum Vincent van Gogh, Amsterdam*

Another important factor in his sad story is what appeared to be hereditary mental instability in the Van Gogh-Carbentus families. Vincent shot himself, and the Red Cross recorded that the youngest brother, Cor, killed himself while serving in the Boer War in South Africa. Perhaps the most tragic case of all was Theo's and Vincent's favourite sister, Wil, who had been active in various feminist organisations. She became suicidal and was committed to the Veldwijk asylum in Ermelo where she had to be force-fed. She was admitted in 1902 and remained there until her death in 1941.

Vincent had also told Dr Peyron at the asylum in Saint-Rémy that his mother's sister was epileptic and that there were many cases of mental disturbance in the family. And Dr Peyron later wrote: 'What has happened to this patient would only be a continuation of what has happened to several members of his family.' In his biography Tralbaut concluded: 'the probability of hereditary influences seems to be overwhelming', while in a lecture he gave to the 1964 French Language Congress of Psychiatry and Neurology, he showed that Vincent's and Theo's mental and physical disabilities were similar in every respect.

*   *   *

Long before Vincent's death, Theo was walking in Montmartre with his friend J.J. Isaacson when he is reported to have said, 'I should not be surprised if my brother were one of the great geniuses and will one day be compared to someone like Beethoven.'

Theo had foreseen the importance of Vincent's art and throughout his life supported him financially to achieve it, but he could hardly have foreseen that a century later Vincent's *Still Life: Vase With Fourteen Sunflowers* (in fact there are 15) would be selling to the Japanese Fire and Marine Insurance Company for over 25 million pounds, *Le Pont de Trinquetaille* for fourteen million, and *Irises* for a world record price of 30 million pounds. From being able to sell only two of his brother's paintings in his lifetime, the two most expensive paintings in the world now bear Vincent's signature.

The irony is that, a century after his death, his work has become so valuable that museums can no longer afford to display it to the public because of the colossal insurance costs. His original work will therefore become less visible to the world as time goes on. A double irony is that you will find his abused image everywhere. There are 'Vincent' potatoes on the market with his face on the plastic bag; there is Van Gogh French wine, self-portrait greeting cards with the message 'Ears to you', and self-portrait birthday cards with the message 'Gogh (American pronounciation "Go") Crazy!' And there is a Dutch chocolate advertising campaign in Italy using 'authentic' Droste chocolate with 'false' Van Gogh self-portraits, showing the painter with an arm in signed plaster, shaving, wearing sunglasses, and one with a clown's red nose.

The Vincent industry has become big business, marketing such inappropriate products as after-shave, umbrellas, sports shoes, T-shirts, sunglasses and beach shorts. Long before the centenary of his death, his image appeared on postage stamps as far afield as Togoland, the Republic of Maldives and Ras Al Khaima. One 'Van Gogh' birthday card takes the ultimate liberty of making him smile when you open the card, yet with Andrej Gromyko, Vincent was one of the saddest looking men I have ever seen. I hope that the realities of his life and that of his brother will filter through the assault of publicity in 1990.

And I wonder how much attention will be paid to Theo in 1991? Of course, for the lack of information on Theo we have partly Vincent to blame. We only know so much about Vincent because Theo kept all his letters, and we know relatively so little about Theo because Vincent kept none of his brother's.

As Vincent had nothing but contempt for photographers, after the age of 18 he never allowed himself be photographed. On the other hand, we have enough self-portraits of him to fill a gallery. It seemed to me odd that, for all his dependence and attachment to Theo, Vincent apparently never painted him, particularly during their two years together in Paris. I telephoned Han van Crimpen, Head of the Van Gogh Museum's Conservation and Documentation Department, and put this thought to him.

His reply surprised me. 'There is one oil painting in our collection, classified as 'a self-portrait of Vincent, Paris, 1886', which I think could be Theo and not Vincent. I cannot believe that this painting is a self-portrait.'

This portrait *Self-Portrait with Felt Hat* has often been described as 'unusual' or 'untypical of Vincent', since it portrays a man in the respectable attire of black felt hat, black coat and scarf. He has a reddish beard, which both the Van Gogh brothers had. I compared a full-page colour reproduction with reproductions of every existing Vincent self-portrait and also with a photograph taken of Theo in 1887 just after the painting was made, and one of Vincent in 1871. Vincent's eyebrows are very pronounced and his eyes are deep-set and intense. But this portrait has the mild eyes and rounded eyebrows of Theo, as well as his finer nose, shape of head and beard.

The more I looked at it, however, the more I began to doubt if it had been painted by Vincent at all. It is not signed and, when compared with

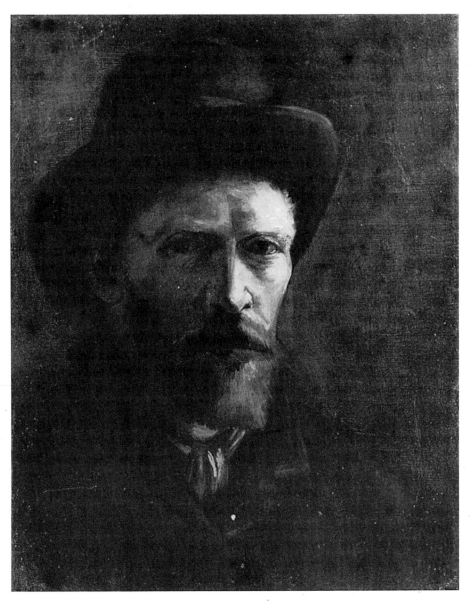

The so-called 'Self-portrait with felt hat', Paris 1886, unsigned. *Vincent van Gogh Foundation/National Museum Vincent van Gogh, Amsterdam*

his other work from around that time, lacks the characteristic brush strokes and bold use of paint.

I rang Han van Crimpen again and asked him if he was sure this painting was indeed by Vincent.

'No, I'm not sure,' he replied. 'It is, in fact, painted in a more traditional way than Vincent was painting at that time.'

I checked the provenance of the work. The huge De la Faille catalogue dates it 'Paris, early 1886'—that is, soon after Vincent landed on Theo from Antwerp. But at an exhibition in London it was dated September-December 1887. My guess is that in the mass of self-portraits inherited by Theo's widow Johanna, this portrait of Theo, by whichever artist (perhaps the Australian Russell who painted such a realistic portrait of Vincent in Paris) was grouped with them by mistake.

It will, no doubt, remain hanging in the Van Gogh Museum as a self-portrait by Vincent van Gogh for some time yet. Perhaps it would be over-optimistic to hope that in January 1991, on the centenary of Theo's death, it can finally be given the title: 'Portrait of Theo, by Vincent'.

9   The Forgotten Niece

One weekend, I was drawn into another Van Gogh family affair, quite unexpectedly.

At a small party in Amsterdam, I met an American author, Gary Schwartz, who had moved to Holland and set up a company to publish works of art history. I told him about my researches and he mentioned having heard of a niece of Vincent's who was living destitute in France somewhere. He could not remember any details, but he did give me the name of an Amsterdam lawyer named Benno Stokvis who he thought could help me.

I called Stokvis the following morning. He was polite but firm: he had no desire to talk to me or anyone else about the Van Gogh family. He sounded afraid of something or someone—I wondered what it was. Unfortunately, he has since died, and as far as I know, his secret has gone to the grave with him.

Stokvis' silence left me with nothing but my curiosity. It forced me back to my old territory—the archives of the Van Gogh Museum. There I was able to find only one slim clue: a reference to an article in a Marseilles newspaper called *Le Provençal*. The subject was someone named Hubertina Normance van Gogh. Was this the niece Gary Schwartz had heard about? The article itself was not in the museum library.

But the name Hubertina did ring a bell. Wasn't that the name of one of Vincent's sisters? A quick check in one of the library books told me it was Elisabeth Huberta. I considered trying to ask the Engineer about this affair but decided it would be premature to do so now. Instead, I went home and put a call through to the offices of *Le Provençal*. The reference to the article had said it had been written by a man named Raymond

Gimel, so when the newspaper switchboard answered the phone I asked for him.

I was in luck. Gimel was the editor of the newspaper and happened to be in his office. His assistant warned me that he was busy and could only spare a minute, but in that minute I learned that some years before in Marseilles he had, quite by accident, encountered the illegitimate daughter of Vincent's sister Elisabeth. Her name was Hubertina and she had been selling calendars door-to-door.

'I can't tell you everything over the telephone,' Gimel said. 'It's a long story and I'm busy now.'

'Could I come down to see you? You can name your day.'

We set a date two weeks away. It was my first free weekend.

This time I took the overnight train, which would at least give me the opportunity to get some sleep. Or so I thought. Even though I had taken care to equip myself with a flask of Glenlivet and a copy of Paul Theroux's *The Great Railway Bazaar*, I couldn't close my eyes. To make things worse, somewhere between Nice and Marseilles the train broke down in a railway siding near Cannes.

For a couple of hours we sat there. I searched out an inspector to find out what the problem was, but he knew about as much as I did. His job was to collect tickets, and that was all that concerned him. I asked whether I could leave the train to walk around. The answer was an emphatic '*Non!*'

So back to my compartment. My flask of malt was nearly empty, I had finished the book somewhere in northern France, and I was slowly going mad. Perhaps this trip was a mistake. Surely I could have accomplished what I wanted with a letter, I told myself.

But writing a letter would have gone against my instincts. After all, a letter to Mrs Maynard in Devon would not have accomplished much. I seemed to get most out of a situation when I handled it personally. Anyway, I had always wanted to see the fish market in Marseilles. The *bouillabaisse* there is supposed to be unequalled.

So here I was, thinking about Vincent and fish soup, and staring at a brick wall. The fish soon gave way to sheep. I must have counted thousands in an effort to force myself to sleep. No luck.

After about three hours, the train suddenly lurched forward. A few seconds later we moved again—this time backwards. I held my breath. Nothing. But then . . . another move forward. Then another move back. This happened about 20 times. After that, nothing. At least the driver had tried.

After five hours or so, the train gave a more promising heave, and this time it kept moving. My spirits immediately improved, and I settled back to re-read my book. On to Marseilles.

We arrived there just before dawn. I walked wearily from the railway station to the already bustling harbour. Fishermen were hard at work, bringing in their catches. Millions of fish, from the tiniest sardine to the great tuna, were piled on the icy marble slabs of the market. I watched for an hour or so, then searched out an appropriate café for the bowl of *bouillabaisse* I had promised myself. It lived up to its reputation, and I continued to watch the harbour as I slowly ate. I remember Vincent's descriptions of harbour life in Antwerp.

Leaving the café, I walked up towards the other end of the city. I had a couple of hours to kill before my appointment with Gimel, so I took my time, stopping at several places for coffee. At 10 a.m. I headed for the office of *Le Provençal*. I had woken up and was looking forward to my conversation with Gimel.

The building where *Le Provençal* has its office is a large one. Later I learned that the newspaper has the biggest circulation of any in the south of France.

Gimel received me in his room. He was a thick-set, well-groomed man with an air about him of the seasoned journalist. He never asked a question that did not have a point to it and he always listened closely to the answer. He seemed more interested in me than I was in what he had to tell me. But eventually we got to the point.

'Mr Gimel, how did you come to know of Hubertina van Gogh?' I couldn't think of a more subtle way to ask the question.

He leaned back in his chair, looked up at the ceiling, and then spoke.

'It was a complete accident, really. One day in the mid-1960s—I'd have to check the year, they blend one into another—I came home from work to find my wife looking terribly upset. She told me that earlier in the afternoon an old woman had come to the house selling calendars for charity. They had looked through the calendar together, and one of the reproductions was of a painting of a cornfield in Provence. It was by Van Gogh. While they were looking at the picture, the woman suddenly said: "My uncle painted that."

'My wife, a little surprised as you might expect, asked the woman what she meant. She said: "That painting is by Vincent van Gogh. My name is Hubertina van Gogh. He was my uncle."

'My wife asked the woman to sit down and talk for a while, which she seemed eager to do. In the course of their chat, the woman told my wife some of the details of her life. It had not been particularly happy. Thus my wife's depression when I got home.'

Armed with the woman's name, and with the information that she lived in a home for poor old people in Marseilles, Gimel tracked her down the next day. He went to see her at the home where she lived, and remembered the scene vividly.

'Her room reminded me of pictures of Van Gogh's room in Arles. It was very stark and simple. The only decorations on the walls were a crucifix and an old calendar of Van Gogh reproductions. Her clothes were old and frayed but, even in her eighties, there was nothing pitiful about her. She had sharp, lively eyes and, in spite of acute deafness, could hear a little with the help of a hearing aid. She spoke excellent French. And her face showed unmistakably the characteristic Van Gogh features.

'I introduced myself and told her that I wanted to do a story about her in *Le Provençal*. She told me most of her life story. I wish I could relate it as movingly as she did.

'In the summer of 1886 Elisabeth Huberta, Vincent van Gogh's younger sister, was on holiday in Normandy with her husband-to-be, a Dutch lawyer named Jean Philippe Theodore du Quesne van Bruchem (Elisabeth had been keeping house for him during his wife's terminal illness). At least, everyone thought they were on holiday. In fact, Elisabeth was many months pregnant. She gave birth to a daughter in the Norman village of Saint-Sauveur-le-Vicomte. That daughter was Hubertina. No one except the parents, and perhaps Elisabeth's mother, knew of the birth.

'When the couple did marry, they had another four children: Jeannette, Theodore, Wilhelmina, and Felix. But little Hubertina was left in Normandy. She was cared for by a young widow named Madame Balley,

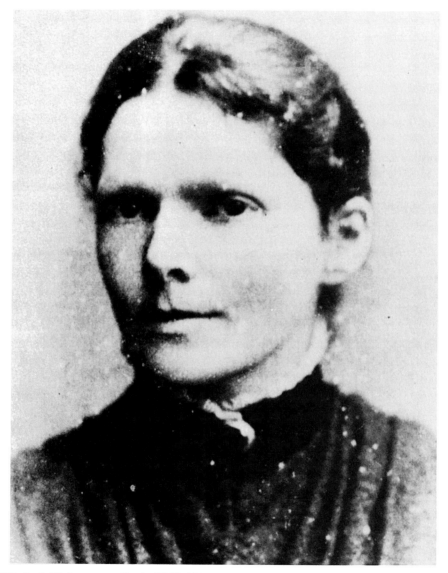

Elisabeth Huberta van Gogh (1859–1936), another of Vincent's sisters, who abandoned her illegitimate daughter, Hubertina, to be brought up in a village in Normandy. *Vincent van Gogh Foundation/National Museum Vincent van Gogh, Amsterdam*

who owned a grocery shop.

'Hubertina told me that she believed du Quesne, her father, had wanted to take her back to Holland, but her mother Elisabeth had refused. Apparently that side of the family was rather more puritanical than the other.

'Hubertina managed somehow to go to school, for she became a teacher. When her uncle was beginning to become famous, she was working in Paris. She was there in 1910, when her mother published a book called *Personal Recollections of Vincent van Gogh.*'

I knew the book well. It was an inconsequential whitewash, designed mainly to save the family face from the more unsavoury aspects of Vincent's personality. No doubt it went over well at respectable dinner parties.

'Hubertina always knew about her family and wondered about them,' Gimel continued. 'She told me: "I knew I had brothers and sisters in Holland, but I didn't know if they knew about me. I would have liked to go to Holland to see them but never dared to. I would have been a stranger to them and maybe an embarrassment—the Van Gogh family being what it was."'

Gimel said that he tried to get Hubertina to elaborate on that last phrase but she changed the subject.

'Hubertina earned a comfortable living until she was 35. Then a severe attack of influenza left her very deaf. She had to give up teaching and couldn't find suitable work for many years. She became destitute and for a long while lived a life that she preferred not to talk about. "I am ashamed of what I was compelled to do to keep alive." She would not elaborate.

'After her father died, Hubertina received a letter from her sister, Jeannette, whom she had never seen. Apparently her father had waited until he was on his deathbed before confiding to his eldest legitimate daughter about the existence of Hubertina. When Jeannette heard that she had an illegitimate sister—who was not going to be provided for in her father's will—she was appalled and felt it was the least she could do to offer Hubertina half her share of the will.

'"I refused," Hubertina told me. "I appreciated Jeannette's thoughtfulness but I did not want to deprive her. After my mother was widowed, she finally did write to me. She asked if I would like to come to her home in Holland as a maidservant." Very charitable of her, don't you think?

'In search of work, Hubertina moved from Paris to Toulon, then south to Nice and Marseilles, where the only work she could find was selling calendars door-to-door for charity. That was how my wife met her.'

When Gimel discussed Hubertina's predicament with some Marseilles artists, they were touched by the irony of the story. So the painters Toussaint d'Orgino, Antoine Ferrari and the brothers Ambrogiani decided they would donate the money earned from one painting a year to helping Vincent's neglected niece. How Vincent would have appreciated that gesture, I thought. It was the sort of thing he would have done.

I asked Gimel if Hubertina had had any contact with the painter's namesake nephew. He recalled that she mentioned having met Dr Van Gogh for the first time in 1951, at an exhibition of Vincent's paintings which was held in Arles. Hubertina said that the Engineer gave her a free ticket of admission to the exhibition and took her out for dinner in Arles. He also bought her a new hearing aid and sent her some money every once in a while.

'The last I heard of her was that she had moved to Lourdes, where she died not long after I met her.'

There was a knock at the door and Gimel's assistant came in to tell him that he had another appointment. He seemed sorry to have to break off, but I had got what I wanted. We shook hands and I left. He asked me to keep him up to date on whatever I was doing with Vincent and, to my surprise, asked if I didn't mind being interviewed and photographed for the next day's edition of *Le Provençal*.

After leaving Gimel's office, I walked slowly through the backstreets of Marseilles, turning Hubertina's sad story over in my mind. On the train back to Nice I decided that the first thing to do back in Holland was to ask Dr Van Gogh what he knew about his illegitimate cousin.

A few days later I was sitting once again in the Engineer's office at the Van Gogh Museum. He had greeted me cordially, having forgotten, or so it seemed, the disagreements of our last visit. His tone remained cordial until I got to the point of my being there.

'Do you know anything about a woman named Hubertina van Gogh?'

He sat back in silence, a little surprised. I think he was trying to decide how to respond. Once again he gave me that penetrating look. Finally he spoke.

'Yes, I knew about her. She is dead now.' His voice was very quiet.

'Did you know her?' I asked

'I met Hubertina for the first time back in the Fifties, at an exhibition of Vincent van Gogh's paintings in Arles. I was just walking through the exhibition when a woman of about my own age approached me.

' "I am your cousin Hubertina," she said. I was shocked. I had no idea that such a person existed. We walked around together and she told me the story of her life. I remember that when I told my wife she said: "Oh, Vincent, what a family the Van Goghs seem to have been." '

I asked him what further contact he had had with Hubertina. He said he had arranged through the Dutch Consul General in Marseilles to send Hubertina 300 guilders (about £75) and a smaller payment every three months. With his help and the contributions of the local painters, Dr Van Gogh said, Hubertina was able to leave the poorhouse and move to a *pension*.

'I continued to send her money for quite a while,' said the Engineer, 'until I began to be blackmailed . . .' He stopped abruptly.

'Did you say blackmail?' I asked.

He hesitated, then spoke with unmistakable anger in his voice. 'Yes, someone tried to blackmail me. I handed over all the correspondence to the Marseilles police.'

'What form did the blackmail take?'

'Oh, it was a bunch of crooks. Don't ask me that. All I want to say is that I washed my hands of the whole affair.' He was making it clear that he had nothing more to say on the subject. I said I must be going and stood up. Walking towards the door, I apologised for concentrating on what seemed to be the more unpleasant side of the Van Gogh family's affairs.

'Oh, that's all right,' replied the Engineer. 'These things are un-important.'

He may have thought them 'unimportant' but I wasn't going to stop until I had found out whatever else I could. After leaving the Engineer, I went back home and telephoned the Marseilles police department. I explained what I wanted and was switched through to someone else. I explained again. I was transferred to yet another official, who listened and did exactly the same thing. After explaining myself to at least half a dozen Marseilles policemen, I finally spoke to the one who was supposed to know about matters of this sort. He listened silently and said that he did not have personal knowledge of the case but would look through the files. He came back about ten seconds later. Clearly he had not looked very hard.

'I am sorry, monsieur, but we do not have records of any case such as the one you describe. Goodbye.'

And that was it. The case rests, mystery to everyone except the Engineer, who has taken his secret to the grave—and someone in the Marseilles police force who, for some reason, does not want to talk about it.

As I hung up, I thought about the Engineer's response to my question about syphilis and hereditary disease in the Van Gogh family. He had dismissed the whole thing. Now, with his cousin Hubertina, he was being similarly evasive. What was the blackmail attempt all about? Why was he so unwilling to talk about it? I was never going to get answers to these questions.

The life of Hubertina van Gogh was made miserable by the hypocrisy of her mother, who refused to acknowledge the existence of a child she had brought into the world. Her birthright was denied her. She was raised by a stranger to whom charity was more important than the 'respectability' which Elisabeth van Gogh so valued. The belief in that kind of respectability seemed to have survived into the present day, in the Engineer's refusal to acknowledge the true nature of Vincent's and Theo's illness.

Hubertina died in 1969. No one is said to have attended her funeral, but a group of painters in Lourdes, where she died, gave a wreath of sunflowers to be placed on her grave. The sunflowers were a reminder of her connection with her uncle. Of him Hubertina had only one thing to say, when she talked to Raymond Gimel: 'We had loneliness in common.'

10   Baby Willem

It was one of the ironies of my involvement with Vincent that the success I had with his story took more and more of my time away from him. I found after doing the article that I had acquired a reputation as a kind of artistic detective. For weeks my letter-box was jammed with mail from people claiming they had found works by, among others, Picasso, Turner and Frans Hals in locations ranging from tool-sheds to outside toilets, although attics obviously were the most common place for finding 'missing masters'. I had no time to spread my energies around the scores of claimants who mistakenly thought that I was their passport to authentication. The reaction was so overwhelming, I had to get an unlisted telephone number for a while.

This reputation—which I did my best to discourage—also meant that I was being given numerous biographical assignments for the magazine. My article on M. C. Escher, which brought to light 30 previously unpublished works and a revealing correspondence with Mick Jagger, was used to accompany the catalogue of a retrospective exhibition of his works at New York's Metropolitan Museum of Art. After that came articles on Vermeer, Hieronymus Bosch, master forger Han van Meegeren, and Karel Appel. I was becoming an instant 'expert' on all these men.

In addition, I had several travel stories to do for the *Holland Herald*. These took me as far away as Indonesia, the West Indies, and South America. And they took time, more than I could spare. But that was my job. Weeks and months slipped by, almost without my knowing it. The one opportunity I did have was a weekend in Paris, in the archive where I had initially failed so completely to find out anything about Agostina

Segatori. This time I was trying to trace descendants of artist friends whose names Vincent had scrawled on the backs of notebooks he had kept while he was living there: Collin, Fantin Latour, Lefèvre, Moisend, Duran, Roll, Harpinguies, Arbey, Brancelet, Risler, Dupré, Guillaumin, the Australian painter Russell, and the sisters Lapointe.

I spent a few days in the city archives, this time without the foul-breathed librarian peering over my shoulder. But my luck was no better. Apart from discovering their addresses in 1886, I came up with absolutely nothing. It was extremely discouraging. I wondered when, if ever, I was going to get an opportunity to do what I really wanted.

It did not come until nearly a year after my trip to Marseilles, and then only through misfortune. About five years before I had been knocked over by a car while crossing the Rozengracht, one of Amsterdam's busiest streets—at a point opposite the house where Rembrandt died in 1669. The accident broke my collarbone and seven ribs, fractured my right leg in two places, and collapsed one of my lungs. I spent three months flat on my back in a hospital bed and left with a metal plate holding the fractured leg together.

It was that metal plate which gave me my opportunity to do some more research on Vincent. In March 1976, I went back to the hospital to have the plate removed, a fairly simple operation. But the weekend after leaving hospital, I spent an evening dancing at a party with my crutches in one hand. The next morning my leg hurt even more than my head, and I went straight to the hospital. They kept me there for three weeks.

I had all my Vincent material brought to me and spent my time reviewing it. What was I going to do after I got out, and what would I have time to do? I would have liked to go back to England, to dig around in more attics and try to find descendants of people whom Vincent knew, but that would be much too time-consuming. No, it looked as if I would have to stay closer to home.

Flicking through my travel journals, I decided that the most interesting question mark in the Netherlands concerned Vincent's stay in The Hague, when he was living with the prostitute, Clasina Maria Hoornik (also referred to as Sien, Christine and Christina), and her two children, five-year-old Maria Wilhelmina and the baby, Willem, born on July 2nd, 1882. After leaving his parents' home, this was the only time in his life that

Vincent would experience anything resembling a family life of his own.

He moved to The Hague on November 28, 1881. He had spent several months at his parents' house in Etten, where he fell in love with his cousin Kee Vos while she was still mourning the death of her husband. She, like Eugénie Loyer, firmly rejected him. But whereas Eugénie's refusal channelled Vincent's passions into the Bible, his cousin Kee's 'No, no, never!' drove him to a prostitute for whom he felt a regard that was dominated by compassion. He told Theo that he felt affection and love for prostitutes: they were his 'sisters' in circumstances and experience. 'I am drawn to the half-faded faces in which I see written: life in its reality has left its mark here.' Thus, when he moved in with Clasina Maria Hoornik it was another significant turning point in his life.

Vincent was attracted to this woman because she could satisfy his sensual needs. But, even more, she represented the kind of poverty and misery that he had tried to serve in the Borinage and to depict in his artistic work since then.

For months Vincent did not mention to Theo in his letters that he was living with Clasina. When he finally did tell him, he explained that she modelled for him and that he was thinking of marrying her.

When the prospect of marriage reached their parents' ears, Theo told Vincent that father Van Gogh was thinking of sending him to a lunatic asylum at Gheel, near Antwerp. Even acquaintances in The Hague, the painter Anton Mauve and the dealer Tersteeg, were appalled when they found out that Vincent was living with this woman. Tersteeg spread the word that Vincent was insane. But Vincent paid no attention.

He was in hospital being treated for gonorrhoea when Clasina gave birth to a son they called Willem. As soon as Vincent was released from the hospital, he visited Clasina and her baby at the hospital in Leiden. He was overcome with emotion.

'What I am most astonished at is the child,' he wrote. 'Although he has been taken with forceps, he was not injured at all. He was lying in his cradle with a worldly-wise air.'

To accommodate his growing family, Vincent used his allowance from Theo to move into a larger apartment in The Hague. He was overjoyed with his experience of family life. He had told Theo often enough that he had always wanted to have a studio with a cradle. 'I work from early till

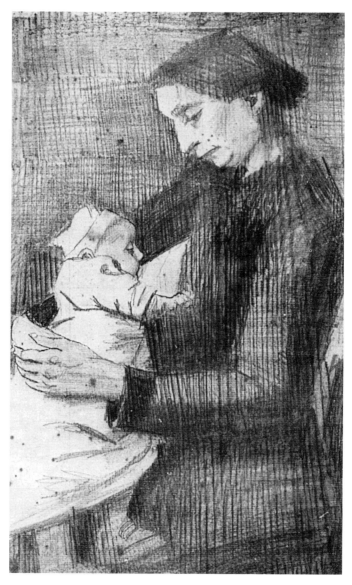

Clasina suckling her child, drawing, The Hague, 1882. *National Museum Kröller-Müller, Otterlo*

late at night and Clasina poses for me.' For Vincent, this was a home of his own and he had a passionate desire to believe in its permanence. He could not look at the cradle without showing emotion, and in his marvellous drawings of the baby Willem we can share something of what he felt. In this unlikely household he found a passionate domesticity that inspired some of his most moving early work.

In successive letters, Theo concentrated on trying to persuade his brother not to marry Clasina, and Vincent continued to plead with Theo not to withdraw the financial support on which he totally depended. He wrote: 'I know how only a short time ago I came home to a house that was not a real home with all the emotions connected with it now, where two great voids stared at me night and day. There was no wife. There was no child.'

In spite of the mounting pressures from his family to leave Clasina, Vincent wrote to Theo: 'When I am with them and the little man comes creeping towards me on all fours, crowing for joy, I haven't the slightest doubt that everything is right. How often that child has comforted me . . . when I am at home he cannot leave me alone for a moment; when I am at work, he pulls at my coat or climbs up against my leg till I take him on my lap . . . he crows at everything, plays quietly with a bit of paper, a bit of string, or an old brush; the child is always happy. If he keeps this disposition all his life, he will be cleverer than I.'

But the Van Gogh family insisted that Vincent practise morality in return for his allowance, and after a year-and-a-half together, Vincent left Clasina, with her daughter and baby. At first glance this might seem an inhuman decision, but a closer look at the letters from this time shows that the reasons were more complex.

Throughout Vincent's correspondence with Theo he is either asking him for money or thanking him for it. From the moment he became a full-time painter, he was totally dependent on Theo's financial support in order to live and buy the materials he required for his work.

When he began to live with Clasina and her family, however, he began to push Theo to increase the allowance. Theo explained that his income had to be divided among no less than six persons. To this Vincent replied: 'The division of your income, directly or indirectly, among no less than six persons is certainly remarkable. But the subdivision of my 150 francs among four human beings, with all the expenses for models, drawing and painting material, house rent, is also rather remarkable, isn't it? If those 150 francs could be increased by the work next year—I reckon the year begins with your visit—that would be delightful. We must find ways and means.'

Theo then suggested the obvious: Why didn't Vincent try and help matters out by selling some of his work himself?—immediately qualifying this by reminding his brother that his ragged appearance was an obstacle in this respect. He told Vincent that both he and his father were ashamed of going out for walks with him because of the way he looked.

Certainly, no more money was forthcoming from Theo and it may have been the economic crisis that helped to move Clasina back in the direction of prostitution—very much against Vincent's will. It was at this point that he decided to leave.

There followed for him three bleak months in the northern province of Drenthe where he mourned the loss of Clasina and the children. He wrote: 'I cannot hide from you that I am overcome by a feeling of great anxiety, depression, a *je ne sais quoi* of discouragement and despair more than I can tell. And if I cannot find comfort, it will be too overwhelming. . . the fate of the woman and the fate of my poor dear little boy and the other child cut my heart to shreds.'

Although he looked on his abandonment of Clasina as his own decision, in a few months he was repeatedly accusing Theo of having put economic pressure on him to force the break. He also launched a vitriolic attack on clergymen, in particular his father, for their lack of human warmth. He compared them unfavourably with pigs, claiming the latter were more in harmony with their surroundings.

What had happened to Clasina Maria Hoornik and the children? She would be dead by now, but were the children still alive? Did they have descendants who might know something of their background? These were the questions I felt compelled to find answers to.

When I got out of hospital, I took an afternoon off and went to the Van Gogh Museum to have a look through the letters Vincent wrote from The Hague and from Drenthe. I discovered that there seemed to be more missing letters or parts of letters, more confusions of dates, than in letters from other periods. This was odd—the letters had for the most part been so concisely assembled and ordered. For some reason Vincent stopped dating his letters during The Hague period.

Someone at the museum suggested I look up the art historian Jan Hulsker, who was the greatest living authority in Holland on Van Gogh. It was Hulsker who assembled, sorted out and rearranged the letters from this period and who drew attention to the fact that the order in which they had originally been published was incorrect. He reordered them in the following way: 191, 195, 196, 192, 194, 197, 198, 193, 199, 200, 202, 203, 204, 201, 205.

It was letter 193 that particularly interested me. Between 193 and 194 there was another—193a—which was withheld from publication by Theo's widow Johanna van Gogh-Bonger in the early editions. But when 193a *was* finally added to the collected letters, by the Engineer, the first part of the letter was missing—as it still is today.

One of the interesting points about this letter was that it was written at the height of the most serious disagreement that Vincent and Theo ever had. It was over Clasina whom Theo was urging Vincent to leave, under threat of cutting off his allowance. Vincent even went so far as to consider terminating his friendship with Theo.

If there were any answers to the questions I wanted to explore, Jan Hulsker would certainly know about them, but when we spoke on the telephone, I explained that I wanted to discuss an entirely different matter and didn't mention Vincent's relationship with Clasina Maria Hoornik. A few months before I had been in Curaçao doing a series of articles. While there I learned of an art-collecting businessman who was said to have an unknown Van Gogh painting. I went to see the man and he told me that in fact he had several Van Goghs, all tucked away in different countries. He was planning to reveal them only gradually, over the years, but said that Jan Hulsker had already seen one of them and was studying it. I asked Hulsker if I could talk to him about these hidden canvases and he invited me to visit him at his home in The Hague.

I drove up to see him a few days later. He is a genial man with silver hair and a polite, restrained manner. We sat down to a glass of dry sherry and talked for a while about the collector in Curaçao. He had been appointed one of the official authenticators for the canvas in question and was currently inclined not to think it authentic. I told him my story about the

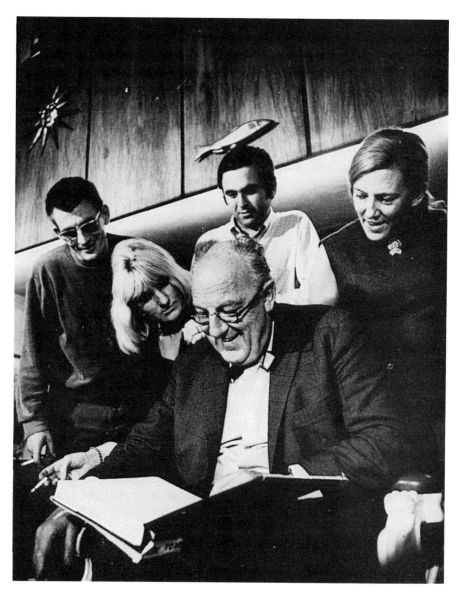

The literary family Hoornik: Ed Hoornik (*seated*) and his wife Mies Bouhuys (*right*).
Photo: Wim Ruigrok, Amsterdam

drawing in Mrs Maynard's attic, and we discussed the problems of authentication.

By the second glass of sherry, I got around to the real point of my visit. I told Hulsker that I was interested in Vincent's Hague period but did not know as much about it as I would like.

'The prostitute he lived with—Clasina Hoornik. What was her background?'

Hulsker told me that she was born in The Hague on February 22nd, 1850. She was the eldest of her parents' 11 children. By the time she moved into the house (since demolished) in the street called Schenkweg, her daughter Marie was five years old. The girl's father was unknown.

I asked Hulsker if he knew what happened to Clasina and her family after Vincent left her. He had researched this matter thoroughly. 'I think the relationship was deteriorating,' he said. 'When Vincent left for Drenthe to mourn the separation, Clasina gave her mother the custody of Maria and handed the baby Willem over to her brother, Pieter Anthonie Hoornik.'

'What became of Clasina?'

'She moved from The Hague to Delft, then Antwerp and finally Rotterdam. She had a really tragic life. To legitimise her children she married Arnoldus Franciscus van Wijk. That was in 1901, when she was 51. Twenty years earlier she had told Vincent she would one day put an end to her life by throwing herself into the water. In 1904 this prediction came true when she drowned herself in the River Schelde. *Sorrow* was the title Vincent gave to the touching drawing he made of her.'

Hulsker told me that Pieter Anthonie Hoornik, Clasina's brother, had a son of his own, who became one of Holland's most noted poets, Ed Hoornik.

'I once asked Ed if he knew that the prostitute Vincent lived with in The Hague was his aunt,' he recalled. 'He was amazed. He had no idea. But I do not know if he pursued the matter further.'

Ed Hoornik died in 1970, but his widow, the Dutch writer and broadcaster, Mies Hoornik-Bouhuys, still lives in Amsterdam. I made an appointment to see her. She lived in a canal house in the Prinsengracht, only a ten-minute walk from my own home in the Brouwersgracht. The Hoornik home differed from its neighbours in having thick ivy framing the windows.

Mies Bouhuys is a charming and intelligent woman. We had some tea and sat down to talk. She was intrigued by the news that I was trying to trace the descendants of Clasina Maria Hoornik—a certain light seemed to come into her eyes. I told her I had just been to see Jan Hulsker who had told me that her late husband, Ed, was the nephew of the prostitute.

'Oh yes, indeed. He told Ed about 20 years ago. I think Ed was greatly amused by the whole thing.

'I remember we were at a cocktail party. Jan Hulsker took Ed aside and said that he had "something to tell him in private, man to man". Ed laughed and told him that he had no secrets from his wife.

'Ed certainly got a surprise—particularly in view of the fact that he had had *Sorrow*, Vincent's nude portrait of Clasina, framed on the bedroom wall for years. Of course, he had no way of knowing that the dejected figure was his aunt!

'Ed was curious—as you are now—to know what happened to his cousin. He had lost contact with Willem who was considerably older than him. So we decided to try and trace him.'

I asked Mies how they went about it.

'Ed had heard that Willem was employed many years before as a designer with the Rijkswaterstaat (State Water Works). And through this body he managed to trace Willem to an old folks' home called the Saint Servaas Bolwerk in Maastricht, in the southern province of Limburg.'

I underlined the name.

Mies and Ed decided to visit Willem there. They drove down together one weekend in the autumn of 1957. After finding the home where Willem was staying, they were shown to his room by one of the staff.

'When we walked into Willem's room, he was sitting at a desk with his back to us. The room was nearly barren of decoration. As we came closer, we saw that Willem had a dozen or so sharpened pencils and several sheets of paper on the desk in front of him. He was drawing. Drawing very intently. It took several moments before he realised that we were standing only a few feet away from him.

'When he saw us, he jumped to his feet. He looked his age—he was 75—but his features were strong and angular, especially when etched against the daylight coming in through the window. There was something vaguely familiar about his face.

'Willem didn't know who we were, but when Ed introduced himself he was visibly moved. The two cousins embraced—Ed was also moved. They had not seen each other since Ed was a boy.

'We all sat down and Willem and Ed began to talk. Ed told Willem about his experiences during the war—he survived Dachau—and about his career as a writer.

'Willem listened attentively. He seemed glad to renew contact with a member of the Hoornik family. Clearly he felt out of touch with his past, and this meeting was a way of renewing that contact.'

I felt that Mies Bouhuys was preparing to tell me something important and I edged forward in my seat. In doing so, I knocked over my teacup, which momentarily put a stop to her narrative as I stood there apologising, and she insisted that I shouldn't worry about it.

When we sat down again, she resumed.

'Ed asked Willem what he had done, how he had come to work in the State Water Works, whether he had married, and so on. Willem looked uncomfortable, as if he had a secret to tell but wasn't sure whether he ought to. He looked at the ground and shuffled his feet back and forth. Then, in a sombre voice, he told Ed that what he was about to tell him he had never told anyone before. I can pass on nearly his exact words, so carefully did I listen. You know how it is with us journalists. When he began to speak, I turned on a little tape recorder in my head. I shall never forget his words, though I've barely thought of them since that day.'

Mies half-closed her eyes as she quoted Willem's words to me.

'I always had the impression that my mother never really wanted to give me over into the care of her brother. She used to visit me secretly at school in The Hague and give me sweets. I remember my stepfather took me to Rotterdam to visit her one day. It must have been around 1900. He thought it important that I have a legal surname, you see, for fear of discrimination when I joined the army. He asked my mother if she would get married so that I would have a legal father.

' "But I know who his father is," said my mother. "He was an artist I lived with nearly 20 years ago in The Hague. His name was Van Gogh, Vincent van Gogh." She turned towards me. "You are called after him," she said. "His middle name was Willem." '

I must have made a noise, because Mies Bouhuys turned to me with a strange look on her face. She didn't comment, but went on with her story.

'Of course,' Willem said, 'the name Vincent van Gogh meant nothing to me then. I only made a note of the name because he was my father. I had no idea how famous he would become later.

'Anyway, my stepfather persuaded my mother to marry a sailor called van Wijk. Van Wijk received 300 guilders in return and went back to sea, I suppose. That is how I became officially Willem van Wijk. But I have always known I was the illegitimate son of Vincent van Gogh.'

Asked why he had kept this secret to himself all his life, Willem replied: 'When I was younger I used to tell myself that one day I would tell the world. But the older I got, the less I wanted to. I have been living in a rather strict community, and I admit that I did not want people and my family to know that my mother was a prostitute. I think it would have made my life unbearable if they had known that here. Not even my wife knew about it. She is dead now.

'For the past few years I have been living from room to room. Not very happily. I rarely see my son and daughter. But I do love to draw. Sometimes I sit with my pencil and wonder . . .'

The expression on Mies' face changed as she seemed to come back to the present. She sat in silence for a moment, then continued.

'I realised after Willem finished speaking why his face looked familiar. There was such a strong resemblance between him and Vincent van Gogh—the high forehead, angular nose, brooding lips. When he held his head at a certain angle the resemblance became even stronger.

'Willem was upset by these memories. We left him quietly and promised to return. We did not speak for most of the drive back up to Amsterdam.'

'And did you ever return?' I asked.

'Ed returned about a year later, early in 1958, just a few months before Willem died. Ed told me that Willem cried openly when he talked about his mother. His last thoughts were of her.'

I asked Mies if Ed had published any of this.

'He always wanted to write about it one day, but never did. He was so busy.'

'And yourself,' I said. 'Did you never discuss it with anyone or write about it?'

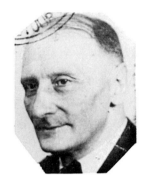

Willem van Wijk (1882–1958), Clasina's illegitimate son. *Collection Willy van Wijk*

Her answer was one I had heard several times in the course of my investigations.

'No one ever asked me.'

'I'm glad I did.'

'What do you think you'll do with what I've told you?'

'I will publish it, but I'm not sure in exactly what form yet.'

'If you would like me not to talk about it to anyone else, I'll be glad to co-operate. It's been sitting with me for so long, I shouldn't have too much difficulty keeping quiet about it now.'

'That's very kind of you. Yes, I would appreciate your keeping it to yourself. Thank you very much. Thank you for talking to me.'

When I left Mies' house, I walked around the canals for a couple of hours to gather my thoughts. The missing sections of letters from The Hague period, and their original disorder, took on a new significance. Were they cut out of the 'official' body of letters deliberately? Was someone in the family trying to hide the true nature of Vincent's involvement with the prostitute Clasina? As far as I was concerned, the importance of this finding could surpass Mrs Maynard's drawing.

I was touched by the reunion between Willem and Ed Hoornik after so many years, moved by the thought of Willem living most of his life with a secret that he felt he couldn't divulge to anyone. But I was moved most of all by the pathos of Vincent's dilemma. He had wanted so desperately to find love, have a family. His descriptions of the joy he felt at seeing the baby Willem crawl across the floor are beautiful. All this was taken away from him by the restrictive moralism of his own family, and even of his friends.

I must have walked around for several hours because, when I next looked at the sky, night was falling. The sun had still been fairly high in the sky when I left Mies Bouhuys. Time to go home. I had to work out what I was going to do with this new information.

First I consulted Jan Hulsker. He told me that, in the course of his research in 1958, he had considered very carefully the possibility of baby Willem being Vincent's son, and had come to the conclusion that he was not.

But I still wanted to find out more about Willem van Wijk, or Willem van Gogh, as he might, in fact, have been. Mies had not said where he was buried.

I also wanted to find Willem's children, to see what they knew about their father and grandfather. Mies knew no particulars of them; I would have to do it all myself.

And after I had found out what I wanted, I would go and talk to Dr Van Gogh.

That night I wrote to the local authority in Maastricht, asking if they had any information about a man called Willem van Wijk, born 1882, died 1958-60, resident of Saint Servaas Bolwerk old folks' home, Maastricht. I went out and posted the letter immediately. I couldn't wait until morning.

I wanted first of all to go to the cemetery where Willem was buried and photograph his gravestone. I'm not sure why I wanted to do this, really. Perhaps because the first thing I had done on my assignment for the magazine was photograph the tiny gravestone of Vincent van Gogh, the boy who had been stillborn a year before his brother, the painter, was born. Or perhaps it was simply the easiest thing to do. In my journeys I had become used to cemeteries.

This cemetery seemed large enough for a city of over 100,000 inhabitants—large enough, I thought, to accommodate the entire province. Thousands of graves, from the humblest stones to the grandest family vaults, were shielded from the sun by weeping willows and tall cypress trees—Vincent's symbol of death.

I rapped loudly on the cemetery-keeper's door. Silence. I rapped again. This time I heard a shuffling noise inside the gatehouse and a clanking that sounded ominously like chains. Then a key was put into the lock from the other side and turned slowly. Finally the door creaked open. There stood a huge man with dark eyes that seemed to be floating in the back of his head. I couldn't tell whether he was looking at me, past me, or through me. It took a moment to gain my composure and tell him the grave I wanted. He replied in a slow, deep monotone:

'Van Wijk, Van Wijk . . . Can't say I recognise the name . . . Come in, please. I'll have a look at the plans.'

I followed him into the gatehouse, a dark and slightly damp-smelling place. He unhooked one of his enormous rusty keys and opened a cupboard, from which he slowly pulled out a dusty register that looked as if it had been there for centuries. I peered over his shoulder as he turned the pages, found the one he needed, and then scanned down the page.

'The grave you want is Lot GG, no. 186. Willem van Wijk, buried November 8th, 1958,' he announced. 'It's over on the other side of the cemetery, and you'll never find it by yourself. If you can wait a minute, I'll walk with you. I have to do something over there.'

As we walked the keeper talked about his job, about how few people he saw. 'You are the first registered visitor that Mr Van Wijk has had. Are you a relative?'

'No, not a relative.'

'A family friend, I suppose . . .'

'You could say that.'

At the end of a long pathway he pointed me in the direction of Lot GG, no. 186. I thanked him and he went on his own way.

Like Vincent's grave in Auvers-sur-Oise, Willem's gravestone was one of the simplest in the cemetery. A slight drizzle had started up and I pulled my collar around my ears. As I stood there, a phrase from one of Vincent's letters came back to me: 'What will be the fate of my poor dear little boy?' I thought again of his descriptions of the baby 'crowing for joy' and tugging at Vincent's smock while he was painting. Now that little boy lay here, unvisited, seemingly forgotten. My breath stuck in my throat.

The happy little boy was the last of Willem that his father had seen. What became of him after that? Did he have a happy life, in spite of his sad secret? Had his secret affected him? What kind of character was he?

To find out, I would have to trace his family and friends. Perhaps they would answer Vincent's question about his 'poor dear little boy.' I made a few photographs of the grave and left.

I drove back into Maastricht and went first to the Saint Servaas Bolwerk, the old folks' home where Willem had lived. The matron, an officious woman in a black tunic, told me that there was no one there who remembered Willem. But she did check the records and told me that he had died of stomach cancer.

My next visit was to the offices of the State Water Works, where Willem had worked as a draughtsman. From the outside the place was exceptionally unfriendly, a gaunt neo-Gothic prison that looked quite out of place in the sunshine. From the inside, it was even worse: full of long dark corridors and creaking doors, and apparently suffering from a shortage of staff.

After asking a few people I ran into in the corridors, I was referred to an information desk on the first floor. There I enquired whether there might be anyone still working there who had known Willem van Wijk. The man behind the desk looked at me a little suspiciously.

'Are you a relative of Van Wijk?'

'No, I'm a journalist doing some research about his family.'

'Van Wijk has been dead almost 20 years, you know. But I'll see what I can do.'

'Thank you very much.' He picked up the telephone, dialled a couple of numbers, and began speaking in the Limburg dialect, which I don't easily understand. After a few minutes he put down the telephone and turned to me.

'If you go up to room 137 there may be someone there who can help you.'

Waiting for me in room 137 were two old men named Anthonie Balthusen and Victor Koekkelkoren. They sat silent and upright in wooden chairs. I introduced myself and explained what I was looking for.

'Van Wijk,' they said almost simultaneously. Apparently it was the custom here to address and refer to people by their last name only—even if, like these two, they have been working together for 25 years.

'Van Wijk,' they said again. I could tell by the way they said the name that their memories were less than favourable. Koekkelkoren was the first to speak.

'If you ask me for good things, there's not much to say.'

I asked whether he had any memories of specific incidents that made him dislike Willem. He shifted nervously in his seat but didn't say a word. I turned to his colleague.

'Do you have anything to say about Van Wijk, Mr Balthusen?'

'There's a lot I could say, but I won't.'

Silence again. I couldn't quite believe their unwillingness to talk to me.

'Is there anyone else who might be able to tell me more about Van Wijk? I've come all the way from Amsterdam.'

They didn't say anything for a few moments. Then Balthusen spoke.

'There was one fellow here at work. He is no longer here. His name is Johannes Feij. I think he knew Van Wijk better than anyone else did. I don't know where he lives now, but it is probably in Maastricht. Talk to him. He might have something to tell you.'

I could tell that they had given me as much as they were going to. I rose and couldn't resist saying: 'Thank you so much for your help, gentlemen.' They didn't see the joke. I gave up and left.

I stopped at the first phone booth I passed and looked up the address of Johannes Feij. He lived near the cemetery which I had already visited. I was about to telephone him when I decided it might be better to drop in unannounced. People seemed so unwilling to talk about Willem . . . maybe if I took him by surprise Johannes Feij would open up more easily. So I drove to the address given in the telephone directory.

Luckily, Feij was at home. A thin, spritely man in his seventies, he was willing to talk and invited me into his house. Over tea and biscuits, he told me about Willem van Wijk.

'I worked under Willem from 1924 to 1938, but knew him for quite a while after that. He was a withdrawn person. Embittered, I would say, and certainly difficult. He kept very much to himself.

'During the war he was a member of the Nationalist Socialist Party and a sympathiser with the Nazis. They had the freedom of his house during the occupation. Of course, this alienated a lot of people. I remember, just after the war, seeing him being transported to the concentration camp at Vught to be tried with other alleged collaborators. But he wasn't confined for very long, I don't think. His wife, Saakje Leistra, left him during the war. I heard that she committed suicide shortly afterwards.

'I always felt with Willem that he had things preying on his mind, but he never talked about them, whatever they were. An odd thing I noticed was that he always signed himself *Willem van Wijk, zich noemende Hoornik* [literally, calling himself Hoornik], a very unusual practice in the Netherlands.'

Feij had the impression that Willem's childhood had not been a very happy one.

'I remember he told me that as a child he was forced to walk for three hours to piano lessons. I think he harboured some resentment towards his family. Yes, I'm sure he did. He told me once that the writer Ed Hoornik was related to him and he would show great interest, I remember, when a new Hoornik book was published. But as far as I know he had no contact with him.'

Feij knew nothing about Willem's mother. Neither did he know where his son and daughter were living. He did, however, give me the name of Mrs Toos van Dijk, who was a neighbour of Willem's before he moved into the old people's home. I visited her next.

Mrs Van Dijk said: 'Willem had a slightly sarcastic humour and was a bit bitter but had an aristocratic air and was very charming. He drew magnificently. His lettering was beautiful.'

She could not tell me much more about Willem. They were good neighbours but didn't know each other well. Nor could she tell me the names of anyone else who might have known him.

I decided next to try and find Willem's son and daughter. To do this I followed the same procedure Paul Chalcroft and I had used in London to track down Kathleen Maynard. I went from Mrs Van Dijk's house to the Maastricht archives to see Willem's death certificate. It took only a few minutes for the registrar to find the certificate. On it were two names: Willy van Wijk and Yosta Eerens-van Wijk. I got a photocopy of the certificate and went out to find a telephone directory.

Now I faced a new problem. If what I had been told was fact, and they were the grandchildren of Vincent van Gogh, how was I going to tell them? What would they say? I was as nervous at that moment as I had been at any time in the whole of my investigations.

Van Wijk is a common name in Holland—like Smith or Jones in America and Britain. So I tried Yosta Eerens-van Wijk first, thinking that it would be easier to find. There was no one of that name in Maastricht. I looked through a few of the nearby towns and, by luck, found the name in the listing for Herten, a village just outside Maastricht. Plucking up my courage, I dialled the number.

A woman's voice answered the phone. I spoke very nervously.

'Hello, Mrs Eerens-van Wijk?'

'Yes, speaking.'

'Good afternoon. My name is Ken Wilkie. I am conducting some research into the Hoornik family and in connection with that research I would be grateful for some information about your father.'

Her reply was immediate and to the point.

'Anything you want to know about my father you had better find out for yourself. You will not get it from me.'

And she rang off.

I called her back immediately.

'Mrs Eerens-van Wijk, I . . .'

Click.

I tried again. This time she gave me the chance to ask her whether she would speak to me for five minutes only. I was quite willing . . .

Receiver down again.

I tried once more. This time her husband came to the phone. His only words were: 'You won't find out anything from this family.'

I couldn't understand it. Yosta Eerens-van Wijk's reaction suggested that she was afraid of something, or was hiding something. What was it? I hoped I would have better luck with Willy, Yosta's brother.

Johannes Feij had told me he heard that Willy moved to somewhere in the Rotterdam area, but he wasn't sure about it. Anyway, it was better than nothing. I got out the Rotterdam phone book and looked up the W. van Wijks. Of course, there were dozens of them. I went to a nearby café for a glass of beer, and returned to the phone booth armed with a pocketful of coins. I knew it might take me an hour's-worth of calls before I got the right W. van Wijk.

I was right, or nearly. I went through many names and numbers, each time asking the question:

193

'Did your father die in Maastricht in 1958? Was he named Willem and was he born in 1882?'

No one was impolite, but some of them clearly thought I was odd. Finally, one man answered positively. He seemed to take the question quite casually. I explained to him that I was doing research into his family and might have something of interest to tell him. If I could possibly pay him a visit . . .

'Yes, yes, please come to my office in Rotterdam next Saturday. I will be there all morning and would be happy to talk to you.'

We made arrangements and I hung up the phone. The difference between his reaction and the reaction of his sister was quite astonishing. I looked forward to meeting him. The two-hour drive back to Amsterdam was a jubilant one.

It was only Wednesday when I went to Maastricht and I had to wait two days. I went back to work but couldn't think about anything but that drive to Rotterdam. When the day arrived, I was up at dawn, even though Rotterdam is not a long drive from Amsterdam and I wasn't due at Willy's office until ten. I tried to prolong everything I did—my morning shower, walking the dog, reading the newspaper—just to kill time until I left. I even drove intentionally slowly down to Rotterdam.

Willy van Wijk's office is in the tree-lined Mathenesserlaan, one of the few streets that escaped the Nazi bombardment in the Second World War. I rang the bell and waited.

When the door opened, I got the shock of my life. The man who introduced himself as Willy van Wijk had distinctive Van Gogh features—the high forehead, large, thin, hooked nose, long head. I masked my amazement as we shook hands and he led the way into his office. But as he made coffee and we talked about the weather, it was all I could think about.

'Would you care for a dash of cognac in your coffee?' he ventured.

'I think I could use it.'

We sat drinking the fortified coffee in silence for a few moments. He was friendly—certainly not threatening the way his sister had been—but I think he could tell I had something on my mind. Finally I asked whether he had known his grandparents. He had not.

I put down my coffee cup.

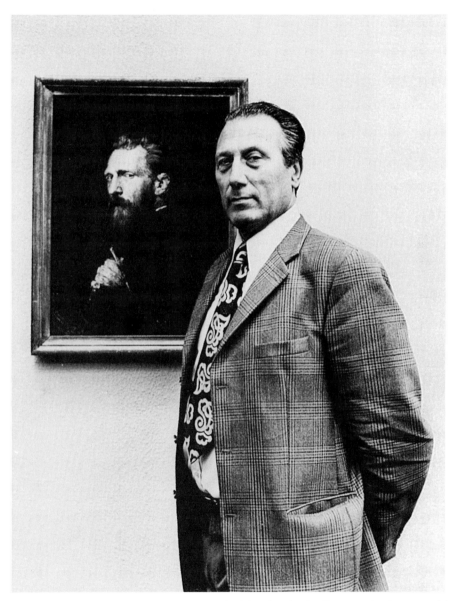

Willy van Wijk, Willem's son, photographed in 1978 in the Van Gogh Museum with a painting of Vincent by the Australian artist John Russell. *Photo: Ted Dukkers*

195

'Mr Van Wijk, my interest in the Hoornik family is in fact related primarily to another family. Can I rely on you not to repeat to anyone what I am about to tell you now?'

'Why, yes. Certainly. But do tell me.'

'There is evidence that your grandfather was Vincent van Gogh.'

Willy fell back into his seat. His jaw had dropped, his eyes were wide open. He was speechless.

I explained how his father had told the story to Ed Hoornik and Hoornik's widow had told it to me. I explained the circumstances in which Vincent had lived in The Hague and about his relationship with the prostitute Clasina. Willy seemed not to worry about having a prostitute in the family. I showed him copies of the drawings Vincent had made of Willy's father when Willem was a baby. Willy, still speechless, looked at the pictures. Finally he spoke.

'My father told me none of this. It's amazing. Incredible. I just can't believe it.'

When the initial shock had worn off, he began to comb his memory for clues.

'I always sensed that there was some mystery surrounding my father's family, but I never had any idea what it was. To tell you the truth, I never became close enough to my father to ask him anything at all personal . . . You know, I think I could use another cognac.'

He poured a trickle into both our cups and continued. 'I remember my father had a drawing he was very attached to. It was of a labourer. I think it was signed. It could well have been "Vincent".'

'Are you absolutely sure?' I asked.

'I remember him saying it meant something special to him, but he wouldn't tell me what.'

'Where is the drawing now?' I asked.

'It's with my sister Yosta in Herten.'

'Are you sure you remember the name Vincent on the drawing?' I wasn't jumping to any conclusions, realising that the sudden entrance of Van Gogh into his life might have affected his memory.

'Well, I can easily phone her and ask.'

He picked up the telephone and dialled his sister's number.

'Hello, Yosta? It's Willy. You know that old drawing of Dad's that you have on your wall? The one he liked so much? Could you do me a favour and check the signature?'

The moments passed very slowly as we waited for Yosta's return to the telephone. I struggled not to get my hopes up. What if Vincent had given Clasina a drawing . . . and she had passed it on to her son . . . and . . . ?

Then Willy spoke into the receiver.

'Hello? Yes, yes . . . Oh, well . . . thanks . . . Yes, no. I just wanted to check. I thought it might have been something else. Yes . . . yes . . . goodbye. Thanks a lot.'

He put down the receiver.

'She says it has some other name on it. Not Vincent. I was mistaken. I'm very sorry. I'm not thinking very straight at the moment.'

'It's all right. You must have Van Gogh on your mind.' I went on to ask Willy about his father's background.

'He had a Catholic upbringing in the Hoornik family, but the woman he married—Saakje Leistra—was a Protestant from the northern province of Friesland. That's really all I know. They were divorced in 1941 and she died four years later.'

I didn't think it appropriate to ask whether she had killed herself, as Johannes Feij had said.

Willy continued: 'Dad was a very creative person, as you know. I remember he designed and made electric trains and warships for me when I was a boy. My sons, one is 27 and the other is 32, don't seem to have any artistic leanings. Neither do I, you know.'

I asked Willy whether he had any photographs of his father. All he had was a passport-type picture and a couple of badly printed snapshots. At least from the passport photo I was able to get an idea of what Willem had looked like later in life. Funnily enough, he looked less like Vincent than his son, Willy.

Willy gladly gave me the photographs and again promised not to talk about our conversation until I gave him the okay. We had a last cognac—this time without the coffee—and I was off.

On the drive back to Amsterdam, I thought about what I had found. Willem van Wijk, or Willem Hoornik, or Willem van Gogh—who was he? A man who had been a Nazi sympathiser during the war. A secretive man who had never talked about 'personal' subjects with his son. A man who was disliked, it would seem, by the men he worked with. A talented artist, but known to one of his few friends as a sad and embittered man.

I realised that I would never know as much about him as I wanted to. He had lived long enough to tell two people his secret—at least that hadn't died with him. All that was left of him now was a cluster of memories—many of them unpleasant—in the minds of the people who had known him.

But there were his children, one of whom, presumably, still didn't know the possible identity of her famous grandfather. They were all his family, apart from Willy's two sons and whatever children Yosta might have. But there was also the Engineer, Dr Van Gogh, who would have been Willem's cousin. Did he know about Willem? If so, he hadn't acknowledged the fact. And he certainly had made no provision for Willy, Vincent's grandson, in the financial settlement of the huge Van Gogh estate. Legally, I assumed, there was nothing that would require him to do so. But wasn't there a moral obligation to acknowledge the existence of this branch of the Van Gogh family? Shouldn't the Engineer at least be informed of what I had been told?

I decided that I would go to see the Engineer. He often worked at his office in the museum on Saturdays, and perhaps I might find him there.

This was without question the most disconcerting part of my investigations. I remembered too well the way in which the Engineer had greeted my questions about Vincent's syphilis, and about mental illness in the family. I had no reason to believe that he would take my present news any more enthusiastically.

As I parked my car near the museum and walked across Museumplein, my palms were sweating the way they used to when I had to recite in class. The Engineer, however, dressed as always in his striped bow tie, greeted me politely as he always did. Perhaps he couldn't believe that this pestering journalist was really going to make trouble for him again. But was there, I thought, a little more strain in the cordiality than there had been before?

After the customary few minutes of small talk, I began explaining to Dr Van Gogh why I was there.

'As you know, sir, I have continued exploring certain questions concerning Vincent van Gogh's life. Most recently I have been interested in the period he spent in The Hague, when he was living with the prostitute named Clasina Maria Hoornik.'

At the word 'prostitute' his eyes narrowed. I gulped and continued talking.

'I was interested in tracing what happened to the woman, and to her children, after Vincent left them. As you know, family pressure forced him to desert Clasina and her children.

'I went to see Jan Hulsker, whom you know well. He told me that Clasina was related to the writer Ed Hoornik and that Hoornik's widow was the writer Mies Bouhuys.'

As I talked, the engineer listened motionless and expressionless. I proceeded to tell him the whole story of what Mies Bouhuys had told me, of my visit to Maastricht, and of my conversation with Willy van Wijk. I concluded by asking him whether he had known of Willem before, and whether he had any plans to contact Willy van Wijk.

The Engineer sat silently. When he spoke, his voice was more agitated than I had ever heard it.

'Now let's get it straight. I don't know anything about this. My only source of information is the letters, and I have published all that have been handed down to me—apart from a few unimportant jottings. My mother never mentioned the name Hoornik to me. She probably didn't know about this or she would have told me.'

'And you,' I asked, 'what do you think of it?'

'Personally I don't think this man Van Wijk was Vincent's son or Vincent would have said so in his letters . . .'

I interrupted him. 'But there are sections missing from the letters he wrote in The Hague . . .'

'That doesn't prove anything. I think it more likely that Clasina wanted to clear herself in her son's eyes when she told him that Vincent was his father. She probably didn't want him to know that she had had so many men.

'If you knew more about that period you would see why Clasina was probably not telling the truth. In the 1880s the upper and lower classes in The Hague had very loose morals. It was only the middle class who exercised moral restraint then.

'I admit that in the 1914 edition of Vincent's letters a lot were left out because Vincent's sisters were still living. But in 1953 I published everything I had. If there are parts of letters and complete letters still missing, I do not know what happened to them.'

The Engineer had been sitting forward in his seat while talking to me. Suddenly he sat back and changed the subject. We talked for a few minutes about Vincent's life in London and other unrelated matters. Obviously the Engineer didn't want to talk to me any longer. I left politely.

The way the Engineer had rejected my findings out of hand was revealing. He disbelieved Clasina simply because she was a prostitute. That, coupled with his statements about the 'loose morals' of the lower classes in The Hague, seemed further reflections of the puritanism he had displayed in our discussion of Vincent's disease.

It is also possible that Vincent may not even have known that he was Willem's father. After all, apart from her daughter Marie and baby Willem, Clasina had had two other illegitimate children who died in infancy, before she met Vincent. As Vincent never mentions them in his correspondence, we assume she had not told him.

Another possibility is that Vincent felt the matter to be so personal that he kept it to himself, as he did the details of his disease. To announce it to his family might well have decided his father to execute his threat of committing his son to the asylum he had lined up in Belgium. Vincent may also have felt, and not without reason, that to make public his fatherhood of this prostitute's child would have meant that his subsistence allowance from Theo would have been cut off, severing the two most important things to him at that time: his means to paint and the means to support his chosen family.

Hulsker argued that in view of the otherwise complete frankness of Vincent's letters to Theo, it is impossible to believe that in this case the painter deliberately deceived his brother. In fact, when he finally told Theo that he had been living with Clasina since the previous January, he proved he already had been deceiving his brother by keeping from him, for months, the fact that he was supporting Clasina and her daughter with the money being sent to him by Theo. Vincent realised he had to tell Theo about it before the news reached him from Anton Mauve or from Tersteeg, the director of Goupil and Company in The Hague, both of whom were in touch with Theo.

A clue to suggest that Vincent could have had contact with Clasina before January appeared in letter 164 to Theo from Etten, in which Vincent described how, after his unsuccessful trip to Amsterdam in late November to try to win Kee, he visited another woman in The Hague. 'She was no longer young,' he wrote, '. . . and she had a child . . .' He wrote further: 'When you wake up in the morning and find yourself not alone, but see there in the morning twilight a fellow creature beside you, it makes the world look so much more friendly. Much more friendly than religious diaries and whitewashed church walls, with which the clergymen are in love . . .' He goes on: '. . . When I think of Kee, I still say, "she and no other"; but it is not just recently that I have had a heart for those women who are condemned and damned by the clergymen, the feeling is even older than my love for Kee.'

We also learn from an even earlier letter (149) that Vincent was in The Hague as early as August 1881, to visit the painter Mauve from whom he would later receive lessons, and in this letter he stated that he had arranged to come back to see Mauve in a relatively short time.

This means that Vincent could have met Clasina early enough to father her child. In the medical dossier of Christina Hoornik recording the birth of Willem at the Academisch Ziekenhuis in Leiden, there is no one registered as being the father. Clasina calls herself Christina. Occupation: Seamstress. The baby was extracted with the aid of forceps and was a normal weight of 3.42 kilogrammes and length 53 centimetres. This suggests conception in late August or early September. If Clasina told Vincent later that he was the baby's father, Vincent might well have had his doubts, due to the nature of her way of life at the time.

My point of going so far into this matter was to see if the story told me by Mies Bouhuys could, in practice, be possible. I found it could, although I have to admit there is also a lot of evidence against it. But unlike Hulsker, who rules out the possibility of Willem van Wijk being Vincent van Gogh's son, I don't accept the case as being closed. For me it remains unresolved.

11 Digging

In June 1989 I at last had an opportunity to pursue my researches in England, in an attempt to track down a lost painting by Van Gogh—a portrait he painted in Antwerp in 1885. I have already described my conversation with Dr Cavenaile, the grandson of the Antwerp doctor who treated Vincent for syphilis. After he had given me the information that explained so much about Vincent's apparent change of character between his time in Nuenen and his arrival in Paris, I asked him if his grandfather had reported anything else of interest that Van Gogh had said to him.

'Well, my grandfather did tell me that before he treated Van Gogh, the painter warned him that he was unable to pay cash. The only way of paying was by painting his portrait. My grandfather agreed,' explained Dr Cavenaile.

'Where is the portrait now? Do you still have it?' I asked.

'No,' replied the doctor. 'Unfortunately the painting has been lost. Not by me, I hasten to add. I remember seeing it when I was a little boy. It was a small oil painting, signed "Vincent". Years later, when I saw the portrait that Van Gogh made of one of his French doctors, Gachet, I was reminded of the portrait of my grandfather.'

I asked Cavenaile how the portrait had been lost.

'It was inherited by my Aunt Jeanne,' he said. 'She married a Jewish corn merchant from Russia called Kleibs. Adolph Kleibs. They had to flee to England from the Germans before the First World War, and they took the portrait with them. I've tried to trace her several times but my efforts have always been in vain. She was last heard of in the 1930s, living in London.'

'Do you know where in London?'

'Some hill. Mussel Hill, I think it was.'

'Muswell Hill, perhaps?'

'Yes, Muswell Hill. That's it. But she moved from there without a trace and hasn't been heard of since.'

'Did they have a family?'

'Yes. Two sons and three daughters, I think. One son I heard went to Canada and one of the daughters, Nadia, was in medicine. But I don't know where she is now. Someone in the family may have the Van Gogh portrait of my grandfather on the wall without realising what it is. I would like to know where my cousin Nadia is . . .'

I decided to dig a little deeper. In the London telephone directory there was not a 'Kleibs' to be seen. One Bob Kleiber but he was no relation. Had they changed the spelling? I wondered. There were two people called 'Kleibe', one in E17 and the other in SE2. They had ancestors from eastern Europe but not from Belgium and no one called 'Adolph'. It occurred to me that in the war years it would not have been surprising if Mr Kleibs had dropped the name 'Adolph' . . . Maybe he changed his 'K' to a more anglified 'C'. But in the London telephone book there were no entries under Cleibs, Cleibe, Cliebs, Cliebe or Clieber.

And that was it. At least I had tried. Dr Cavenaile died and I let the matter rest for a while. But it was far from the end of the story. During an interview with the BBC's *World At One*, I told John Spicer about my vain search for the missing Van Gogh of Muswell Hill.

The morning after the programme was sent out, I was summoned out of my shower in Amsterdam. It was John Spicer on the phone from London.

'We've found your family, Ken,' he exclaimed. 'Can you get to a studio?'

'I haven't even got to my underwear yet, John,' I replied.

'OK. Don't worry. Hold the line. We'll do a three-way telephone conversation. I'm going to put you through to Mrs Clives. She says she is a relation. And that her husband changed his name from Kleibs to Clives.'

It is just as well the *World At One* is not televised. Still naked and dripping from the shower, I asked Mrs Clives where she lived.

'Muswell Hill, ' she said. 'Jeanne's daughter, Nadia, was my sister-in-law. I would never have known anything about this, you know, had it not been for my next-door neighbour coming in yesterday and saying, "Doreen, Serge changed his name from Kleibs to Clives, didn't he? I've just heard an interview on the BBC with someone in Holland trying to trace your family in connection with a lost Van Gogh . . ."'

'Do you know if the family brought a painting, a portrait of a man, over to England with them in 1914?' I asked her.

'No,' said Mrs Clives, 'I'm certain they didn't. They had to flee in a hurry. They had hardly any belongings with them.'

The BBC interview had to be kept short, but I had made a note of Mrs Clives' address and telephone number, and planned to look her up at the next opportunity. Now, several years later, I was on my way.

The London bus laboriously edged its way out of the Thames valley and up to Muswell Hill, a place I had never been to but had heard graphically ridiculed years before by Spike Milligan.

Doreen Clives was an active 84-year-old lady living in a large terraced house on a rise overlooking Alexandra Park. Over a glass of sherry she cast her mind back. 'My husband, Serge, died in 1979. He was born in Antwerp in 1905. His father was a Russian Jew and the whole family had to flee Belgium for their lives when the Germans invaded the country in 1914.'

Mrs Clives showed me a document dated May 31st, 1940. It was a carbon copy of an application by her husband to be exempted from the Aliens Movement Restriction Order of 1940—after he had already been resident in London for 26 years. From this paper I read that Serge's father was Michael Adolph Kleibs, born in Nicolaiev, Russia, and his mother was Jeanne Marie Colette Cavenaile, born in Antwerp. Serge had a brother, Robert John, also born in Antwerp and already by 1940 a naturalised Canadian, an older sister, Nadia Micheline, married to a doctor in Kent, and a younger sister, born in London, Marguerite Muriel Frankia, known as Peggy.

'When Adolph died, Jeanne went back to Belgium and took Peggy with her,' said Mrs Clives. 'Then the Second World War broke out. The Germans invaded Belgium again and were rounding up all the Jewish people. Peggy was teaching English in Namur, and in the chaos of the

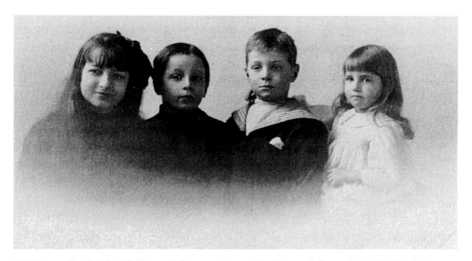

Children of Adolph Kleibs and Jeanne Cavenaile. From left to right: Nadia, Robert, Serge, Vera. The photo was taken in Antwerp before the First World War. The youngest child, Peggy, was born after they had fled to London. *Collection Mrs Doreen Clives*

invasion Jeanne couldn't reach her, hard as she tried. Finally, she fled, for the second time in her life, to London. We hoped Peggy would find a way back to England but she never came back. We never heard from her again. We assumed she had perished, either in Namur or in a concentration camp. Jeanne was in a terrible state. She was a very sweet and kind person. She stayed with us during the first part of the war, but when the bombing became very intense she moved in with her daughter Nadia. After that she moved into a flat in Onslow Gardens, and she finally died in Sussex in 1964.

'Adolph had arrived in London with nothing and became very successful on the Stock Exchange. All their children were clever. Nadia was a paediatrician, Bob had moved to Ontario and my husband was an architect. But they are all dead now.'

After absorbing the family background, I began to ask Mrs Clives about the missing Van Gogh portrait of Dr Cavenaile.

'I can tell you for certain that no paintings came with the Kleibs family to England,' she said. 'They often marvelled at how lucky they had been to escape with their lives. As Jeanne told me when I was looking after her after the war, you don't think of taking valuables with you when you are running for your lives. And another fact was, of course, that in 1914 Van Gogh was not recognised and the family would not be aware of the painting's future value. You knew there were two portraits, didn't you?'

'Well, I saw a large knee-length oil in Dr Cavenaile's grandson's consulting room. But it was not painted by Van Gogh, and it portrayed the doctor at a much more advanced age than when he treated Van Gogh in 1885,' I said.

'Well, Nadia told me that Van Gogh had made two portraits of Dr Cavenaile' said Mrs Clives. 'The larger one hung in the dining-room on the first floor of the doctor's house at number 2, rue de Hollande, and the other was hanging somewhere else in the house. They had to leave the paintings behind, together with other valuables that were too clumsy to carry.'

'At number 2 rue de Hollande?'

'Yes. At their home, 2 rue de Hollande.'

I told Mrs Clives that I would be going to Antwerp to investigate the matter more fully. What I was most interested in at this stage was a photograph, if such existed, of Dr Cavenaile around 1885, the year in which Van Gogh had painted him. I asked her if there was a photo album anywhere in the family.

'I have a few old snaps in a box upstairs,' she said. 'I'll show you what I've got.' On top of the pile was a photo of Mrs Clives' own grandfather. 'He was a stonemason who worked on the erection of the Albert Memorial,' she said. Underneath was a photo of Adolph and Jeanne Kleibs, taken shortly after their arrival in London, a beautiful passport photo of Peggy in her late teens and a photo of Nadia, Serge and Bob as children with another little sister, Vera, who died very young.

'Was there a family album?' I asked.

'Yes, there was one,' said Mrs Clives. 'When Nadia died, the old family photo album was passed on to her daughter, Jane. Jane lived with her family in Fiji for some years . . .'

'The family album's in the Fiji Islands?'

'Oh no, Jane's back in England now. She lives in a village in Kent.'

The only possible time to visit Jane during my stay in England was

Wednesday, June 28th, the day of a national rail strike. I was fortunate in being able to borrow a car from my long-suffering friends in London, Jim and Nel Mailer. If asked today what is the most unpleasant way of spending a morning in London, I can confidently answer that it is driving from west London, through the centre in a south-easterly direction to Kent, in a heatwave during a rail strike. It took three hours to get out of London.

By the time I arrived at Jane's cottage there was no one in, but my depression was alleviated by a note from Jane on the door, saying she was at another address nearby. I was delighted to be invited to join Jane and her friend John for lunch. My initial feeling of being an intruder on the doorstep of John's beautiful old cottage, accentuated by crashing my head against one of the ceiling's ancient wooden beams, soon dispersed over lunch as I absorbed the ambiance.

When the conversation touched on the subject of descendants, John pointed to the miniature painting on the wall. 'That's Samuel Pepys' wife,' he said. 'I am a direct descendant of her, you know. It's an exquisite little miniature, don't you think?'

What I was to hear next, however, really made me pause. I was explaining to Jane how I had traced her initially from the name of a doctor on the back of an Antwerp sketchbook of Vincent van Gogh.

'There's an original photograph of Dr Cavenaile in my family album,' she said. 'Come along and we'll have a look.'

From John's cottage we walked past the churchyard to Jane's house. She then placed on the table one of the most beautiful old photograph albums I have seen. It was ornately inscribed with the word 'Anvers', the French name for Antwerp.

It opened with a rare collection of Russian studio portraits of the Kleibs family, more exotic and theatrical than their European equivalents from the second half of the nineteenth century. There was a magnificent one of Adolph, Jane's grandfather, posing in a large mirror; there was a portrait of an armless painter friend of Dr Cavenaile, pictured before his easel with brush between toes; there was Dr Cavenaile's wife from Amsterdam, and at last the doctor himself. Interestingly for me, the photograph appeared to show him in his mid-40s. As he would have been 44 when Vincent painted his portrait in the Autumn of 1885, I was looking at the doctor as he must appear in the missing portrait.

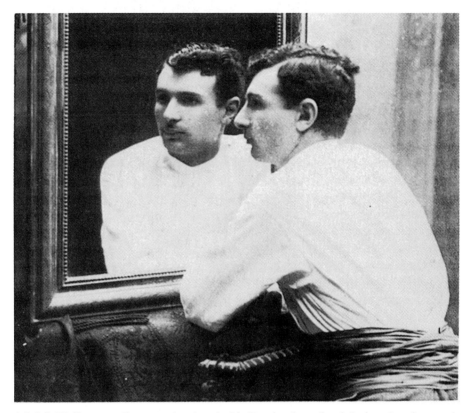

Adolph Kleibs, a studio portrait taken in his Russian homeland during the nineteenth century. *Private collection*

Jane's mother, Nadia, had been the eldest of the Kleibs children, and Jane told me her mother clearly remembered the portrait of her grandfather, signed 'Vincent', on the living room wall at number 2 rue de Hollande in Antwerp.

'Yes, it was definitely left behind. The family had to leave almost everything. But they buried the painting in the garden with a few other valuables too clumsy to carry.'

'You say they buried the portrait?' I said aghast.

'Yes. Mother told me several times that they buried it in the garden just before they left.'

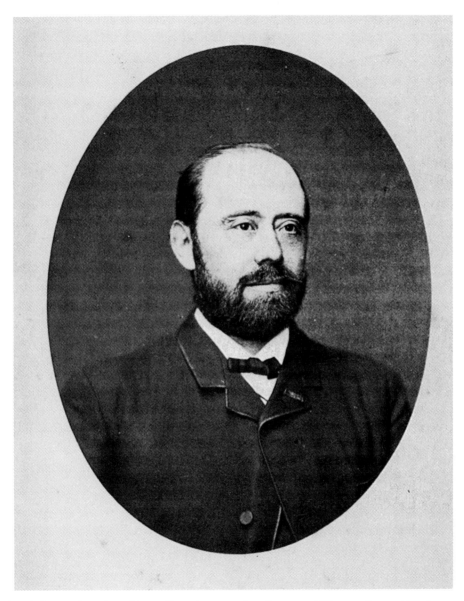

Dr Hubertus Amadeus Cavenaile as he was when he treated Vincent for syphilis in Antwerp. *Private collection*

'And they never dug it up after the war?'

'No. Grandmother Jeanne returned to Belgium before the Second World War, but not to rue de Hollande which was no longer her property, of course. And she returned to London again in 1940, where she remained until her death.'

Jane did not know in what kind of container the painting was stowed away.

'As far as you know, the portrait by Vincent of your great-grandfather could still be buried in this garden in Antwerp?' I concluded.

'Yes, it could.'

It looked as if my digging into Van Gogh was destined to take a realistic turn. During the five-hour drive back to London to collect my baggage and take the last plane to Amsterdam, I had plenty of time to contemplate my next move. It had been a hectic but interesting and fruitful day. Jane had loaned me the photographic material I requested, including the portrait of Dr Cavenaile that would be essential in identifying Van Gogh's painting of the doctor—if I ever found it.

I knew that before and during the two World Wars, it was not an uncommon thing for people fleeing the Germans to bury valuables, particularly paintings. Rembrandt's *Nightwatch* was hidden away in an underground cave, Van Goghs were buried in sand dunes, and the old villa in which I live in the Netherlands has a garden that may still conceal valuables buried by the family who were forced to move out by the Germans.

But was number 2 rue de Hollande still standing? It might have been demolished. After all, it was in the centre of the city.

A few days later I was in Antwerp with a street map looking for Hollandstraat (the street spellings are now in Flemish). I was glad to see that the area did not appear to have undergone any major demolition or rebuilding during this century.

For this escapade I had been joined by two friends and kindred spirits: the writer, satirist, and my neighbour Kees van Kooten, and a journalist colleague at *Holland Herald*, Roderic Leigh, two of the very few people I had confided in and who had offered to help me. In the boot of the car were three spades and a metal detector—a large, professional-looking model, the kind you see people using to comb the beaches of California.

True, we were looking for a lost painting, but as I had learned from the family that Vincent's *Dr Cavenaile* had been buried with silver and other metallic valuables, a metal detector was essential equipment.

We found ourselves at the far end of Hollandstraat and followed the even numbers up the street . . . 30, 28, 26, 24, 22, 20, 18 . . . 12, 10, 8 . . . we were nearing the end. I prayed that the end house had not been hacked off. Fortunately not. There it was: the first house in rue de Hollande, on the corner of St Gumarisstraat. A three-storey town house in the style of the mid-nineteenth century. Confirmation that I had the right address was on the outside wall in Hollandstraat: a plaque dedicated to Antwerp's doctorial dynasty of Cavenaile. It stated: 'Armand Jules Cavenaile, 13 Juillet 1882'. And the initials AC were ornately engraved on the corner gable above what had once been the entrance. Vincent's doctor, Hubertus Amadeus Cavenaile, had set up his practice there in 1883, two years before treating Vincent for syphilis.

At first sight from the outside, the upper floors of the house looked as if

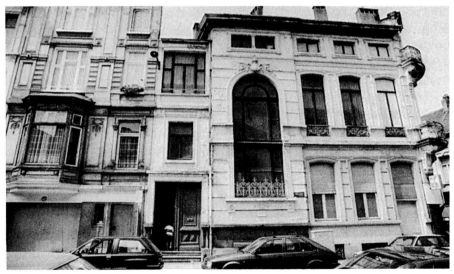

Number 2 rue de Hollande, where Dr Cavenaile had his practice. The building is largely as it was in 1885. Part of the ground floor is now a carpet shop. *Photo: the author*

211

they had not been occupied since the Kleibs family fled in August 1914, the month of the German invasion of Belgium and, ironically, the year of the first Van Gogh exhibition in Antwerp. The grey-white paint was peeling off the outside walls. From behind one of the grime-streaked curtainless windows, I saw a black cat looking down at us, obviously not used to his dirty windows being gazed at like this.

The neglected look of the place held promise of other things forgotten. Equally encouraging was the abandoned-looking service entrance, a large double door with no bell, locked, and a jammed letter-box. At ground level, there were two indentures in the wall which had once supported metal bands that Vincent might well have used, in November 1885, to scrape the mud off his down-at-the-heel boots, after walking from his lodgings at 224 Longue rue des Images.

The Hollandstraat side of the house remained in its original state, but the ground floor on the St Gumarisstraat side had been totally gutted and renovated. It housed a carpet and paint shop—not entirely inappropriate, bearing in mind that we were looking for a painting down below.

We agreed that the course of action depended a lot on the owner of the house. I was worried that if I explained the whole story—that there might be at least one Van Gogh buried in the back garden—the owner might refuse access and start digging himself. If the painting was still underground and in one piece, the owner of the property might well be the legal owner, but in my opinion it would be morally wrong to exclude the rights of the descendants of the Kleibs family who had been persecuted by the Germans in the First World War for being part Russian, and again in the Second World War for being part Jewish.

In 1914 there was a war raging between the Russians and the Germans. The Russians had been defeated by the German forces at the Battle of Tannenburg on August 26, and on September 6 had begun the retreat from East Prussia. When the Germans moved into Antwerp, had they found Adolph Kleibs they could have shot him on sight, and probably his wife Jeanne Cavenaile and their three children too.

First of all we had to decide how to present ourselves to the current occupants. As both Kees and Roderic were talented character actors and I could be cast as a not-too-verbal plumber's apprentice, another approach might have been with spades in hand: 'Good morning. We're from the research department of the European Plumbing Standardisation Authority. Prior to the installation of your new pipes in 1993, we've come to take some measurements . . .' Thereby gaining access. Perhaps.

We settled instead for the restrained-and-cautiously-innocent-to-the-point-of-naïveté approach. In other words, our usual impulsive selves. Nodding and mumbling, 'Let's improvise,' we entered the carpet and paint shop.

There were no lights on inside. Only two men, whispering among the Persian carpets, their voices muffled by the thick pile all around. As Kees and Roderic nervously tapped their fingers on rolls of linoleum, I explained, fumbling for words until I could gauge some reaction, who we were and that we were not in the shop to buy a carpet, which was probably obvious anyway.

One of the men, Freddy Freyssen, was the new owner and the other, Robert Vansant, the manager. We had arrived at a fortunate time, as the Freyssens were leaving that night for Italy and the Vansants had just returned from holiday. I began to tell the story of how Vincent van Gogh had been a patient of Dr Cavenaile. They knew about the house belonging to the Cavenaile family but not about the link with Van Gogh. Within a few minutes the entire families Freyssen and Vansant had joined us. Of course they all recognised Kees who, as he put it, is 'world-famous in Belgium', but he reassured them that there were no film cameras waiting round the corner. Instead he encouraged them to listen to my little tale.

Freddy Freyssen's mother was there, too. She had lived in the neighbourhood, she said, for more than 35 years. She didn't know anything about Vincent van Gogh being treated here either. There was good humour in the air. When Mrs Freyssen learned I had been born in Scotland, she spluttered out: 'It's a braw bricht moonlicht nicht the nicht (It's a fine bright moonlight night tonight).' Effortlessly, of course, as the Flemish soft 'g' is almost identical in pronunciation to the 'ch' in the Scottish 'loch'—and the first 'g' in Van Gogh, for that matter.

'The English can't say that, can they?' asked Mrs Freyssen.

'No. In the same way as the Germans have trouble pronouncing the fishing port of Scheveningen,' I replied.

It was in this convivial climate that I sailed on to explain the chain of

213

events and people in Belgium and England that had finally led me to their carpet shop. I showed the families the original photographs of Dr Cavenaile and the Russian portrait of Adolph Kleibs looking into a mirror. It then seemed in the natural drift of the story to tell them: 'Adolph's family in England told me that in the hasty departure from Antwerp, with the Germans on the outskirts of the city, the portrait of Dr Cavenaile by Vincent was taken off the living room wall and buried in the garden with other valuables that were too bulky to take with them to London. And, to their knowledge, there has never been an attempt to retrieve them.'

A short silence followed as everyone looked at each other. Then came action. It was as if we all knew what to do without a briefing.

I'll get the keys to the Hollandstraat entrance,' said Robert. 'It leads to the back garden. Well, it's more of a courtyard than a garden. It hasn't been used for as long as I can remember.'

As Robert wrestled with the lock for about ten minutes, Kees, Roderic and I stood patiently with our spades and metal detector. To the curious cat at the upstairs window we must have looked like a mine disposal squad from the front line.

'This is impossible,' said Robert, writhing at the keyhole. 'The lock is completely rusted and I don't seem to have the right key, either.'

Although we couldn't get in, I felt heartened by this development as the apparent neglect of this part of the building seemed to increase the chances of retrieving the treasure.

'Don't worry!' shouted Robert. 'There's another way into the courtyard by a back staircase. Follow me.'

We filed after him, equipment on shoulders. This 'other way' was the Antwerpian town house equivalent of scaling the north face of the Eiger. It took us, circuitously, up through every remaining part of the old house.

'It's been a beautiful house in its day,' I said, falling at that instant through part of the staircase.

'Yes, the detailing is magnificent,' said Kees, holding a part of the banister in one hand.

The stairway was covered in old rolls of linoleum, cast-off carpets and miscellaneous bits of furniture. Robert was far ahead. Roderic was the leading figure of our trio on the staircase.

'If you follow me you'll be all right,' he said as a roll of linoleum avalanched down the stairs, bonking him on the head. He lurched against half a hall-stand, a coat hook of which caught one of my camera straps and almost strangled me as I was admiring the engraved staircase window.

We searched every room of every landing and all were utterly empty, not even a cat to be seen. At the top of the house we branched off into a passage leading down a back staircase and out into the little courtyard.

At the entrance to the courtyard was a stair that led down to the basement, a stair so decayed that it shook when you looked at it. In the gloom at the bottom one could just discern an old mattress and bits of furniture half-submerged in water. It gave off a spine-numbing smell of cold mould which aroused the beavering instincts of Roderic; he disappeared with a torch into the damp catacombs.

The courtyard was small and square, covered for the most part with cracked, dirty yellow tiles which could have been 100 years old or 40—no one in the family knew. Part of the courtyard around the rain-pipe against the wall had been dug up and concreted over, and there was an old pile of bricks stacked up in one corner. At the other side of the yard there was a large stone manhole cover which Robert said was the entrance to a disused cesspit. It was sealed off. The courtyard was flanked by high brick walls, covered in plaster which was now powdering off.

Detective-Inspector Kees Van Kooten began to scan the courtyard for signs of buried metal. The machine was so ferrous-sensitive that it would register a high-pitched squeak at even a suggestion of rust. As Kees moved like a water diviner from tile to tile, I noticed that we were being watched from above by the cat, perched on a rooftop above us.

Suddenly, near the middle of the courtyard, the metal detector came to life with a strong, high-pitched bleep. We shared the electric excitement in silence, stunned. Finally Kees said: 'There's something metallic down there. Shall we see if there's earth under this tile?'

We looked at Robert. It was his courtyard. But he had disappeared. He was back in a few seconds, however. As soon as he heard the bleep he had run off to fetch a hammer and chisel.

The first tile was carefully chipped away and removed to reveal, not surprisingly, earth. A second tile was dislodged. Then a third. With every thrust of Kees's spade, the dig gained momentum. With the rapid teamwork of chisel and shovel, the hole deepened. Stone splinters were flying all over the place. To the cats above us—there were now three—we must have looked like bone-crazy dogs.

The Freyssen family, about to leave for Italy, dropped in to wish us luck in our attack on their back yard. 'It's not hard to guess what a speculative topic will be on that holiday,' said Kees.

The signal on the metal detector was getting stronger. Abruptly, Kees's shovel hit something hard, flat, smooth and black. We looked at each other with a 'This is it' expression, beads of sweat dripping off eyebrows into the hole. Was this the container of valuables? Was Vincent's Dr Cavenaile about to be unearthed? Further scraping revealed a slab of black marble. Bumping our heads together over the hole, we heaved it out.

Kees's face went brain-grey as if he had seen a ghost. He picked up something from the soil under the slab of marble.

'What is it? What is it?' I asked, nearly falling into the hole to see what he had found.

In the palm of his hand lay the soiled yellow plastic face of a child's wristwatch, with cat's ears, blue eyes, red nose and laughing mouth. The hands still moved and were fastened to the cat's nose by a metal pin which had been picked up by the detector.

'This is an incredible coincidence,' said Kees, who went on to explain: 'A few years ago our cat died and my wife buried her in the back garden. When she went to put the shovel back in the shed, she saw, lying on the ground in front of her, a plastic child's watch in the shape of a cat's head, with two plastic ears just like this one. It did not belong to our children nor to any of their friends, nor to any of the children from the school next door . . .'

This story appeared in one of Kees's best-selling books called *Koot Digs Himself*, and the end of the story, 'The Death of My Cat' was as follows:

'Does it go?' I ask.

'Yes,' she says. 'That's very strange. It's keeping the correct time.'

Speechless, we stare at the cat face. Then I take her wrist and hold it to my ear . . .

The watch is purring.

It was hot, humid and dusty. There was a pause in the digging when Monique Vansant and her daughter brought us some lemonade. We tried to work out when and how this laughing puss could have been buried. Judging by the old tiles we had removed, the watch dated from the early days of plastic, maybe even before the Second World War, but perhaps more recent.

'I wonder why anyone would be digging here?' I asked.

'Maybe to fix this pipe,' said Kees, scraping the earth away from a stone sewer pipe which led underground towards the cesspit whose lid we had already noticed.

'That cesspit,' I said. 'If it has been out of use for a long time, maybe back in 1914 Adolph Kleibs hid the painting in there, perhaps thinking the Germans would be unlikely to open that up, fearing the germs. I think it's worth having a look. What do you think?'

'Let's do it,' said Kees.

The large stone slab was well sealed over the pit. I had to hurl the hammer with all my weight to break the vacuum. When I did hammer through the seal, the resulting stench was so intense that it was as imperceptible as an extraordinarily high-pitched note. It began to register behind my ears and the outside edges of my feet before rising through the groin and bronchial tubes to poison my nasal membranes and cloud my judgement. I keeled over slightly in slow-motion and smiled faintly at Kees.

'Do you smell gas?' I apparently said.

'It's all right, Ken. You're doing fine. A few more blows and we'll lever it up,' he replied. The smell dispersed. As we were about to heave open the slab, I thought of Auguste Mariette, the French archaeological digger who, in 1851, opened a chamber of the Apis tombs at Saqqara in Egypt, which had been walled up during the reign of Ramses II in the thirteenth century BC. The first thing Mariette saw, impressed on the sand floor, was the footprint of the last priest to leave the tomb before it was sealed off from the world 3,000 years before. If a footprint could remain in a beautiful tomb for 3,000 years, why couldn't a Van Gogh painting survive in a sealed cesspit for 75 years? I thought.

Kees levering with the spade, Robert with the chisel, I heaved up the great stone of destiny and held it open with stretched tendons.

We peered over the edge. The pit was round and quite deep. There was some water in the bottom, but shallow enough to leave some things uncovered. Resting on a heap of netting was an empty-looking bottle.

'That could be an empty bottle of sealing fluid,' said Kees, which would suggest that the pit was sealed from the inside . . .

As my eyes got adjusted to the darkness below, I saw something wooden.

'Kees! That looks like a wooden frame. The frame of a painting, perhaps!' I shouted.

'Robert, hold my legs,' said Kees, kneeling at the edge of the cesspit. 'I'm going down head-first.'

Robert clamped Kees by the calves and he literally dived down. He hung upside-down, flailing around with his arms but couldn't quite reach the wooden frame.

'Lower, Robert,' he ordered. He grabbed the frame and dislodged it slightly from the netting. 'It's not a frame,' he concluded. 'It's part of a fence. Haul me up, Robert!'

'I can't,' said Robert.

'I can't let the lid go or you've had it,' I said.

'Roderic! . . . Where's Roderic? He's not still in the basement, is he? He never came back from the basement.'

With a lightning change of grip on Kees's legs, and a massive heave, Robert pulled Kees out of the pit and we lowered the lid back over the hole.

I went round to the top of the cellar stairway. From far into the bowels of the basement I could hear a distant cry of 'Help!'

'It's all right, we can hear you.'

'It's not all right. The torch battery has failed and I can't see to get back.'

'Take a reading from my voice and try to make in that direction!' I yelled.

Within five minutes he emerged from the darkness, looking like Andrej Gromyko after a month of solitary confinement.

Although it was painful to contemplate, I couldn't ignore the possibility that the painting had been dug up, perhaps by workmen, at some stage during the last 75 years, and then sold, thrown out, taken into another family or put up in some attic. We had already ferreted about in every corner of every room of the house, except the attic. Roderic, smeared in grime like a soldier in camouflage, said he had seen a hole in the ceiling on the top floor that looked like the entrance to an attic. But there was no stairway.

'There is an attic in the house, sure enough,' confirmed Robert, 'but I've never been up there. I'll get a ladder. Let's go.'

Kees and I shovelled the earth and stones back into the hole in the courtyard. I noticed that the audience of cats had left their wall. The show was over.

We filed up the stairs like miners emerging from a pit in the Borinage. By the time we got to the top of the house, the basement beaver was already nosing around the rafters. There was no electricity so Roderic was using a lighter.

'Postcards and envelopes!' he tried to shout with dust-lined lungs. 'Old cards.'

'Who are they addressed to?' I asked.

'Can't see. The lighter fuel is nearly used up. You can almost feel the dust in the air up here.'

Hearing this, Kees disappeared and came back with two new torches and consolation presents for the Vansants. As the shops were closed, it remains a mystery where he got them. The attic was windowless and cat-black. Even the sky-light was sealed off with tar. The banging and crunching of our feet were muffled by the thick velvety carpet of dust that had accumulated since the house was built the previous century. The local inhabitants, the spiders, must have had heart attacks at the invasion of this trio of coughing and sneezing art detectives, tripping over loose bricks and beams and meshing our heads in their webs.

Everything we touched created more dust, or turned to dust in our hands. There were old medicine bottles, samples of string, half of an old felt hat. Concealed in a cocoon of dust like a giant caterpillar was an army kitbag which contained a change of army clothing from the First World War, most of which crumbled into fragments when pulled out of the bag.

There was no correspondence addressed to Cavenaile or Kleibs. All the cards were addressed to a Julius Friedenthal, Antwerp—no street address or number on any of them. The writing on the cards concerned Mr

Friedenthal's string business, although he apparently did not believe in tying up his correspondence. Most of them had been sent from Germany from 1889 to 1923.

We scoured every lung-clogging inch of the attic, examining every stray piece of linoleum or wood. But no paintings. Monique Vansant invited us to their house next door for coffee, where we sat like three Al Jolson stand-ins, under the disapproving gaze of Robert's great-grandmother and a sneering self-portrait of Franz Hals in reproduction on the wall. We hadn't found what we were looking for, of course, but for all the dust and dirt there was not a speck of pessimism in the air. On the contrary.

'Rubens' House tomorrow, Ken?' said Kees.

The Vansant cats, who I am convinced knew exactly where to find what we were looking for, strolled in to inspect the cat-faced wristwatch lying on the table, then left discreetly.

Weeks later, I received a telephone call in Holland from Robert Vansant in Antwerp.

'Hello, Ken. I have some new information that you might be interested in,' he said.

'You've found the painting?'

'No, not yet. But I learned yesterday from an old neighbour, Mrs Roos, that the Cavenaile house on the corner and the one next door were originally one house. Both were number 2 rue de Hollande.'

'Don't tell me. And the house next door has a big garden?'

'Yes. It did.'

'Well, I'd better rally the diggers again.'

'I'm afraid there's not much point,' said Robert. 'The garden was completely built over with an extension to our carpet shop.'

'So you might be working on top of a Van Gogh,' I said. 'What are you going to do now? Planning any renovations?'

'I don't know,' replied Robert. 'What would you do?'

'I have to finish this book.'

THE END?

220

Chronology
of Van Gogh's Life

1851	Zundert	May: The Reverend Theodorus van Gogh, from Benschop near Utrecht, marries Anna Cornelia Carbentus, from The Hague.
1852		March 30: Birth and death of the first Vincent.
1853		March 30: Birth of Vincent, the future painter.
1857		May 1: Birth of Theo.
1864	Zevenbergen	October 1: Vincent goes to boarding school.
1866	Tilburg	September 15: Attends another boarding school.
1869	The Hague	July 30: Begins apprenticeship at his Uncle Cent's art gallery, Goupil and Company.
1872		August: Begins to correspond with Theo at school in Oisterwijk, near the new family home in Helvoirt.
1873	Brussels	January 1: Works at Brussels branch of Goupil.
	London	June 13: Transferred to Goupil's London branch in Covent Garden. Lodges with Mrs Sarah Ursula Loyer at 87 Hackford Road.
1874		June: Rebuffed in his love for Mrs Loyer's daughter, Eugénie. Becomes melancholic and turns to religion.
	Paris	October: Transferred to Goupil's head office in Paris.
	London	December: Returns to London branch of Goupil.
1875	Paris	May 15: Sent back to Goupil head office in Paris against his will.
1876	Paris	April 1: Dismissed from Goupil.

	Ramsgate	April 17: Assistant teacher with Mr William Stokes.
	London	June: Walks 70 miles from Ramsgate to London.
		July 1: Becomes 'a sort of curate' with the Rev. Thomas Slade-Jones at Isleworth.
		November: Delivers first sermon from pulpit in Richmond.
		December: Returns to parents' home at Etten.
1877	Dordrecht	January: Hired as a clerk in a bookshop.
	Amsterdam	May: Studies for theological school with Professor Mendes da Costa.
1878	Etten	July: Quits Latin and Greek studies and returns to Etten.
	Brussels	August 25: Enters missionary school.
1879	Wasmes	January: Failing to qualify, moves to the Borinage region of southern Belgium, working as mission preacher with mining families.
		July: Dismissed for his unconventional behaviour.
	Cuesmes	August: Continues missionary work on his own account.
1880	Brussels	September: Registers at Royal Academy of Fine Arts and meets Van Rappard.
1881	Etten	April: Returning to family parsonage, falls in love with his cousin Kee Vos-Stricker who rejects him.
	The Hague	August: Visits his cousin Anton Mauve, an important artist of The Hague school.
		November 28: Spends a month in The Hague studying with Mauve.
		December 25: After bitter argument with father, leaves parents' home in Etten.
1882	The Hague	January: sets up house with Clasina Maria Hoornik and her daughter.
		April: Breaks with Mauve.

		June 7: Hospitalised for three weeks with gonorrhea.
		July 2: Clasina gives birth to a boy, Willem.
		August 4: Pastor Van Gogh and family move from Etten to Nuenen.
1883	Drenthe	September 11: Leaves Clasina and family and concentrates on painting.
1884	Nuenen	January: Visits Clasina again. Cares for injured mother. Meets neighbour Margot Begemann who falls in love with him.
		August: Margot attempts suicide with strychnine while with Vincent.
1885		March 26: His father dies of heart attack.
		April: Works on *The Potato Eaters*.
	Antwerp	November: Leaves Nuenen in wake of scandals. Treated for syphilis by Dr Cavenaile of whom he paints at least one portrait in place of payment. Makes first of many self-portraits.
1886		January: Studies Rubens.
		January 18: Enrols at Academy.
	Paris	February 27: Moves in with Theo and his girlfriend 'S'.
		March: Attends Cormon's studio. Meets Emile Bernard, Toulouse-Lautrec, Gauguin, Pissarro, Signac, Degas, Guillaumin. Exhibits work in Café-brasserie du Tambourin, run by Agostina Segatori, an Italian.
1888	Arles	February 21: In Provence he plans to establish an 'artists' co-operative'.
		May 29: Visits Saintes-Maries-de-la-Mer.
		September 18: Moves into 'The Yellow House'.
		October 20: Gauguin arrives and moves in with him.
		December 23, 24: Cuts off lobe of ear in a mental crisis. Hospitalised. Gauguin leaves.

		Theo announces engagement to Johanna Bonger.
1889		January 17: Paints portrait of Dr Rey.
		April 17: Theo marries.
	Saint-Rémy	About May 8: Voluntarily enters the Saint-Paul-de-Mausole asylum.
1890		January: Albert Aurier praises Vincent's work in the *Mercure de France*.
		February 1: Birth of Theo's son, Vincent.
		February 14: Theo sells one of Vincent's paintings, *The Red Vines*, to Anna Boch for 400 francs.
		May 17: Vincent visits Theo, Johanna and baby Vincent in Paris.
	Auvers-sur-Oise	May 21: Lodges at inn owned by Gustav Ravoux.
		June 4: Works on portrait of Dr Gachet.
		June 20: Paints doctor's daughter, Marguerite, at piano.
		July 6: Visits Theo, Aurier and Toulouse-Lautrec in Paris.
		July 27: Shoots himself in the chest but staggers back to inn.
		July 29: Dies at dawn.
	Paris	October: Suffering from the same disease as his brother and under severe stress, Theo's mental health collapses and he is admitted to a clinic at Auteuil, near Paris. On the evidence of Dr Frederik van Eeden, Theo is certified insane and committed to a mental hospital in Utrecht.
1891	Utrecht	January 25: Theo dies.
1914		Johanna van Gogh-Bonger has Theo's bones transferred to a grave beside Vincent's at Auvers-sur-Oise.
1978	Laren	Theo's son Vincent dies, aged 88.